Seasons of Love

TONY AND LOIS EVANS

WORD PUBLISHING
Nashville
A Thomas Nelson Company

Unless otherwise indicated, Scripture quotations used in this book are from the New
American Standard Bible. Copyright ©1960, 1962, 1963, 1968,
1971, 1972, 1973, 1975, 1977 by The Lockman Foundation,
La Habra, California. Used by permission.

Scripture quotations indicated KJV are from the King James Version of the Bible.

A portion of this material is taken from:
Sexual Purity by Tony Evans. Copyright © 1995 by Anthony T. Evans.
Moody Press. Used by permission.

The Battle Is the Lord's by Tony Evans. Copyright © 1998 by Anthony T. Evans.
Moody Press. Used by permission.

No More Excuses by Tony Evans. Copyright © 1996 by Anthony T. Evans.
Used by permission of Good News Publishers/Crossway Books,
Wheaton, Illinois 60187.

"Stand By Your Man" by Lois Evans from *Promises, Promises.* Copyright © 1996 by
Multnomah Publishers, Inc.
Used by permission.

Library of Congress Cataloging-in-Publication Data

Evans, Anthony T.
Seasons of love / Tony and Lois Evans.
p. cm.
ISBN 0-8499-1412-4
1. Spouses—Prayer books and devotions—English.   I. Evans, Lois, 1949–   .
II. Title.

BV4596.M3E93   1998
242'.644–dc21   98-20990
                                             CIP

Printed in the United States of America
9 0 1 2 3 4 5 9 BVG 9 8 7 6 5 4 3 2

*We gratefully dedicate this book
to our parents,*

James Basil and Annie Eleen Cannings

and

Arthur Sherman and Evelyn Lucille Evans.

*Thank you for modeling to us
the love, commitment, dedication,
faithfulness, and grace of a God-centered marriage.*

WITH GRATITUDE

We want to say a special word of thanks to our friend and editor, Philip Rawley, for his excellent help in the preparation of this manuscript and to Joey Paul and the editorial team at Word Publishing for their encouragement and quality work on this project.

INTRODUCTION

The institution of marriage has fallen on hard times today. Marital misery, conflict, spousal abuse, and divorce are on the rise while marital joy and happiness are on the decline.

Most of these and other problems can be traced to the reality that the world, rather than its divine Author, has increasingly set the standards for marriage. The thesis that guides this devotional book is that since God made marriage, He's the One who has to make it work.

As of this writing, we have been married for twenty-eight years. During this time we have had to face and communicate our way through financial struggles, job and ministry pressures, personality differences, child-rearing trials, and a myriad of other challenges that are the common lot of married couples.

Sometimes people ask us how we have made it thus far. Our answer is always the same: "He who began a good work in [us] will perfect it" (Phil. 1:6). God does not begin things He does not plan to finish, and marriage is one of those things.

Twenty-eight years ago, we promised to weather the good and the bad, and to do it together. There was no provision for allowing circumstances, no matter how difficult, to overrule that commitment.

Yet it is not just our human tenacity that has allowed us to weather the challenges the years have brought our way. The key is that Jesus Christ and His Word are the foundation of our lives. He is the centerpiece of our relationship. He occupies the throne of our lives, and as such He is the One who makes the joys and pleasures of this wonderful union called marriage so meaningful to us.

Over these years, God has given us many truths that have undergirded our relationship. *Seasons of Love* is our way of sharing these truths with you so that, with the help of the Holy Spirit, you will be able to experience the blessing of His presence in your home.

It is our prayer that the two of you will get together for a few minutes each day to meet with God and that the daily principles shared in this book will help you grow in your relationship to each other and to God.

If you will join together regularly as a couple, with sincerity of heart, to meet with the Author of your relationship, we can assure you that your marriage and home life will begin to experience His powerful hand.

It is our hope that God will use these daily devotionals for couples to help you enhance the spiritual, emotional, and personal development of your marriage relationship. Then you will find joy and delight in all the seasons of love!

—Tony and Lois Evans

PUTTING CHRIST'S POWER TO WORK

I can do all things through Him who strengthens me.

—PHILIPPIANS 4:13

〜⟨✧⟩〜

Many men and women tell their biggest lie on their wedding day! They stand before a minister, family, and friends and say, "I do." But before long, they don't. The promises they made at the wedding are forgotten as their marriage dissolves into an unhappy union.

Some Christian couples sit in a pew on Sunday morning singing that their God is "so high I can't get over Him, so low I can't get under Him, so wide I can't get around Him," but they don't believe He can put their marriage back together.

Given the fact that our own strength is limited, it's not hard to understand why marriages are having a hard time surviving the pressures of the twentieth century. But we don't have to rely on our own finite power. With Christ as our enabler, we can do all things because He has promised to give us the strength.

We have all the spiritual ability we need to accomplish whatever God asks us to do. And since God's command is that a husband and wife commit themselves to each other for life, every Christian couple has the ability to accomplish God's will for their marriage.

There is no area in which God's power needs to be more graphically demonstrated than in marriage. The problems and challenges involved in marriage should cause us to seek and apply the power of God.

A dynamic, loving marriage is a great witness to our families, friends, and coworkers of the truth of Scripture and the reality of the God we say we serve. Most couples really want their marriages to be fulfilling and joyful. They just don't know where to find the power to pull that off. Why not show them how it's done—and then point them to Christ when they ask how they can have a marriage like yours.

PRAY ABOUT IT

Since God made marriage, He can make it work. Claim that power for your marriage, beginning today.

THE IMPORTANCE OF OUR ATTITUDE

I have learned to be content in whatever circumstances I am.

—PHILIPPIANS 4:11

〜〜〜〜〜

Many of the struggles that we have as husbands and wives are tied directly to our attitudes, and sometimes we don't even realize this source of a problem.

Because of our attitudes we react to things in a particular way that may not necessarily be Christian or godly.

You probably have heard people say, "That's just the way I am." Perhaps you have said this yourself. We get set in our ways and things have to be a certain way, or we develop an attitude.

Over the years, Tony has told countless numbers of sermon illustrations about me. That's part of being a pastor's wife! Tony has pointed out one particular trait I have that I have to admit to, and that is being obsessive compulsive. Things have to be done a particular way at a particular time, or my attitude does a flip. I have a feeling I am not the only person who is like this!

For us obsessive-compulsive people, learning to have a proper attitude when things aren't going our way is an adjustment that requires the daily help of the Holy Spirit. Because we were born into a certain environment and were raised to do things in a certain way that we thought was the gospel truth, as Christians we have to work to adjust to whatever circumstances we find ourselves in. That requires a growth process, but the apostle Paul reminded us that it can be done.

Bring two people together who were raised in different backgrounds with different mind-sets, and it is easy to see why marriage requires such a great adjustment in our attitudes. Each partner brings a set of expectations and needs into a marriage. We naturally want to get our desired goals accomplished, get our needs met, and receive the attention we need.

But God wants us to react supernaturally, not naturally. He wants us to develop biblical attitudes. And with His help, we can do it.—LOIS

PRAY ABOUT IT

Ask God to do an "attitude adjustment" in your heart today. Remember, you can do all things through Him who strengthens you (see Phil. 4:13).

WHEN ALL ELSE FAILS . . .

Be subject to one another in the fear of Christ.

—EPHESIANS 5:21

❦

Would it surprise you to learn that many married people don't know how to be married? What I mean is that they have never taken the time to study God's instruction manual on marriage. The Bible provides clear guidelines for making good, stable marriages, but too many couples are looking for help in all the wrong places.

I'm afraid a lot of people subscribe to the popular version of love and marriage, which says that two people can know they are truly in love when they feel chills, thrills, and butterflies in their stomachs. With eyes only for each other, the infatuated pair promises undying love and rushes to the altar.

But marriage doesn't work like that. The longer they are married, the more some couples act like they were married by the secretary of war instead of the justice of the peace!

A well-known illustration tells of the way marriages can deteriorate over the years. The comments are those of a husband whose wife has caught a cold during the successive years of their marriage. As a newlywed, he says, "Sugar dumpling, this cold is making you mighty uncomfortable. Won't you let your lover boy take his baby to the doctor to get rid of that nasty cough?" As time goes on, his patience—and his focus on his wife's comfort—gradually shift until, by the seventh year, he responds to his wife's cough by complaining, "Woman, do something about that cold before you give me pneumonia!"

A humorous story, but it makes a serious point. If we're not careful, we can move from concern for our spouse to concern for ourselves.

Things don't have to fall apart after the honeymoon. Commit yourselves to spend time each day in God's Word together. Open the "instruction manual" and find out how this beautiful thing called marriage is supposed to work.

PRAY ABOUT IT
Today, ask God to restore that newlywed sense of excitement to your marriage.

HOW TO HAVE A "MISSIONARY MARRIAGE"

This mystery is great; but I am speaking with reference to Christ and the church.

—EPHESIANS 5:32

In Genesis 2 we find a detailed account of God's creation of man and woman, and of marriage. In these creation events God provided a model of things to come, because later the Bible describes marriage as an illustration of Christ's union with the church.

Knowing that our marriage is a model of the eternal union of the believer and Christ gives us a very special reason for improving the *quality* of our marriages.

Everyone agrees that a good marriage is more pleasant and beneficial than an unhappy one. But equally important, your marriage may be the tool the Holy Spirit uses to win someone to Christ.

On the other hand, your marriage may cause another person to turn away from God's offer of salvation.

That in itself should be reason enough for us to learn to be godly mates and live the abundant life in the context of a growing, Christ-centered marriage. We never know exactly who may be watching our lives. But we know that many unbelievers keep a close eye on Christians, trying to decide whether these followers of Jesus have anything going for themselves that's worth finding out about.

You've probably heard about "missionary dating," the idea that a Christian can date a non-Christian to win him or her to Christ. That rarely works, but "missionary marriage" does!

Make your marriage a brightly burning light for Christ, and somebody else will be drawn to the flame.

TALK ABOUT IT

On a scale of one to ten, is your marriage a one (cold and dark) or a ten (bright and glowing)?

GET A JOB

The LORD God took the man and put him into the Garden of Eden to cultivate it and to keep it.

—GENESIS 2:15

⟨ornament⟩

The opening chapters of the Book of Genesis give us a lot of information about what God had in mind when He created marriage. God had a definite job in mind for Adam when He created him. The first man was to tend and cultivate the Garden of Eden, a pleasant job in a fertile garden where there were no weeds, no destructive insects, and no droughts.

Now, we need to point out that Adam was still single at this juncture. Adam had to learn how to work and be productive before God gave him a helper. Adam had to learn how to handle responsibility in the workplace before he was ready for the responsibility of marriage and a family.

Do you see a pattern unfolding here? It's clear from the order in which the events of Genesis 2 took place that God wants a husband to work and be responsible, to be the provider for his wife and family.

This pattern stayed pretty simple and straightforward in the agricultural society of biblical times, in which husbands and fathers typically worked in the fields, close to home. Things have become a whole lot more complicated in our day as many women have taken a place in the work force and in some cases earn more money than their husbands.

But the biblical priority has not changed. God has still given the man the primary responsibility to provide for his family. In fact, Paul said in 1 Timothy 5:8 that a man who refuses to provide for his family is worse than an unbeliever.

When a Christian man makes his wife and family feel well cared for and protected, regardless of the size of his salary, he is reflecting God's care of His own and demonstrating that he is serious about being a husband and father who pleases God.

THINK ABOUT IT

God gave man his physical strength to use in working hard, serving, and protecting his wife, not to use in dominating her.

A SUITABLE HELPER

Then the LORD God said, "It is not good for the man to be alone; I will make him a helper suitable for him."

—GENESIS 2:18

A man boarded an airplane one day and noticed that the man seated next to him was wearing his wedding ring on his right hand. He couldn't contain his curiosity, so he asked the man, "Aren't you wearing your wedding ring on the wrong hand?"

"No," came the reply. "I married the wrong woman."

There are certainly some men (and women) who feel that way about their spouses. As one man said, "I thought my marriage would be ideal. But now it's become an ordeal, and I want a new deal."

One of the most important things a husband must learn is how to cherish his wife as the helper God created her to be. God made Eve to correspond perfectly to Adam, to complement and complete him.

The word *helper* means "one who is brought alongside to assist." Throughout the Bible, women were given one basic responsibility: to help. But when Adam and Eve fell, marriage fell with them. From that point on, the roles of husband and wife would be complicated by our sinfulness.

One result of the fall is that instead of being helpers in the home many women have been forced to become mother, father, and breadwinner because no husband is present. But in a home where the husband is committed to love and to lead, his wife is free to become a helper. And when that happens, a husband has the best friend he can ever have.

I want to challenge you, my Christian brother, to become the head of your home as God intended and to free your wife to be the helper she was made to be. Get those basic roles in place, and the two of you will become an unstoppable team for the Lord!

TALK ABOUT IT

In what ways are you helping and encouraging each other to fulfill your God-given roles? Are there areas in which you may be hindering each other? What can you do to address these needs?

A HUSBAND'S GREATEST NEED

Let the wife see to it that she respect her husband.

—EPHESIANS 5:33

---

*D*id you know that God never *commanded* wives to love their husbands? Certainly, God does *expect* wives to love their husbands. But His basic command is for wives to *respect* their husbands.

There's no denying that men have strong egos. Therefore, they have a great need for recognition. Just as women have a need to be loved, men have a need to be respected. That is why Peter told wives not to use their tongues to turn disobedient husbands around but rather to use reverence (see 1 Pet. 3:1–2).

When a man's wife gives him respect, he is more likely to return that respect with the love and security she seeks. The greatest thing a wife can do for her husband is to follow the example of the matriarch Sarah, who, according to Peter, called Abraham "lord," recognizing his position as head of the home and as a demonstration of sincere respect (see 1 Pet. 3:6).

In fact, God honored Sarah so much that He gave her a child when she was ninety years old. Now that's a real miracle—and God will honor your submission as well.

Respect is particularly needed by men who have grown up being disrespected. Many men don't receive respect at their jobs or in the culture, where they are still looked at as inferior no matter what their age. So there needs to be a place where they know they are respected. That place should be the home.

Demonstrating this kind of respect involves submission on a wife's part. I know this is an unpopular word. But in the Bible, submission is a positive force to accomplish good, not a technique to diminish the status or value of women. The word means to place oneself under the authority of another.

Again, we are talking about a husband and wife fulfilling God's desire for their marriage. When a wife gets lined up under God by respecting her husband, it clears the way for God to work on her husband and file down his rough spots. And God can do a better job!

PRAY ABOUT IT

For the wife: Pray that God will help you respect your husband and submit to his leadership. For the husband: Ask God to make you a man who is worthy of his wife's respect.

WHAT MAKES A MAN?

The LORD God commanded the man, saying, "From any tree of the garden you may eat freely; but from the tree of the knowledge of good and evil you shall not eat."

—GENESIS 2:16–17

W hen God called Adam on the carpet for his sin, Adam tried to pin the blame on God Himself. Adam said, "It was the woman You gave me who caused this mess" (see Gen. 3:6).

But God wasn't buying that attempt to pass the buck. Adam knew exactly what God had commanded concerning the forbidden fruit. The conversation God had with Adam points out a weakness in many homes today. Too many Christian husbands don't really know what God has said about their responsibility to their wives, to their children, and to God Himself.

This is often a problem of male identity that can begin even before marriage. That is, men in our culture tend to draw their identity not from God's Word but from either their friends, their coworkers, the athletes they admire, or the images they see on television.

But since these are usually distortions of biblical manhood, a man who takes his manhood cues from the culture is headed for problems. You can tell when a man has this problem, because he finds his identity in clothes, cars, cash, or romantic conquests.

God's definition of manhood is in direct conflict with the cultural idea of what makes a man. Biblical manhood is the ability to put divine truth into action at home and on the job. No amount of strength, good looks, or liquid assets can improve a man's performance from God's perspective.

But before a man can put biblical truth into action, he has to *know* the truth. Husband, if God is going to hold you accountable for what happens in your marriage and your home, you'd better get into the Book and find out what God has said. Then teach it to your family. You'll never have any greater joy than leading your wife and children in the discovery of, and obedience to, God's revealed Word.

TALK ABOUT IT

When is your best time for family devotions? Take advantage of the family's regular routines to build in time for Bible reading and prayer.

THE PERFECT EXAMPLE OF SUBMISSION

Being found in appearance as a man, [Jesus] humbled Himself by becoming obedient to the point of death, even death on a cross.

—PHILIPPIANS 2:8

s a Christian woman and wife, I draw a great deal of encouragement and strength from the example of my mother. She had a lot of struggles to overcome as she reared eight children while putting a lot of her dreams and goals on hold. She submitted to God's will for her life. What a role model! Philippians 2:5–11 tells us that Jesus was and is God Himself, equal in essence with the Father. But to accomplish our salvation, Jesus voluntarily laid aside the independent use of His deity and placed Himself under the authority of His Father.

Jesus joyfully submitted to the Father's will, even though it meant going to the cross and suffering the most humiliating and painful kind of death. When I think of our Lord hanging on the cross for our sins, I realize that the submission He asks of me is not only possible for me to do but can be done with joy.

So when it comes to submission, I have the examples of Jesus Himself and of my mother. Jesus is not asking me to do anything He did not do or that I have not seen modeled (see Matt. 28:20). In addition, it helps me to remember that submission in marriage is not just a one-sided relationship. As the leader in our home, Tony is called to submit to Christ (see 1 Cor. 11:3). A wife may say, "I know what the Bible teaches about the wife's submission. But my husband isn't keeping up his part of the bargain by loving me as Christ loves the church."

There is no denying that this problem makes godly submission more difficult. But the Bible says we Christian wives are to submit to our husbands "as to the Lord" (Eph. 5:22; see also 1 Pet. 3:1–6). I can submit to Christ without reservation, and I can trust Him to honor my submission to Tony.

Some women fear that if they practice submission, they will never accomplish anything on their own. But submission does not mean a woman ceases to use the gifts God has given her. Instead, it involves using those gifts alongside, or in concert with, her husband to accomplish God's agenda for her marriage and family.—LOIS

PRAY ABOUT IT
Both husband and wife can pray that they will reflect the attitude of Jesus Christ toward each other.

CELEBRATE THE DIFFERENCE

She shall be called Woman, because she was taken out of Man.

—GENESIS 2:23

One of the most frequent comments I hear in marital counseling is this complaint from a couple that isn't getting along: "We are not compatible. We are as different as night and day."

In light of God's design for marriage, this is one of the most uninformed statements a husband or wife can make. Of course the two are different. God planned them to be different. The reason a husband and wife need each other is because they are different.

One of the sweetest blessings God has given me is a woman who has a personality totally different from mine. I'm an outgoing, exuberant, public personality while Lois is poised and serene.

Because we have contrasting personalities, when I'm too outgoing, her reserve pulls me back. And when she is too reserved, my enthusiasm pulls her forward. Occasionally this causes friction, but those are minor distractions. Our goal remains to make our God-given differences work for us instead of against us, to be enhanced by our differences, both personally and in the ministry.

When God brought Eve to Adam, he recognized immediately how distinctly different she was from him—and he was excited about those differences. Adam also knew that Eve was part of him; she made him complete and drove his loneliness away.

Adam called Eve "bone of my bones, and flesh of my flesh" (Gen. 2:23). She was his helpmate and completer. Theirs was truly a match made in heaven!

Now, it's true that the presence of sin has clouded this understanding. However, if we would look for what God is trying to teach us through the mate He has given us, we would be growing instead of griping.—TONY

THINK ABOUT IT

It's a good thing you are very different as husband and wife. If you were both the same, one of you would be unnecessary!

OOOOWEEE!

The LORD God fashioned into a woman the rib which He had taken from the man, and brought her to the man.

❧

*I*n order to prepare the first man for marriage, God began to teach Adam that he needed something he didn't have. God did it by putting Adam to work naming the animals. Before long, Adam noticed that for every ram there was a ewe, and for every rooster there was a hen. For all of the animals there were corresponding mates, but there was no one to fulfill Adam's needs.

So as Adam named species after species of animal, he began to experience the need for a partner. Then the Lord put Adam to sleep, opened his side, removed a rib, closed up the flesh, and made a woman from the rib.

Then, having created Eve, God brought her to Adam. When Adam awoke and saw God's choice for him, he said words that are literally translated, "This is now."

That seems like a strange thing to say until we understand that the spirit behind Adam's declaration is joyous astonishment. This phrase could be translated, "Ooooweee!" Here was the solution to Adam's need.

There are some tremendously important lessons here for us as husbands. My Christian brother, that woman God gave you is not just a nice addition to your life. You *need* her, and she has a right to supersede all other loves and relationships in your life except your love for Christ.

Another lesson is that manhood is not the ability to make it alone. God planned for a man to be made complete through marriage to a specific woman. Lifetime faithfulness, dedicating yourself in marriage to one woman, is more than a prerequisite for marital survival. It is essential to your growth and development as a man.

From the moment God created woman, Adam had a rib missing, and Eve had the rib that belonged to Adam. Marriage gave Adam back what he had lost and gave Eve what she had not possessed. In God's perfect plan, they made each other complete.—TONY

THINK ABOUT IT

Genuine manhood is the ability to see your need for a specific helper to complete you, not to compete with you, and to commit yourself to her alone.

A WOMAN'S EMOTIONAL "WIRING"

Be kind to one another, tender-hearted, forgiving each other.

—EPHESIANS 4:32

❧

God made a woman to be a responder. He made her a little softer, a little warmer, a little more intricately fashioned. In other words, when a husband demonstrates toward his wife the exclusive, self-sacrificing love the Bible talks about, she will respond to that love. As a result, the very thing a husband wants, he receives by giving and serving, not by demanding.

God does not want a wife to love her husband and respond to him because he demands it. God wants a wife to respond because a husband overloads her emotional circuits with loving care, because he wears her out with love and attention.

I tell many men who come to me for marital counseling, "Stop pushing so hard and start loving a little more. Stop complaining so much and start loving a little harder."

A husband may say, "I'm trying. Why isn't my wife responding?" It has to do with the different emotional "wiring" of men and women. A man can become angry with his wife at ten o'clock and be ready to kiss and make up by ten thirty.

On the other hand, if a woman becomes angry with her husband at ten in the morning, she may still be angry at ten that night. And sometimes, she's still mad at ten the night after that! Her emotions take much longer to stabilize.

A husband can shorten that recovery time significantly if he learns how to love with or without response, no matter how difficult the process.

For many husbands, loving like this will require an apology and a new start, perhaps saying, "I haven't loved you the way I am supposed to love you, and I know it has affected our relationship. But I'm going to change. I'm going to love you deeply the way you need to be loved."

Whether this means a new commitment for a husband or the continuation of a commitment already made, it is worth making.

TALK ABOUT IT

A man has truly come to understand what genuine love is . . . if he can love even when he doesn't feel like loving.

GET EXCITED ABOUT OPPOSITION!

Consider it all joy, my brethren, when you encounter various trials, knowing that the testing of your faith produces endurance.

I enjoy a good game of basketball. I'm unstoppable . . . when I play alone. When there is no opposition, I can make any play and hit any shot. But some years ago, I had an opportunity to go one-on-one with a star member of the Dallas Mavericks basketball team. Suddenly, I wasn't playing so well!

My basketball ability isn't tested when I play without opposition. The test is how good I am when I go up to shoot and find six-and-a-half-feet worth of opposition staring me in the face.

But that's the way the game of basketball is designed to be played. Having to face strong opposition and having to learn how to cooperate with teammates to overcome that opposition should make me a better player, not a poorer one.

That's the way it is with marriage. Life's trials are not designed to destroy your union. On the contrary, it's in learning how to face and overcome opposition and tough times together that you and your mate grow closer to each other and to God. Until you face opposition as a couple, you will never really know how strong your marriage is.

Sure, the enemy will take aim at your marriage. Did you ever notice that Satan didn't bother Adam before Eve was created? As long as Adam was single, Satan left him alone. But as soon as Adam was united with Eve, the attack was launched.

Why? Because Satan's long-term goal is to destroy the family, not just the individual. That's why his attacks are focused on the husband-wife relationship, because by destroying that he can get the family as well.

But God has a wonderful way of turning Satan's attacks into faith-building trials. So the next time you and your spouse bump into opposition, get excited. God is about to grow your marriage!—TONY

THINK ABOUT IT
A little girl once asked her grandmother why her wedding ring was so thick. The grandmother replied, "That's because when I got married, marriages were made to last."

13

STAYING OUT OF DEBT

Know well the condition of your flocks, and pay attention to your herds.
—PROVERBS 27:23

When the Bible tells us not to go into debt, that does not mean we are never to have any financial obligations. It doesn't mean that we can never borrow money for a house or something we need.

Having bills is not how the Bible defines debt. Instead, debt is the inability to pay the financial obligations we have made. It is being in such financial bondage that we are hampered in our ability to use our resources in a way that honors God and supports His work.

Part of being on top of your finances is understanding how easy it is to fall into the debt trap. People fall into debt for one or more of four basic reasons:

1. They are ignorant of God's principles of finance. They don't know what God has said about money and debt, so they don't know how to put His Word into practice. As a result they wind up doing what everybody else is doing, and they fall into financial bondage.

2. They have given in to self-indulgence, impulse spending, and a desire to have more no matter what the cost. The Bible calls these things *greed*, which leads to unwise decisions.

3. They have practiced poor planning. It's amazing how many couples I talk to who have no answer when I ask them to tell me about their financial plan for living within their budget and staying out of debt. And when people don't plan, they plan to fail.

4. They are the victims of a financial catastrophe. This is one area they may not be able to help, something that is beyond their control.

Are you in debt right now? Identifying the cause of your debt is the first step toward doing something about it.—TONY

PRAY ABOUT IT

The next time you face a major purchase, promise each other that you will pray about it for twenty-four hours before buying.

YOU CAN RESTORE THE LUSTER

Remember therefore from where you have fallen, and repent and do the deeds you did at first.

—REVELATION 2:5

❧

Couples sometimes ask me if lackluster marriages can be revived. The answer is a resounding *yes!* As long as both of you are still breathing, there is real hope. The formula for restoring a marriage is the same formula Jesus Christ gave to the church for restoring the passion of its initial love for Him.

That formula came in Christ's words to the church at Ephesus, which had been reduced to loveless rituals. Christ offered the members a way to revive their first love: remember, repent, and return. The same principles can revive a marriage.

First, a couple needs to *remember,* to reflect on the early days of their marriage when each season of love was sweet and when love ruled their lives.

Husband, do you remember how you used to open the car door for your sweetheart? Now she's lucky to get into the car before you drive off! How about your conversation? You could talk to her for hours when you were dating. Now you grunt a few words over the newspaper or the blaring TV.

Wife, do you remember how much you enjoyed cooking your husband's favorite meals? Now he's liable to get anything that's quick and easy. You used to compliment him and build him up. Now he hears mostly about his shortcomings.

If you remember how your relationship was, you'll know it can be that way again.

Second, the formula calls for *repentance.* To confess that you are wrong is tough, especially when words are not enough. To repent means to change direction. In this case, the right direction is probably toward the early stage of your marriage, when your relationship with one another took precedence over your careers, your friends, and even your own interests.

Finally, a couple needs to *return* to the "works" they did at first. That means recapturing something of that earlier relationship. You can't return to the past, but you can bring the works of the past into the present and the future simply by redoing them in a consistent, loving fashion.—TONY

PRAY ABOUT IT

Offer this prayer to the Lord today: "Dear God, help my marriage to regain its first love—and begin the process of restoration with me."

POSTING A GUARD

The peace of God, which surpasses all comprehension, shall guard your hearts and your minds in Christ Jesus.

—PHILIPPIANS 4:7

*I*n his classic book *True Spirituality,* the late Francis Schaeffer said that the true spiritual battle and the loss of victory are always in the thought world. When I am plagued by negative, destructive thoughts, I work at replacing them with positive, uplifting ones. This is not always easy to do, especially for people who have established a pattern of pessimism, but it is possible. *All* things are possible with God.

As a wife and mother, I have found several great antidotes for gloomy thoughts in my home. Sharing Tony's life and ministry helps me keep my mind and heart centered on the good things God is doing in our lives. Another cure is spending uninterrupted time in Bible study. Store God's Word in your heart and mind through reading, memorizing, and quoting Scripture such as Jeremiah 29:11, Romans 8:28, and Philippians 4:6,13.

Another way to combat negative thoughts is to develop a regular meeting time with a prayer partner so you can encourage one another. Finally, be careful not to overwork or overschedule yourself. There needs to be a balance.

The wonderful thing to me about the fourth chapter of Philippians is that it shows how the changing circumstances of Paul's life did not affect the inner contentment he enjoyed. What Paul possessed was not self-sufficiency but divine sufficiency, a calm acceptance of life's pressures. He had allowed the peace of Christ to do "sentry duty" around his heart and mind.

Our thoughts are like measles—they're catching. What type of thoughts and attitudes are your spouse and children catching from you?—LOIS

TALK ABOUT IT

What is the atmosphere of your marriage and home? Is it dark and gloomy or positive and Christ-centered?

PICKING UP THAT ROCK

*Ask, and it shall be given to you; seek, and you shall find; knock,
and it shall be opened to you.*

—MATTHEW 7:7

O ne day a little boy was trying to pick up a rock, but he couldn't budge it. His father was watching the boy struggle, so he decided this was a good time for a lesson. "Son, pick up the rock."

"I can't, Dad," the boy replied. "It's too heavy."

But his father insisted, "Sure you can, son. Pick up the rock."

So the boy grabbed the rock, puffing and straining, but he couldn't pick it up. "It's too heavy, Dad."

"Son, the reason you can't pick up the rock is because you're not using all your strength." This really puzzled the boy. He answered in frustration, "But Daddy, I *am* using all my strength!"

"No, you're not," came the reply. "You haven't asked me to help you." And with that, the father leaned over and picked up the rock.

I think I know where that same rock is, because I've tried to pick it up a few times myself! How about you? Are you huffing and puffing, grunting and groaning in frustration, trying to move a boulder in your life when Jesus is sitting there saying, "You haven't asked Me to help yet"?

Why do we struggle so much when God is waiting to manifest His power in our lives? Why does it take some of us so long to learn that God is able to do far beyond anything we can ask or imagine? I think the answer lies in Ephesians 3:20. Paul says God is able, but notice that it's "according to the power that works within us." If there is nothing happening inside of us, we can't call for God to help with the mess on the outside. Our problem so often is that we have spent too little time in the presence of God—getting to know Him, seeking His face, grasping His greatness. And little time in God's presence produces little power in our lives. Much time in His presence produces much power. It's really that simple.—TONY

PRAY ABOUT IT

The disciples said, "Lord, teach us to pray" (Luke 11:1). Many people want to pray but never plan to pray. Don't just talk about asking, seeking, and knocking. Do it!

ADDING A POSITIVE TO YOUR NEGATIVE

Words from the mouth of a wise man are gracious.

—ECCLESIASTES 10:12

I don't like negativism. I don't like to be around negative people, because their attitudes might rub off on me. Now don't get me wrong. I didn't say I try to keep away from everything negative. If there's a need or a complaint, I want to face it and get it resolved. But there's a difference between a person who has something negative to bring up and being a negative person.

A negative person is someone who only sees what's wrong, not what's right. And negative people typically never have a solution to the problem they are upset about. They just know they're never happy—and they don't know what anyone can do to help them be happy. That's the disease of negativism.

Let me give you an example of the difference between pointing out and fixing a problem, and simply dwelling on the negative.

In Ephesians 4:25–32, Paul told the liars, thieves, and bad-mouthers among these believers to quit lying, stealing, and tearing people down with their words. But Paul also offered solutions: work for your money, speak the truth, and make sure your words are healing, not damaging.

Negativism is lethal, especially in a marriage. If all a mate hears is what's wrong, what doesn't work, and why nothing ever looks good, the negative partner is mixing up a recipe for trouble.

My brother, when you come home at night after you and your wife have worked all day, don't come in as if the king has arrived and everything is supposed to stop. Take note of what needs to be done and help get it done.

For instance, there's a world of difference between these two questions: "When will dinner be ready?" and "How can I help get dinner ready?" Things like this can have a tremendous impact on the emotional climate in the house. A positive spirit says, "Here's the problem, and here's how I want to help us solve it."—TONY

THINK ABOUT IT

Promise yourself that you won't offer a criticism until you can also communicate a way of solving it.

TILL DEBT DO US PART

Godliness actually is a means of great gain, when accompanied by contentment.

—I TIMOTHY 6:6

---

oes this scenario sound familiar to you? A newlywed couple sets off to establish their life together. They may bring car payments, a little college debt, and some wedding bills into the marriage, but everything looks to be under control. Then they buy a house, a purchase that takes them right to the edge of their financial capability. But they're both young and energetic, so they are willing to work hard to pay for it.

But then the wife decides she can't live in an unfurnished house. They need furniture, even though they can barely afford the house payment. So they take the plunge for furniture, and now they're in well over their heads financially. It's a good thing they both have good jobs.

But after a while, the wife discovers she's pregnant. That brings on a whole new round of bills, so her husband starts working more to pay for the things they need for the baby, plus the house and the furniture. However, that means he's coming home later and spending less time with his wife just when she needs him the most. So she gets mad . . .

Well, you get the idea. The pressure of debt is squeezing many marriages today, and the results can be disastrous. Someone has said that when it comes to money, there are three categories of people: the "haves," the "have nots," and the "have not paid for what they have."

I'd like to suggest a fourth category: "content with what they have." The Bible teaches that taking on more financial obligations than you can handle is a sign that something is wrong spiritually.

Money is tainted: 'taint mine, 'taint yours. Everything we have belongs to God. He has promised to meet our needs. Until we can be content with His provision, debt will continue to be a noose around the neck of our marriages.

Is debt a problem in your house? Start getting a handle on it today. Ask God to give you contentment. He will!

TALK ABOUT IT
Don't let money ruin your marriage!

IT'S A MATTER OF HONOR

Offer to God a sacrifice of thanksgiving, and pay your vows to the Most High.

—PSALM 50:14

⁂

Lois and I made a basic commitment when we got married and established our home, and God has enabled us to honor this vow we made to Him. The rule we agreed on is this: At no time would any money come into our home for which God did not get the minimum tithe of 10 percent—and He would get His portion first.

Today's verse is a powerful reminder that God is the source of our blessings and that we owe our thanks to Him for what we have.

What happens when we honor God? Here's the promise God makes in Psalm 50:15: "Call upon Me in the day of trouble; I shall rescue you, and you will honor Me." When you honor God, when you make His glory and His work your priority, He becomes your greatest helper in your time of need, whether it's a financial crisis or a spiritual need.

"If you give Me what's Mine," God says, "then when you call upon Me about a problem with what is yours, because you brought Me into the equation by honoring Me, I will hear you when you have need of Me."

Now, I'm not talking about making a deal in which you say, "OK, God, I'll give Your portion to You, and You fill my bank account." God doesn't make deals, but He does honor those who honor Him.

You and your spouse may say, "We trust God." That's great. But remember, trusting God involves taking a step of faith. A farmer cannot say, "I trust that I'm going to have a good harvest" and then never plant any seed. Neither can a Christian say, "I trust God to supply my needs" and then never give to Him. Honor God and watch Him work.—TONY

THINK ABOUT IT

Prove God's faithfulness in your life. Make a vow to honor Him first with your finances.

BELIEVING THE WRONG MESSAGE

The wicked borrows and does not pay back.

—PSALM 37:21

***

*A*s far as the Bible is concerned, debt is a spiritual issue before it is a financial issue. It is a violation of God's Word to take on debts that we do not take proper responsibility for—not only repaying the obligation, but repaying it in a timely way. How we handle our money is a matter of our character, not just our checkbook.

Ecclesiastes 5:5 says it is better not to take a vow than to take a vow and not pay it. That principle has a direct application to our finances.

Why do so many Christian couples get themselves into debts they can't repay? I think it's a problem of believing the wrong messages. See, everybody out there has a marketing plan to sell you his or her product. These people want to convince you that you deserve, want to have, and ought to have what they are selling.

But God's Word tells us not to take on obligations we can't meet from the resources He has given us. So the question is, whom are you and your mate going to believe?

My encouragement to you is to believe God when He says He knows your needs before you even ask Him and that He will supply.

It's true that God may permit a catastrophe to come into your life, something that throws your finances for a real setback. But even in these situations, God is still working His sovereign plan for you.

The problem for most of us is that we create our own financial catastrophes because we believe the wrong messages.

So I want to ask you again, whom are you going to believe?—TONY

PRAY ABOUT IT

We can pray like the father whose boy needed healing. He said to Jesus, "I do believe. Help my unbelief!" (Mark 9:24).

HE'S STRONG WHEN I AM WEAK

[Jesus] has said to me, "My grace is sufficient for you, for power is perfected in weakness."
—2 CORINTHIANS 12:9

*Y*our attitude impacts your whole lifestyle. It determines your perspective on life, and it also affects others. You can influence other people either toward a more fulfilling Christian experience or toward a crippling one. Your attitude determines how you deal with the challenges or problems God sends your way—or whether you even try.

I remember one occasion when God taught me this lesson. A dear Christian sister called me and very graciously asked me to speak to her group.

I accepted the speaking engagement. And further, I made up my mind that I was not simply going to speak on a subject I had already studied and had in my file drawer. I was going to stretch out and prepare something new.

But when the time came to prepare, I started talking to myself. *You know, you didn't have to accept this engagement. You can't do this. You don't have a thing to say on that subject.*

Did I ever develop an attitude! I not only talked to myself, I began to *answer* myself. *You're right; you can't do this. You don't have the time. Ask your friend who speaks all the time to come and take your place.*

This was my struggle. I knew my thinking had to change. So I told Satan no and told the Lord, "Yes, in Your power I am going to give this preparation all the gusto I have."

My attitude of fear and uncertainty and doubt only began to change when I realized the Lord had given me this ministry opportunity and with His help I had better get started. As I began to study my subject, God gave me a message and the power to deliver it when the time came.—LOIS

THINK ABOUT IT

A popular chorus reminds us that God's strength is perfect when we are out of strength ourselves. God wants us to turn to Him in our weakness because only then do we discover His perfect strength.

WHAT'S YOUR PLAN?

A certain nobleman went to a distant country . . . and he called ten of his slaves, and gave them ten minas, and said to them, "Do business with this until I come back."

—LUKE 19:12–13

*O*ne of the most obvious yet most often overlooked ways to practice good financial stewardship is to know where your money is going and have a plan to cover your needs.

We call this plan a budget, and it's essential to the proper management of the resources God entrusts to us. Most married couples don't plan to get into financial trouble. They just don't have a plan *not* to get into trouble.

The main point of the parable Jesus told in Luke 19:11–27 is about doing kingdom business with the king's resources, how we should manage our God-given gifts and abilities, including the money God allows us to have.

Read the entire parable, and you'll see that when the nobleman returned, he had words of praise for the servants who had a plan of their own and put his money to good use. The only servant rebuked by the nobleman was the one who had no plan. He simply hid the money away in a handkerchief.

One of the reasons we get into financial messes as couples and families is that we have failed to put a God-honoring plan in place to manage our money. The world has set our financial agenda, so God is not able to bless us according to His principles.

If you follow everyone else's way of handling your money, then don't be surprised if you wind up in the same mess everyone else is in. The Bible says that one of the ways you know things aren't going right in your finances is when you are in bondage to the bank or to some other lender.

Having a budget that includes your giving to the Lord is a great way to stay out of the debt trap.

TALK ABOUT IT

Do you know where your money is going each month? Budget your money yourself, before others budget it for you.

DON'T ROB GOD

"Bring the whole tithe into the storehouse, . . . and test Me now in this . . . ," says the LORD of hosts, "if I will not open for you the windows of heaven."

—MALACHI 3:10

⁂

*P*erhaps you heard the story about the man who fell deathly ill. He told his preacher, "Pastor, I'm dying. I want you to pray for me that I will get better. And if God does a miracle and I get better, I will give the church a hundred thousand dollars."

Well, that preacher went to work, praying that God would do a miracle for this sick man. And God raised him up from his sick bed. But week after week went by, then month after month, and the church did not receive a check from the man.

So the pastor went to the man's house and reminded him of his promise. "When you were sick, you said you would give the church a hundred thousand dollars if God made you well."

"I said that?" the man asked.

The pastor said, "Yes, you said that when you were sick."

The man shook his head and said, "Well, that shows you how sick I was."

A lot of people make all kinds of promises when they are in trouble or when they need something. But when it comes time to follow through on the promises, there is no action. The Bible calls that robbing God. Some believers have been robbing God month after month, year after year, and then they wonder why things aren't going too well for them financially.

Prayer alone won't help the couple who is robbing God. Having the pastor call won't do the job. Even the bank won't be able to help, because when you rob God, He puts holes in your pockets or purse. Even a raise or a promotion doesn't help because the washing machine is going to break down, the roof is going to leak, and the car is going to act up.

That's the bad news. But the good news is that if we will be faithful in giving God the firstfruits of our income, He will be freed up to bless us.

PRAY ABOUT IT
If you feel like you're putting your money in a bag with holes, ask God to show you how to sew up the holes.

WHAT DID YOU SAY?

Let your speech always be with grace, seasoned, as it were, with salt.

—COLOSSIANS 4:6

A good percentage of marital problems and breakdowns can be traced to the absence of good communication. This need shows up in a lot of ways, but people often see the symptoms instead of seeing the problem.

For instance, a husband may say, "My wife and I can't get along" when he means, "We can't communicate."

Or a wife may say, "We don't know how to be intimate with one another" without realizing that intimacy starts with communication, not with the physical act of sex.

You might say, "But we didn't have this kind of conflict when we were dating." Of course not. And do you know why? Because you were lying to each other when you were dating! You were covering up the negative stuff, trying to impress and win the other person.

Isn't it true that you weren't about to tell that sweet thing all the stuff that made you mad when you were dating? Tell the truth and shame the devil!

But when you two got married, you found out the real deal. And that jolt of reality can often lead to a jamming of the lines in marital communication. You talk past each other instead of to each other.

One of the greatest challenges and joys of marriage is learning to speak the language of love. Paul gave us a great way to practice; he said we should bathe our words in grace.

Are your words bathed in grace—or soaked in sarcasm?

THINK ABOUT IT

Marital communication is like dynamite. It can be used to build or to blast, to open a road or to block a path.

COMMUNICATION DOESN'T JUST HAPPEN

You are Christ's body, and individually members of it.

—I CORINTHIANS 12:27

⁘

*O*ne of the apostle Paul's favorite analogies for the Christian life was the human body. As believers in Jesus Christ, we are all members of His body. That means we are vitally connected to each other, the way the big toe is vitally connected to the brain. You learned that the night you stubbed your toe on the coffee table in the dark!

Good communication within the members of your body is vital to your health and even to your survival. Communication is also vital among the members of Christ's body.

Now think about your marriage. Jesus said that when a man and woman are joined in marriage, "they are no longer two, but one flesh" (Matt. 19:6). That means to survive and thrive, you need to communicate with each other.

Too many couples think good communication will just happen because they both have mouths that work and they speak the same language. But communication takes work, because a marriage brings together two different people with different personalities and a different set of experiences and assumptions.

Now the two of you are living together in the same house, and you are engaged in the exciting process of becoming one flesh. It's time to start connecting.

Let us talk to the man of the house for a minute. Do you know how you can improve your communication skills almost overnight? Work as hard to communicate with your wife now as you did when you were trying to win her.

Back then, you jumped to turn off the TV if she called and wanted to talk. You had no problem finding cards that said what was on your heart. The flowers and candy were frequent. You talked about your plans and dreams.

Why stop now? Turn off the ball game, look your wife in the eyes, and tell her you want to talk. When she gets up off the floor, you'll be on your way!

PRAY ABOUT IT

Husband, ask God to give you an unquenchable desire to communicate with your wife.

TELLING THE TRUTH

Speak truth, each one of you, with his neighbor, for we are members of one another.
—EPHESIANS 4:25

*I*f you want to improve the communication in your marriage and your family, here's a bedrock commitment you need to make: Tell the truth. Now when we talk about telling the truth, we don't mean saying everything that comes to your mind to everyone regardless of the consequences. That's not truth-telling in the biblical sense. That's just running off at the mouth!

Truth corresponds to reality. It's the right word spoken at the right time. It's what needs to be said when it needs to be heard.

That means telling the truth can be painful, but if so it's an infliction of pain that is intended to bring healing.

Whenever we hear a wife say, "I really can't tell my husband the truth. He doesn't want to hear it. He just shuts me out," we know there is a marriage in trouble.

Whenever we hear a husband say, "Every time I tell my wife the truth about something unpleasant, she blows a fuse or gives me the cold shoulder," we can mark that marriage down as a troubled one.

The Bible teaches that if we are going to have harmony and peace in our homes and individual lives, we must be people committed to the truth. We must also create an environment in our marriages and homes that is conducive for people to tell the truth. Parents sometimes almost invite their children to lie by threatening, "If this [whatever it is] ever happens, I'm going to lower the boom on you. You'll be grounded until you go to college!"

As a result, when "this" happens, the child makes up a story to cover the truth. Parents can help their children tell the truth by accompanying their rules with an attitude that they are willing to listen.

When couples and families practice the truth, good things happen. Lines of communication open up. And God brings blessing because He loves truth.

PRAY ABOUT IT

Pray that God will make your home a place where the truth is the first thing that comes out of your mouth.

HOW TO BE GOOD AND ANGRY

Be angry, and yet do not sin.

—EPHESIANS 4:26

⁂

Anger is not an illegitimate emotion. It's OK to be angry in the right way at the right time. We know that anger is a legitimate emotion because Paul makes a distinction between being angry and committing sin. Anger is the arousal of an internal displeasure because something or someone has displeased us. We're unhappy about what has been done or said, or left undone or unsaid, and we get angry.

If you ever get angry, you're in good company. God gets mad too. The Bible says God is angry at wicked people every day. When Jesus Christ went into the temple in Jerusalem and saw the merchants and moneychangers misusing God's house of worship He became so angry He made a whip and broke up the temple "flea market."

Anger is a normal human emotion. God built it into us so that when we see sin and wrong happening, we will be stirred to do something about it.

But when it is mishandled or expressed inappropriately, anger can become destructive and sinful. One way anger can become sin is when it moves to a plan to hurt the one who made you angry. At that point it is not just your internal emotion of upset or grief but an attitude that seeks revenge. A spirit of revenge is wrong for us because only God is qualified to judge a situation and perfectly exact punishment (see Rom. 12:19).

Anger also becomes sin when we attack the wrong thing. One man said, "When my wife and I have an argument, she gets historical."

His friend said, "Don't you mean hysterical?"

"No," the man said, "I mean historical. She goes back to the beginning and brings up everything I ever did."

Anger is only properly addressed when you're dealing with the problem that caused the anger.

THINK ABOUT IT
If you keep your anger boiling just under the surface of your life, it won't take much to make it erupt.

DON'T JUST GO TO BED MAD (DAY 1)

Do not let the sun go down on your anger.

—EPHESIANS 4:26

The Bible says that anger unleashed wrongfully is hard to overcome. According to Proverbs 18:19, "A brother offended is harder to be won than a strong city." How many times have you wished you could take back what you said or did?

Some people say, "I just explode, and then it's all over." Well, so does a shotgun. But when the smoke clears, a shotgun blast leaves some serious damage behind!

People who know it's wrong to explode may deal with their anger by stuffing it, suppressing it, pretending nothing is wrong, or letting it build up. But the Bible says there is an appropriate way to express and deal with anger. The key is to learn the proper timing.

Ephesians 4:26 gives us the parameters of that time to do something about anger, but Paul is not necessarily saying that no matter what happens in a day, we just need to kiss and make up and get it all over before we go to bed.

There are some conflicts that simply can't be resolved completely in one day. Paul wasn't necessarily telling us not to go to bed until the problem is fixed.

One man said, "The Bible says not to go to bed angry. My wife and I haven't been to sleep in three weeks."

That's not the idea. But neither is the answer to just go to bed mad. Instead, don't let the sun go down without addressing the issue. That may involve settling things if it's a marital spat or a child who doesn't like a rule. But if the problem is really serious, obeying the Bible may involve simply agreeing to deal with it tomorrow. The point is that the issue that caused the anger won't be ignored or swept under the rug. It's on the family agenda.

TALK ABOUT IT

Is there something that should be on your marital or family agenda for discussion and resolution? If so, don't just go to bed mad! Deal with it, now!

DON'T JUST GO TO BED MAD (DAY 2)

Do not give the devil an opportunity.

—EPHESIANS 4:27

Yesterday we talked about dealing with anger in a timely and appropriate way. Today we want to see the reasons we need to take action rather than letting the anger build up.

One reason for dealing with our anger is that the Bible commands us to do so. It's an issue of obedience.

Another reason is that harboring anger doesn't get us anywhere. When you and your spouse or you and your children go to bed without resolving the problem—or at least agreeing to address the problem—this thing grows overnight. So the next day, you wake up with the same stuff to face, only now it's grown to twice its size.

Here's another reason for not going to bed mad: When you do, you invite the devil to jump right into the middle of the situation. You are giving him an access he shouldn't have into your heart and mind, and while you're sleeping he's in your subconscious mind building a workshop.

If you are a believer in Jesus Christ, Satan cannot touch you in terms of your eternal destiny. You are secure in Christ. But he sure can mess up your daily walk with God, your marriage, and your family when you give him an opening into your heart through unresolved anger.

The problem is that Satan is never satisfied with just a little corner of your life. Once he secures a foothold he starts building a fortress (see 2 Cor. 10:4). Soon he multiplies your unresolved anger into all kinds of other problems.

The best way to prevent this is to shut the devil out before he gets a foot in the door. Resolve anger, and enjoy God's peace.

PRAY ABOUT IT

Tell God today that you want nothing to do with the works or the ways of the devil, and ask the Holy Spirit to help you keep anger from spoiling your marriage or family.

LEAVING, CLEAVING, BECOMING ONE FLESH (DAY 1)

For this cause a man shall leave his father and his mother, and shall cleave to his wife; and they shall become one flesh.

—GENESIS 2:24

꧁꧂

*Y*ou and I can't improve on God's idea for anything—and that goes double for marriage! For the next three days, we want to look at the beauty and simplicity of God's basic plan for marriage: leave, cleave, and become one. Notice the reason for the closeness of the marriage union. A man is to join himself totally to his wife "for this cause," because woman "was taken out of Man" (Gen. 2:23). Woman came from man's flesh, and a man and wife are to become one flesh again.

The tragedy today is that a lot of people have these words read at their weddings but they don't know all that is involved. In particular, too many young women who get married have not really left Mama emotionally.

And too many young men don't realize marriage means subjugating all their previous relationships. That includes not only relationships with Mama and Daddy but also with friends. A man who thinks that marriage won't change his activities and his hang-out time with all of his buddies doesn't understand what marriage is all about.

Ask yourselves: Is your mate a nice addition to your life, or is he or she your *life?*

Husbands, you must be willing to break with anything or anyone necessary to show your wife there is nothing more important to you than loving her and spending time with her. This is what God asks men to do because a husband and wife are one flesh, and because one of a woman's greatest needs in marriage is a sense of security.

A wife needs to know she's number one to her husband! When a man can make that commitment and keep it, he will begin to understand what marriage is all about.

THINK ABOUT IT

A secure wife is free to love and please her husband, motivating him to love her all the more!

LEAVING, CLEAVING, BECOMING ONE FLESH (DAY 2)

[A husband and wife] are no longer two, but one flesh.

—MATTHEW 19:6

W hen He pronounced the original wedding vows between Adam and Eve, God said that a man must leave his family and cleave to his wife so that they become one flesh (see Gen. 2:24). This instruction was addressed to men, but of course the leaving and cleaving in marriage go both ways.

Today we want to discuss the second part of God's instructions—what it means for a married couple to cleave to each other. The word *cleave* itself means to stick to something like glue or to attach oneself in a vise-like grip. It's a graphic picture of the union that is to take place between a husband and wife. But cleaving involves much more than a physical coupling of two bodies. It means a totality of union with a whole person.

If we are not careful, too often our "Let me love you" words to our spouses actually mean "Let me please me." We men are particularly vulnerable to this error.

Our culture teaches men to use women for their own pleasure. So it's easy for a man to bring that mind-set into marriage—where it is devastating. And of course, wives can become self-centered too. But that's the devil's plan, not God's. Cleaving to your spouse means you have made a total commitment to your partner—not only to his or her body, but also to heart, mind, and soul as well.

Husbands, to cleave to your wife means that you work hard at pleasing her, not yourself. She needs to know that nothing will ever cause you to pull away from her and tear apart that love relationship.

Wives, cleaving to your husband includes respecting and supporting him in his efforts to lead the marriage and the family. One of a man's greatest emotional needs is respect.

Cleaving is costly, but the reward is an intimacy of life that rivals anything on earth!

PRAY ABOUT IT

If you or your spouse are still "glued" to Mama, Daddy, or some other relationship, pray that God will apply His "solvent" and help you dissolve that tie!

LEAVING, CLEAVING, BECOMING ONE FLESH (DAY 3)

The wife does not have authority over her own body, but the husband does; and likewise also the husband does not have authority over his own body, but the wife does.

—1 CORINTHIANS 7:4

⁂

We don't know of any verse in the Bible that teaches more clearly the one-flesh relationship of marriage. In 1 Corinthians 7, Paul set down a fundamental principle of marriage for all believers: A husband and wife are no longer two bodies but one; so each partner has equal authority over the one body that makes up their marriage.

Today we are finishing up our brief look at God's formula for marriage: leave, cleave, become one flesh (see Gen. 2:24). These few words are easy to repeat, but putting this plan into action is a long-term process. It takes a lifetime to become totally "one flesh" in marriage. That is why marriage is "till death do us part."

Obviously, becoming one flesh in marriage includes sexual faithfulness. It also involves a sensitivity to your partner. Paul said, "No one ever hated his own flesh, but nourishes and cherishes it" (Eph. 5:29). Two people who are truly one flesh will be incredibly sensitive to each other's needs and desires.

This is why Paul said each member of a marriage has authority over the partner's body. A husband and wife are to meet each other's needs. The only exception, other than for some sort of physical reason, is for a definite, limited season of prayer that both partners agree to ahead of time (see 2 Cor. 7:5).

But becoming one flesh goes beyond the physical. We believe God has made the husband responsible to help his wife remove the blemishes in her life just as Jesus Christ loves and cleanses the church of which He is the Head (see Eph. 5:25–27). A man can only fulfill that important and demanding role in his marriage when he is truly one flesh and one spirit with his wife.

Go back to Genesis 2:24, and you'll see that when it comes to being one flesh, the pronoun God uses changes from "he" to "they." God promises to take two people and make them one when they do things His way.

THINK ABOUT IT

If a husband leaves and cleaves the way God intended, his wife will respond the way he (and God) wants her to respond.

CLIMATE CONTROL FOR YOUR MARRIAGE

Your wife shall be like a fruitful vine, within your house.

—PSALM 128:3

***

Today's verse give us a fascinating look at the responsive nature of women and how that nature affects the home. A man who "fears the LORD" and "walks in His ways" (vv. 1–2) will find his wife blossoming like a fruitful grapevine.

In a favorable climate, grapevines need no coaxing to grow. Given the right environment, they will grow and produce grapes from which wine (a drink symbolizing celebration and happiness in biblical times) is made.

But grapevines do need the right care and attention and even pruning to make them fully productive. It is much the same in marriage. The husband is responsible for creating a climate in which his wife can grow and flourish. He needs to be the climate-setter, and when he gets that temperature control set right, he can expect a joyful response from his wife. But to create the right climate, a husband must be at home enough to maintain an ideal temperature. The husband who is rarely at home frustrates his wife and damages her self-confidence. And when he is home, a husband must be ready to give his time and attention to his wife so he can know what she needs in order to grow and flourish.

The west wall of a house in which we once lived was covered with a vine. Each summer, the rain and sunlight caused that vine to grow with incredible speed. In no time at all, the vine had to be trimmed and then trimmed again. It delighted us with its exuberant growth because it was in the right place with just enough of everything it needed to grow.

So it is with a wife who finds her husband providing the right climate. She will delight her husband with her love, providing him with the joy he needs and desires. The better and more constant the climate, the better, faster, and more consistent the wife's growth will be. And as she grows and is fulfilled, her husband will benefit from her growth.

PRAY ABOUT IT

What's the temperature in your marriage? Ask God to help you put that thermostat on the right setting. If you want a summer wife, don't bring home winter weather.

LOVE YOURSELF, LOVE YOUR WIFE

Husbands ought also to love their own wives as their own bodies.

—EPHESIANS 5:28

⌘

The apostle Paul gave husbands an easy-to-understand guideline for providing the kind of nurturing love that wives need and deserve. Simply stated, a man should do for his wife those things that he would like to have done for himself. Most men don't slap their own bodies around, even when their bodies displease them. And when a man accidentally hurts himself—cutting himself while shaving, for example—he takes great care to stop the bleeding and ease his discomfort.

In the same way, if a man causes his wife emotional pain, he ought to tenderly treat her wound to the best of his ability. Apart from this kind of loving care that recognizes a wife's emotional makeup, Peter says that men's prayers will be hindered (see 1 Pet. 3:7). That is, God determines whether He will communicate with a husband based on that husband's willingness to treat his wife in a sensitive and loving way.

That's a potent reason to keep our marriages in good emotional shape. When we husbands cause our wives emotional pain, both of us suffer. It's not like a husband gets any benefit from failing to nurture his wife.

Paul adds another motivation in Ephesians 5 for husbands to care for their wives. We men are called to nurture and cherish our wives the way Christ does the church. And we know that Christ loved the church even when that love took Him to the cross.

Since a husband and wife are one in Christ, joined together by God, to be at odds with one another is to be in sin. And sin always breaks fellowship with God as well as fellowship between people.

But a husband can restore fellowship, and intimacy, in his marriage by treating his wife with the same kind of love he has received from Jesus Christ.

TALK ABOUT IT

One great way a husband can learn how his wife wants to be treated is to ask her. Most women are very capable of articulating their needs and desires.

AVOIDING THE SQUEEZE

Do not be conformed to this world, but be transformed by the renewing of your mind.

—ROMANS 12:2

---

*O*ur spiritual condition is changed in an instant when we receive Christ and become joint heirs with Him; at that point we become entitled to everything He has. However, we are still capable of sin after conversion. So regardless of how long we have been Christians, we need to be constantly aware of what goes into the computer system called our minds.

No doubt you're familiar with the computer term *gigo*. It stands for "garbage in, garbage out." In other words, if you put bad information into your mind, you will get bad information out of it. Bad actions and reactions follow naturally.

If movies, television, and magazines are programming your mind, that can be very dangerous. I am not saying there's anything wrong with keeping up with the news, watching a good movie, or reading a good magazine. The question is whether these things are impairing your ability to think for yourself and to think biblically. For us as women, if Madison Avenue is influencing the way we think, then our efforts will be concentrated on promoting our outer beauty rather than our inner beauty (see 1 Pet. 3:3–4).

This is not to condemn a woman's attempts to look attractive, since we are a reflection of His glory. And we have a great role model in the woman of Proverbs 31. But if we would immerse ourselves in the Word even half the time we spend decorating ourselves, we would definitely have God's attitude toward beauty as opposed to the world's attitude.

We need to reject the world's attempts to form us or manipulate us, both as individuals and as a married couple. We need to keep in mind that the things of this world are temporary while the things of God are eternal. We sometimes give far more value to this world than it deserves. Let's make sure our minds are not being squeezed into the world's mode of thinking.—LOIS

THINK ABOUT IT

If we want to have authentic outer beauty, then Christ has to be Lord of our inner experience. We must keep a watch on the gate to our soul, which is our mind. How we think on the inside will determine the attractiveness of our beauty on the outside.

THE KEY TO REAL POWER

A cord of three strands is not quickly torn apart.

—ECCLESIASTES 4:12

The Trinity is made up of three coequal Persons who are one in essence: God the Father, God the Son, and God the Holy Spirit. Christian marriage is designed to be an earthly, although admittedly imperfect, replica of the divine Trinity. It consists of three persons who are one: a man, a woman, and Jesus Christ.

It is Christ's resurrection power operating in the lives of a believing couple that gives them the ability to establish a loving marriage. Without Christ's presence at the center of a marriage, the other two people in the relationship are operating at a serious handicap.

But this incredible power is only available to people who have repented of their sin and trusted Christ as their Savior. Could it be that your marriage has not tasted of this power because one or the other of you, or perhaps both of you, have never received Christ as your Savior and Lord?

God sent His Son to earth to die on the cross as a substitute for your sin. Whenever men or women respond to Christ in faith, trusting Him alone as Savior, He not only forgives them but empowers them to live new lives. And when Christ makes you new, He includes your marriage in that new life.

Do you long for forgiveness, eternal life, and new power for daily living? You can have it if you believe Christ died for your sins, was buried, and rose from the dead on the third day (see 1 Cor. 15:3–4). When you give Him your life, you will experience life to the full. And you will have the potential—and the power—to experience marriage as God planned it.

God made marriage, and He can make it work. We challenge you to commit yourselves to the Lord. Let Him save you from sin and give you new life. And then allow Him to remake your marriage.

PRAY ABOUT IT

Admit to God that you are a sinner, ask His forgiveness, and tell Him you want to trust Jesus alone for your salvation.

HE IS ABUNDANTLY ABLE

Now to Him who is able to do exceeding abundantly beyond all that we ask or think, according to the power that works within us, to Him be the glory in the church.

—EPHESIANS 3:20–21

---

*D*o you get the idea that Paul believed God is able to do anything that may be needed in your life or marriage? This is one of the Bible's greatest statements of God's power. God is able—*abundantly able!* It doesn't matter what you put after that, because once you bring God into the formula, you have set aside all the normal expectations and limitations that human beings bring up.

God is able, not because He has to try to be able or because He simply wants to be able. God can't be anything but able. He is all-powerful by nature. He can't be any other way.

It doesn't matter what problem or challenge you are facing in your marriage or family today, God is able. If there is a wall of some sort between you and your spouse, God is able to help you tear that wall down. If a wayward child is giving you problems and disrupting your home, God is able to call that child back to Himself and restore peace in your home.

I can say that God is able because I read it in the Bible, which is the infallible, errorless Word of God. But I can also say it because God has proven Himself able in my life and ministry since the day I committed my life to Him. Anything that has been accomplished in my life can be explained by the fact that God is abundantly able to do anything and everything.

One day a young woman came to my office at church and asked, "Do you really believe all this stuff you preach?"

It was no problem to say, "Yes, I believe it." I have seen God's power at work in me. It is not just words on the page. I can talk about what my eyes have seen and my ears have heard of God's faithfulness.

What are you up against today? God is able!—TONY

THINK ABOUT IT
Since God is able, no need that you have is beyond Him.

IT'S OK TO BE DIFFERENT

This I say therefore . . . that you walk no longer just as the Gentiles walk.
—EPHESIANS 4:17

We all face tremendous pressure to be like everyone else. No one wants to feel like the odd person out. I remember that growing up, I was always the one left out at school because I was a Christian. And I can assure you, the pressure to conform was great.

When I was a girl, I sometimes got tired of being known as a Christian and as a Cannings (my maiden name), because my father and grandfather were well known in the community where I grew up. When I fussed to my mother, she would always share verses such as Ephesians 4:17 with me. Or she would remind me that the Christian life is not supposed to be easy (see 2 Tim. 3:12). Of course, I didn't want to hear that back then. But what stabilizing truths these have become for my life.

I know that the pressure to conform hits most of us very hard in our marriages. Once you determine that your marriage is going to be patterned after Christ, the enemy will unleash his attacks on you. Christian wives can really feel the pressure not to be different, because the world has such different expectations of women these days. To be a biblical wife and mother can subject us to pressure, sometimes even from other Christians!

There is real security then in knowing that we are not called to be popular but called to be like Him. Being different because we belong to Christ is not always easy. But it becomes easier as we put the Scripture into practice and grow and develop in the Lord.

We may not be very popular, but then we weren't promised popularity on this earth.—LOIS

THINK ABOUT IT

We can either do what everybody else is doing or put into action the power we have within us through Christ to be in the world, but not of the world (see John 15:19). Remember, your manual for living is God's Word, not the latest magazine.

A THIMBLE OR A RESERVOIR?

I will not let you go unless you bless me.

—GENESIS 32:26

*Y*ou probably know that the Pacific Ocean is the largest body of water in the world. If you were to fill a thimble from the Pacific Ocean, that thimble would be full of genuine Pacific Ocean water. There just wouldn't be very much of it in relation to what is available in the ocean. The same principle would hold true if you took a bucketful of water from the Pacific Ocean. Once the bucket is full, you'll get no more water in it even though the ocean has a lot more water to give.

Then somebody might say, "I want more. I'm going to dig my own reservoir and fill it with water from the Pacific Ocean." Well, the deeper that person digs the reservoir, the more the ocean will fill it. It's impossible to dig deep enough or far enough, though, to exhaust the ocean's supply.

The same thing is true with God. So many Christians are happy with a little bit of God. All they know is, "I'm saved, and I'm going to sit here until I go to heaven."

If you're satisfied with a little bit of God, that is all the experience of God you are ever going to get. We're not talking about salvation here but the power God has promised us to live victorious, overcoming Christian lives.

Once Jacob got hold of God and God got hold of Jacob in that famous wrestling match, the patriarch realized who he was grappling with. And he was doggedly determined that he would not let go until God had done something supernatural for him.

We need to do some grappling with God ourselves. We need to quit being satisfied with ordinary Christian lives, with average marriages. Let's reach out to take hold of God and discover the One who can fill not only our reservoir but the universe with Himself.

PRAY ABOUT IT

If you want more than a thimbleful of God, say, "Lord, expand my capacity so that I can have more of You."

FIXING THE BROKEN PLACES

Keep fervent in your love for one another, because love covers a multitude of sins.
—1 PETER 4:8

I have a steel plate in my lower right leg, a souvenir from my earlier football days. I had just made an interception from my linebacker spot when I was hit with a cross-body blow. My right leg stayed planted on the ground, and I heard a loud crack. The two bones in my lower leg were shattered.

The ambulance came onto the football field and rushed me to the hospital, where a surgeon opened up my leg, put the bones back together, and screwed a steel plate onto the bones to hold them in place. That was in 1970, and the plate has been there ever since.

The ugly scar on my leg is a reminder of the excruciating pain of that injury. My leg had a multitude of broken places, but the surgeon knew exactly what he was doing. He made the right incision at the right place at the right time, and he used the right instruments. The result is that today, my formerly shattered right leg is stronger than my left leg that has never been broken.

Love can do the same thing for people with broken places, people whose lives have been shattered by sin. Now don't misunderstand. We're not talking about a coverup. Sin always has to be dealt with. But the idea here is that love does not broadcast the other person's sin or constantly remind the person of his or her sin or refuse to give him or her another chance.

Instead, love "bears all things" (1 Cor. 13:7) by forgiving the sinner as we remember we are forgiven people ourselves.

What better place to practice the healing ministry of love than in your home? Every marriage needs forgiveness to survive and thrive. Godly love can put the broken pieces back together and affix a steel plate over the weak area, making it stronger than it was before.—TONY

TALK ABOUT IT
Take turns as spouses sharing what the other person can do to bring healing to the hurts in your life.

ARE YOU AN IMPLODER OR A BUILDER?

Let no unwholesome word proceed from your mouth, but only such a word as is good for edification according to the need of the moment, that it may give grace to those who hear.

—EPHESIANS 4:29

❦

few years ago, a historic building in downtown Dallas was imploded after all efforts to salvage it had failed. The implosion occurred early on a Sunday morning and was televised locally. It was an impressive sight watching this multistory building quiver and then collapse in a matter of seconds. All it took was for the workmen to weaken some key support beams and plant some charges in strategic places.

In the same way, it's possible to "implode" a mate's spirit with a few well-chosen words spoken in anger or from a spirit of revenge. "Unwholesome" words can eat away a person's spirit and self-worth. The word *unwholesome* here means "rotten."

Paul was saying that this kind of speech belongs in the garbage can with yesterday's leftovers.

Profanity is a good example of unwholesome words. I hope your home isn't polluted by unholy speech that degrades the person it is directed against and creates a stink.

Another example of unwholesome words are the cuts and put-downs that are so popular today. A lot of people do this stuff in a joking way. But if you have ever been on the receiving end of one of these barbs, you know they're not always funny. Instead of tearing down your mate with your words, make it your commitment to build him or her up. We build people up when we speak appropriate, grace-producing words. Even when correction or rebuke is called for, we need to frame our words in a way that leaves the *person* standing while still handling the problem.

The difference between the right word and the wrong word is the difference between lightning and a lightning bug—in other words, all the difference in the world! If you're wiring someone up for a verbal implosion today, better defuse those explosives!

PRAY ABOUT IT

Ask God to control your tongue and teach you how to use your words to build up, not tear down. Then speak a kind word to your mate.

THINKING LIKE CHRIST

All things that I have heard from My Father I have made known to you.

—JOHN 15:15

⁂

Have you ever thought about what it means when the Bible says, "We have the mind of Christ" (1 Cor. 2:16)? That is a staggering reality! This means, as Tony and the other theologians would say, that we have the ability to think God's thoughts after Him. It means that we have the capacity to think about things the way Jesus Christ would think about them. Paul called it having the same attitude as Christ (see Phil. 2:5).

Since we have the mind of Christ, we don't have to think the way we used to think. We don't have to see people the way we used to see them. And we don't have to approach life with the same attitudes we used to exhibit. Think what would happen to our marriages if we would respond to our spouses with the mind and attitude of Christ. So much delicious spiritual fruit would begin to grow and mature in our lives that our relationship as a couple would take on a whole new flavor.

I know that even with the mind of Christ at our disposal, we are still very imperfect people who can easily lapse back into our old way of thinking and acting. But the Scripture is clear about the resources available to us in Christ. Here are some ingredients you can begin using today to develop a Christlike mind and attitude:

- Meditate on God's Word (Ps. 1:2–3).
- Seek God's will (Matt. 26:39).
- Bear the burdens of others (Gal. 6:2).
- Resist the devil (Matt. 4:1–11, James 4:7).
- Learn to control your mental focus (Phil. 4:8).
- Be careful how you view life (Rom. 8:6).
- Look for God's purpose in everything (Rom. 8:28).
- Seek His strength in your weakness (2 Cor. 12:9).   —LOIS

THINK ABOUT IT
When Christ's mind dominates our minds, then we will be truly in our right minds!

HOW TO BE CONTENT WHERE YOU ARE

Godliness is profitable for all things.

—I TIMOTHY 4:8

One Sunday a man came to church looking very sad and despondent. The pastor noticed him and asked, "Why are you so sad?" "Well, two weeks ago my uncle died and left me seventy-five thousand dollars. Then a week ago my aunt died and left me fifty thousand dollars."

The pastor said, "Wait a minute. Two weeks ago your uncle died and left you seventy-five thousand dollars. Last week your aunt died and left you fifty thousand dollars. Why are you so sad?"

"Because nobody died this week."

Greed is an ugly thing. The greedy person sees money as an end in itself. The greedy person demands the best without regard to need and always says, "I want more." The cure for greed is to be content with what you have and to develop the attitude of a giver. The Bible calls this being a good steward of God's gifts. Biblical stewardship is more than just the check you drop in the offering plate on Sunday. It involves the part you keep for yourself as well as the part you give to God.

That's what Paul said in 1 Timothy 6:6–7, a powerful passage on greed and stewardship. It reminds us that one reason we can be content is that when we leave this place, our wallets stay here.

It's not wrong to want to better ourselves. But if we cannot be content with where we are until God takes us where we want to be, we are greedy. So many Christian couples are knocking themselves out to get ahead and pile up the toys. They're missing an important part of the formula Paul gave us: *godliness* plus contentment equals gain. We tend to skip over that first part of the equation.

What is godliness anyway? It's focusing our minds and hearts so completely on being like Jesus Christ in how we think and what we do that when people look at us they get a clear picture of what Christ is like. We can't follow Christ wholeheartedly and chase the pot of gold at the end of the rainbow at the same time.

PRAY ABOUT IT

Ask forgiveness for any discontentment in your life and request a grateful spirit for all that God has already done for you.

TURNING YOUR TRIALS INTO TRIUMPHS

In the world you have tribulation, but take courage; I have overcome the world.

—JOHN 16:33

ᴵf you're not in the middle of a trial right now, just hang around. The next one is probably on the way. Jesus basically promised us that trials will come! No one, none of us, can dodge trials. So we need to find out what resources God has given us to deal with them.

Trials are adverse circumstances that God allows or even brings about in the lives of His children to deepen our faith in Him. Trials can come from a number of directions. Sometimes they come simply because we live in a sin-cursed world and the curse rubs off on us. So we become the victim of a crime or accident or illness that crashes into our individual lives or our marriage.

Sometimes trials are the result of our own sin. We yield to a temptation that leads to circumstances that are tough to deal with. At other times, God may send us a trial to teach us a specific lesson. And don't forget that the enemy can attack us with trials for the purpose of bringing about our spiritual defeat.

The good news is you're not out there alone, because no matter what the source of your trial, Jesus has the situation well in hand. He has already overcome *anything* you and your mate can possibly face in this world.

The best place to learn how to deal with trials is right in the middle of one. That's why Jesus told His disciples to get into a boat and row out to the middle of the Sea of Galilee (see Matt. 14:22). He knew the storm was coming, but He wanted the Twelve to learn the encouraging truth that He had total authority over their trials. He wants us to get that message too.

THINK ABOUT IT
Trials are not designed to sink your boat but to help you improve your navigation skills.

THIS WORLD IS "NUTHIN'"

What does it profit a man to gain the whole world, and forfeit his soul?

—MARK 8:36

A few years ago, former heavyweight boxing champ Muhammad Ali was interviewed by a major sports magazine. You may know that Ali suffers from Parkinson's disease and has been reduced to a slow and painful shuffle. His speech is also affected.

The article told how it used to be when Ali was the champ. At one point in the story he made this statement: "I had the world, and it wasn't nuthin'."

That's the message the Bible wants you and me to get! This world is "nuthin'" compared to what God has in store for us. That's why Paul reminded believers who are rich not to get the big head or to fall in love with their wealth (see 1 Tim. 6:17–19).

Now, Paul wasn't jumping on rich folks, and neither am I. If God has blessed your work, I rejoice for you. Some of God's best stewards are wealthy believers who handle their wealth for His glory. And God's people don't need to be getting ulcers because they're jealous over how God is blessing someone else.

But wealth does bring responsibility—and notice that Paul didn't set any monetary amounts here. Compared to the rest of the world, we Americans are wealthy. So don't check out on me here.

Paul also told us in 1 Timothy 6:17 not to "fix [our] hope" on money so that it controls us and quenches our desire for godliness.

Instead, we're to fixate on the God who gives us these things to enjoy; He will never leave us or let us down. God is not a tight-fisted miser who hoards His blessings. When we are pleasing to Him, He delights in giving us good things to enjoy.

God places His resources in our hands so we might use them to do good, to help others, and to bring Him glory. And as we do, we are laying up for ourselves treasure in heaven.

PRAY ABOUT IT

Ask God to help you see your checkbook through the eyes of faithful stewards.

WHAT IT TAKES TO BE A WINNER (DAY 1)

Run in such a way that you may win.

—I CORINTHIANS 9:24

⌘

A concert pianist was once asked, "How did you come to play the piano so well?" "By neglecting anything that did not contribute to it," she answered. Now this pianist was not saying that other things were wrong. They just didn't contribute to her goal of being the best at her chosen craft, so she left them off.

There is nothing wrong with wanting to be the best. There is nothing wrong with wanting to be a winner. We just need to make sure we're competing in the right game to win the right prize. The only prize worth giving our lives to is Jesus' commendation, "Well done, good and faithful servant."

So let me ask you, what's your passion as individuals and as a couple? What is it that makes you look forward to getting out of bed tomorrow?

My passion is to be a winner for God. I want to close my eyes every night knowing that I did my best for Him as a pastor, father, and husband. I'm running the Christian race to win, not just to place or show!

The apostle Paul had that kind of passion. He wasn't satisfied just to be back in the pack of runners. A winner breaks from the pack, intent on winning the race.

But if we're going to run to win, we need to make some decisions. Speaking about the Isthmian Games, an event held every two years that was similar to the Olympics, Paul said, "Everyone who competes in the games exercises self-control in all things" (1 Cor. 9:25).

If you wanted to win a wreath at the Isthmian Games, you had to be ready to exercise a lot of self-control. Why? Because you can't live any way you want and still be a winner!

THINK ABOUT IT

Paul said, "One thing I do" (Phil. 3:13), not "Many things I play around with." Is that true for you and your mate? What must you let go of to get closer to God and to one another?

WHAT IT TAKES TO BE A WINNER (DAY 2)

Let us also lay aside every encumbrance, . . . and let us run with endurance the race set before us.

—HEBREWS 12:1

❧

*A*ncient athletes were willing to discipline their bodies for months to win a simple garland of greenery that was placed on their heads at the winner's stand.

As Christians, we are also running for a kind of prize, but it's much greater than a strand of ivy that soon fades to brown. How much more should we be willing to discipline ourselves to win the eternal prize of God's approval in time and eternity?

The reason some believers are not running as winners is that they get hung up on some side issue and lose sight of the prize. Athletes understand that their training is just a means to a much larger end. They are after the gold.

Committed athletes want this prize so badly that it controls their lives. Their sleeping and eating habits change. Their relationships change. Everything changes because the serious athlete has his or her eye on the prize.

Our commitment to Christ needs to guide our decisions too. For instance, if you are committed to making your marriage all that God wants it to be, you won't have to struggle very long trying to decide whether you should pick up the TV remote for the evening or spend time talking with and listening to your mate.

Once you get the larger goal in sight, it will help you make the daily decisions you need to make to get there.

Encumbrances are the things holding you back from being a winner for God, from receiving His approval. It could be too much television and not enough time with your family. It could be that God gets too little of your attention.

Whatever the encumbrance is, it's worth getting rid of because of the prize we're running toward: "the upward call of God in Christ Jesus" (Phil. 3:14).

TALK ABOUT IT
If you're feeling really brave today, ask your mate whether in his or her eyes you are living like a winner in your marriage.

NOT PERFECT, JUST AUTHENTIC

Let your statement be, "Yes, yes," or "No, no,"; and anything beyond these is of evil.
—MATTHEW 5:37

Authenticity is a big buzzword these days. Everybody seems to be talking about the need to be authentic in our dealings and in our relationships. But the the concept of authenticity is nothing new. Jesus spoke about it in the Sermon on the Mount, the first great sermon of His public ministry. Today's verse captures the heart of what it means to be an authentic person.

As believers, we should be people whose everyday speech is totally reliable. When we say yes, that's what we mean. The same is true when we say no. Our spouses, children, and coworkers shouldn't have to wonder whether we are telling the truth or whether we will stand behind what we say.

There's no better place to learn authenticity than at home. It's hard to fool those you live with. Your family will usually know if what you are doing and saying on the outside matches who you are on the inside.

Jesus Himself is the perfect model of authenticity. He was the perfect Son of God, so it was impossible that He could be anything but totally truthful.

You may say, "But I can't be perfect like Jesus." That's true. No one can. But authenticity doesn't demand perfection.

In fact, one of the traits of authentic people is that they are the first to admit they aren't perfect. So when they blow it, they don't pass over or excuse the mistake. They call it what it is.

The apostle Nathanael was an authentic person. Jesus looked into Nathanael's heart and said of him, "Behold, an Israelite indeed, in whom is no guile!" (John 1:47).

Nathanael wasn't perfect, but he had an undivided heart. He was free of guile or deceit. With Nathanael, what you saw was what you got. Could the same be said of you and me today?

PRAY ABOUT IT
Pray that God will help you be the kind of person whose heart and mouth are on the same channel!

DO YOU HAVE A PLAN OR A SCHEME?

A faithful man will abound with blessings, but he who makes haste to be rich will not go unpunished.

—PROVERBS 28:20

*D*o you have a financial plan in place that God can bless? We're not necessarily talking about your investments. What we mean is a plan that gives God His rightful place in your finances, one that allows you to take care of your needs without having to live in debt.

We're also talking about a plan that includes discipline so that one or both of you don't try to pursue your every want and desire.

The Bible teaches that wise management pleases God. If you don't have a plan that God can bless, you won't get the full benefit of what you earn. He may even take away what you have because you're messing up what He gave you.

Every dime you bring home was given to you by God. And while only a portion goes directly to His storehouse, the local church, all of your money is to be managed for His glory.

A lot of people don't want to manage their money; they want to luck their way into wealth. And the primary way a lot of God's people are trying to do this is through get-rich-quick games like the lottery.

Let us spell it out: The lottery is a pagan, unrighteous way of trying to make progress that is born out of a hellish desire to get rich quick.

God opposes any scheme that is designed to help you get rich overnight, because that means you don't have to work for what you have. To get rich overnight does not require any faithfulness or productivity. Every time you go into a gas station or store and buy a lottery ticket, you are saying, "God, I don't trust You. I've got to luck my way to success."

When you do that, you miss God's activity in your life and forfeit His power. God wants you to have a plan, not a scheme.

PRAY ABOUT IT

If you don't have a plan, ask God to give you one. Open His Word and pray that He will show you His truth.

BRICKS OR CATHEDRALS?

Here is what I have seen to be good and fitting: to eat, to drink and enjoy oneself in all one's labor in which he toils.

—ECCLESIASTES 5:18

❦

A man was walking down the street one day and passed a construction project. He asked one of the workers, "What are you doing?" He answered, "I'm laying bricks."

Another laborer was working a few feet away, so the man asked him, "What are you doing?"

The second man said, "I'm building a cathedral."

Some men lay bricks while others build cathedrals. The difference is in your perspective on work. Are you content to lay bricks, or do you want to build a cathedral? There are a lot of excuses men give about work. The lazy man says, "I don't want to work." The frustrated man says, "I don't like my job." The purposeless man says, "My job is not getting me where I want to go." And of course, the man who's broke speaks for all of us when he says, "I'm not making enough."

It's unfortunate that we live in a world where people are finding ways to get out of work, because work is a gift from God. You won't hear that fact many places these days, but it's true. Work existed before sin existed. So if you believe that work came about because of Adam's sin, you've missed it. Work was always a part of God's plan. Genesis 1 shows us God Himself at work.

The first thing the Bible says is that "God created the heavens and the earth." He was busy from the beginning. God's Spirit was busy "moving over the surface of the waters" (v. 2). Then God was busy giving names to the entities He had created, making "the expanse" (v. 7), gathering "the waters below the heavens . . . into one place" thus letting "the dry land appear" (v. 9). He organized His creation and placed the sun, moon, and stars in the heavens (v. 17).

Before there was ever sin or even mankind, God expressed Himself by doing productive work. God is the ultimate Worker!

PRAY ABOUT IT
Have you thanked God for your work lately? Think about the alternatives, and then praise Him for your job!

CHOOSE FOR YOURSELF

The serpent was more crafty than any beast of the field which the LORD God had made. And he said to the woman, "Indeed, has God said . . . ?"

—GENESIS 3:1

The first conversation in history between a human being and Satan was about God. The real issue in Eden was not whether Eve would eat a piece of fruit. The issue was whom she would obey. That's the issue for all of us. We have to decide under whose authority we will place ourselves.

Who will be Lord of *your* life?

When Eve ate the fruit and gave it to Adam to eat, they were saying, in essence, "Satan, you are lord of our lives. We submit to your authority."

Notice that Satan waited until he could tempt Adam and Eve together. He knew that if he could get this husband and wife to yield to him, he would have access to their offspring. And tragically, his strategy worked.

So the issue for mankind from the beginning has been whom we will serve, God or Satan. Satan wants to bring as many people as possible under his control because Satan is at war with God, and now we are at war with Satan.

Sometimes people wonder why God did not just annihilate Satan after his rebellion. That's a complex question, but one reason seems to be that God is giving every person an opportunity to choose, the way Satan had an opportunity to choose. Joshua said to the people of his day, "Choose for yourselves today whom you will serve" (Josh. 24:15).

That was also the question Job faced. In all of his suffering, would Job obey God or curse Him?

We all face that decision. When you accept Jesus Christ as your Savior and place yourself under His Lordship, you reverse the choice Adam and Eve made in the Garden of Eden when they placed themselves under Satan's control.

PRAY ABOUT IT
We need to reaffirm Jesus' Lordship in our personal and family lives every day. Tell Him you want Him to be Lord of your life today.

HOW TO BE A PROBLEM TO SATAN

[Christ] is also head of the body, the church; and He is the beginning, the first-born from the dead; so that He Himself might come to have first place in everything.

—COLOSSIANS 1:18

W hen you come to Christ, you leave Satan's kingdom and come over to God's kingdom (see Col. 1:13). That makes you a problem to Satan. When you commit your life to Jesus Christ, not only has Satan lost you, he loses anyone you touch. If we men learn how to be godly husbands and fathers, Satan may lose whole families. If all of us learn how to be witnesses for Christ, Satan may lose some of our friends or coworkers.

Satan cannot touch our salvation, but he can neutralize the effectiveness of our faith. He will do whatever he has to do to keep us from building God's kingdom.

Now, because Satan is very clever, he doesn't usually come at us with his guns blazing in a frontal attack. That would be too obvious. His warfare techniques are much more subtle and effective. He simply gets us so busy that we don't have time to pursue God's will.

Satan can keep you so tired that you don't have the energy to serve God. He will keep you too entertained or too distracted or too whatever to do much for the Lord. That's Satan's strategy. He wants to break up homes to set a bad example for the children and start a ripple effect that will move from generation to generation.

The only answer to Satan's attacks is to totally commit to the Lord Jesus Christ everything we are and everything we do. He deserves and demands that commitment. Colossians 1:16–18 teaches that Christ deserves our all because "all things have been created by Him and for Him" and "He is before all things, and in Him all things hold together."

The simple fact is that no area of our lives lies outside of Jesus Christ's control. You cannot keep any area of your life to yourself because all things were created by Christ and for Christ. He deserves it all.

THINK ABOUT IT
The only way to keep part of your life for yourself is to take it away from Christ.

ARGUING BY GOD'S RULES

Let your speech always be with grace, seasoned, as it were, with salt, so that you may know how you should respond to each person.

—COLOSSIANS 4:6

❧

*H*ere's a resolution for you to make today as a couple: Resolve that you won't waste your disagreements! What we mean by that is, agree together that you won't allow your arguments to simply deteriorate into hurtful words or accusations or name-calling. Promise each other that you won't argue unless each side presents at least one possible solution to the problem.

You may be thinking, "That's a lot of work. I'd just rather get what I have to say off my chest." It may be a lot of work to bend over backward in an attempt to communicate fairly and avoid hurting your spouse. But one thing is certain. When you bend over backward, you never have to worry about falling on your face! Yes, it takes work to disagree agreeably with each other. But consider the possible alternatives: screaming and hollering, angry words and thoughts, put-downs, or frosty silences. These things don't have to happen if you follow God's rules for your speech, rules such as "Let no unwholesome word proceed from your mouth" and "Let all bitterness and wrath and anger . . . be put away from you" (Eph. 4:29, 31).

Instead, the Bible advises us to season our words with salt. Salt is a preservative that keeps rottenness from setting in. If you'll salt down your words before you say them, you'll preserve your relationship and avoid the kind of words that can spoil a love relationship. Besides, rotten words grieve the Holy Spirit (see Eph. 4:30), and a grieved Holy Spirit is like corrosion on a battery's terminals. When your battery gets corroded, you lose access to the power. The Holy Spirit is the power of the Christian life. If you use rotten and unwholesome words around your house, don't be surprised if you have no power in your spiritual life.

Maybe you didn't know you could use God's rules for healthy communication even when you're disagreeing with one another. But the fact is, that's when you need God's rules the most!

PRAY ABOUT IT
Get down on your knees together today and ask God to help you be kind and tender-hearted toward one another (see Eph. 4:32) even when you're arguing.

A DOMESTIC PEACE INITIATIVE

Forgive us our debts, as we also have forgiven our debtors.

—MATTHEW 6:12

T he Berlin Wall was torn down in 1989—but there is still a "Berlin Wall" standing in too many Christian homes. That's the invisible wall running through the middle of many homes, dividing husband from wife. Neither one looks over the wall or crosses over it except to argue. Or maybe there is no communication over the wall at all. Maybe there's just a sullen, silent truce because neither party is willing to compromise or offer a peace initiative.

Now, if your marriage is not like that, praise God. But in case it is, we want to offer you a word of hope. And even if the scenario above does not describe your marriage, what we want to share with you today can help keep that from happening.

It's time to dismantle the wall. It's time to make peace. You say, "But we don't love each other anymore. We sleep in different beds."

OK, then love your neighbor!

But you answer, "Well, we're not even neighbors; we're enemies." Then love your enemy. It doesn't matter how you slice the bologna, the Bible has you covered.

Here's a key to keeping the peace and the love alive between two people who have joined their lives together: Each of you has to be gracious enough to wipe the mental slate clean. The Bible calls this forgiveness.

Forgiving is a hard thing to do, especially if you've been hurt emotionally. And since you're not a computer, you can't just erase the hurt from your memory.

We're not suggesting that you forget the past ever happened. The Bible doesn't focus on forgetting a wrong but on refusing to hold that wrong against the other person—just as we would not want God to hold our sins against us.

Forgiveness restores and maintains intimate fellowship and opens the way for God's blessings to flow into our lives. As long as the two of you can forgive each other, you've got a powerful tool for blessing. Don't let anything mess with that.

PRAY ABOUT IT
Praying together—out loud—is a wonderful way to worship the Lord and maintain intimacy. It's hard to pray with someone you're carrying a grudge against!

DOING THE RIGHT THINGS

God is faithful, who will not allow you to be tempted beyond what you are able.

—I CORINTHIANS 10:13

I am often asked by other women, "How is a woman supposed to find the time and energy to support her husband, fulfill her own duties, and still maintain her first love for the Lord?"

I wish I had an easy answer to that question, but I don't think such an answer exists. After years as a pastor's wife, a mother of four, and the administrator of a national ministry, I'm still learning how to balance all of these callings.

But one thing God has taught me over the years is the importance of letting Him set my priorities for me. As I look back, I can see a definite pattern to my life. When I am doing the things God wants me to do, I can get everything done in the allotted time with a sense of energy and joy. But when I try to do only what *I* want to do or what others demand that I do, then my joy is gone and I don't have the stamina I need to get it all done.

The more time we spend in God's presence seeking and learning His will, the more productive we will become in what He wants us to accomplish. The more we pursue Him, the clearer His will becomes to us and the more effectively we function as His people.

Today's verse reminds us that God promises He will not give us more to handle than we can bear. The problem comes when *we* take on more than we can bear.

It's so easy to do that, isn't it? We want to do so many good things. But no one can do it all. You and I don't need to worry about all the things we *could* be doing. Let's just concentrate on those things that God has called us to do.—LOIS

THINK ABOUT IT

It's up to us to drop the things from our lives that are not part of what God wants us to do.

NOURISHING THOSE LITTLE SPROUTS

Your children [will be] like olive plants around your table.

—PSALM 128:3

*T*n this classic psalm describing the family that pleases the Lord, the writer likens children to olive plants. Why? Olive trees were very important in biblical days because olive oil had a lot of uses. One reason children were so valued in biblical days was that a man knew if he dealt right with his kids, his own future would be secured when he was old. In helping his children grow into productive adults, he found his joy and some of his own success.

Notice that the psalmist compared the olive plants to children, not adults. Young trees, like young children, need extra care and attention as they grow and develop. We sometimes jokingly refer to our kids as little "sprouts." That metaphor is popular because there's a lot of truth to it. A sprout is eager to grow, but it must be packed in good soil and carefully tended. Its growth can be stunted if the proper care is withheld.

Similarly, our children are filled with potential that needs to be developed and brought to full growth. Dad and Mom, you won't know how well your children are growing up around your table unless you are at the table too!

I'm convinced there are a lot of boys today who would grow into productive adults if they only had the right men at home challenging them in the right way. The same thing needs to be said about girls and their mothers. The problem is there aren't enough parents, particularly fathers, in the homes to challenge and guide their children.

Dad, you're the thermostat of the home. It's up to you primarily to set and maintain the right temperature for little olive plants to grow.—TONY

TALK ABOUT IT
Dad and Mom, how is the temperature in your home? Is the atmosphere conducive to your kids' spiritual nourishment?

FAMILIES THAT MAKE AN IMPACT

The LORD bless you from Zion. . . . Indeed, may you see your children's children.
—PSALM 128:5–6

❦

*T*his great psalm makes it clear that a God-pleasing family is maintained within the community of believers. Zion was Israel's place of worship. Hebrews 12:22 uses Zion to refer to our place of worship too. If you want the blessing of Zion to rest on your family, see to it that your family is a vital part of your local church, the kind of participants a pastor doesn't have to prod into taking the lead spiritually.

We have too many "hitchhikers" in our churches today. Hitchhikers don't invest in the car or buy the gas. They just want a free ride. And you'd better not have an accident, or they may sue you!

Our churches are also plagued by "McChristians." They want drive-through Christianity—no getting out, no going inside, no commitment, no sacrifice, no inconvenience. Just drive by, order what you want, and leave the work for someone else. But that's not what God wants for our families, because He knows that godly families can't survive and thrive in isolation. We need the nurture of the assembled body of Christ. When our families are properly nurtured in the body of Christ, they are ready to turn around and make a powerful impact on the community.

If we can get our homes and our churches right, our neighborhoods will have peace and our cities will be better places in which to live. We must be involved in our churches and then in our communities. Taking an interest and a place of leadership in the community, no matter how small that involvement may be, gives us the chance to help others and witness to our faith.

What's the result? When we operate our families according to God's principles, we get to "see [our] children's children" (Ps. 128:6). Our influence is passed on to our grandchildren. In other words, we build a legacy.

PRAY ABOUT IT
Dad, Psalm 128:1–2 reveals that this godly legacy begins with you and your spiritual life. Pray that God will enable you to fear Him, walk in His ways, and lead your family to do the same.

GROWING INTO GRACE

Grow in the grace and knowledge of our Lord and Savior Jesus Christ.
—2 PETER 3:18

I have had the opportunity to visit a lot of interesting places. Three places especially stand out in my mind. I had always thought of the Grand Canyon as a hole in the ground until I stood on the precipice of that crater. It was breathtaking. If you have been there, you know what I mean.

A second place that grabbed my attention was Niagara Falls. I had seen it plenty of times on television, but hearing that water roaring with unstoppable force was mesmerizing to me.

But number one on my list of unforgettable sights is the Taj Mahal in India. It is situated in such a way that as you approach it you really can't see it very well. All you see is a white building in the distance with an entrance like a keyhole. As you go through that entrance you encounter another opening, and the view expands a little bit. But when you pass through that last opening, you are literally glued to the ground by what you see. The beauty of that palace is nothing short of staggering.

Seeing these wonders from a distance and then close up is like trying to comprehend God's grace. If you only peer at grace from a distance, it's just another theological concept that's nice but hardly overwhelming. However, the closer you get, the more mind-boggling God's grace becomes. If you ever get a handle on grace, it will revolutionize your spiritual life—and even your marriage.

Peter told us to grow in grace. Why? Because by growing in our understanding and application of grace we maximize our spiritual potential to the glory of God. We serve God because of the grace He extended to us at salvation. The Christian life is loving, accepting, forgiving grace from beginning to end—much like marriage!—TONY

PRAY ABOUT IT
Pray that grace will capture and dominate your relationship.

ARE YOU SEEING CRACKS IN YOUR WALL?

If the foundations are destroyed, what can the righteous do?
—PSALM 11:3

few years ago, an ugly crack appeared in our bedroom wall. So I called a painter, who replaced the defective plaster and repainted the wall. It looked great. I was happy, Lois was happy, the painter was happy. I paid him, and he left.

But about a month later the crack reappeared, uglier than ever. Now preachers don't get mad, but I was somewhat "evangelically ticked off." I called the painter back and asked him to fix my problem. He apologized, redid the work, and everything was fine . . . for a while. But then that crack came back—and brought lots of other cracks with it. At this point I concluded I needed a new painter. The new man looked at my wall and shocked me by saying, "I'm sorry, sir. I can't help you, because you don't have a problem with cracks in your wall."

I looked up at the cracks in the wall then at this "crackpot" telling me my problem wasn't cracks in the wall. I said, "Excuse me, but I can see a crack, you can see a crack, in fact, all God's children can see a crack."

"Oh yes," he replied, "you have a crack, but that's not your problem. Your problem is a shifting foundation on your house. Until you stabilize your foundation, you will forever be repairing cracks in your wall."

What a perfect metaphor for the condition of America today. We can see "cracks" everywhere: social cracks, political cracks, moral cracks, even crack-cocaine cracks.

But until we stabilize the foundation, no amount of programs, government grants, or elections will be able to repair the cracks in our cultural walls. And there is no place where the foundation needs to be stabilized more than in the home.

Strong families hold the key to a strong society. But you can't have strong families without God as their foundation. So let me ask you today: What are you doing to stabilize the spiritual foundation of your home?—TONY

THINK ABOUT IT
It's the basic stuff that keeps a family strong: prayer, God's Word, worshiping together. Do the basics right, and a lot of other things will take care of themselves.

BECOMING GOD'S IMITATORS

Be imitators of me, just as I also am of Christ.

—I CORINTHIANS 11:1

❦

*D*o you have anybody imitating you? That's part of what is supposed to be happening if we obey Jesus' command telling us to "make disciples" (Matt. 28:19). Disciples learn from the people discipling them, just as students learn from the example of their teachers and children imitate their parents.

The danger for most of us is not that we will suddenly plunge off the deep end and lapse into gross sin or toss our faith aside, although that can happen. A more prevalent danger is that we will continue to take in the truth and simply sit comfortably on it until we are so spiritually bloated we can't move.

We must exercise, using what we are learning to change our own lives and help bring other people along in the faith. Otherwise, what we are taking in stops nourishing even us.

It's possible for us humans to eat so much that what we are eating for nourishment actually begins to work against us. This can happen in the spiritual realm. In fact, it happens all the time. Discipleship is designed to keep the fat off by allowing us to burn spiritual calories as we put into practice the truth of God.

Paul was the preeminent discipler. He could urge the believers in Corinth to follow him because he was following the Lord. I love the charge he gave to his disciple Timothy in 2 Timothy 2:1–2: "You therefore, my son, be strong in the grace that is in Christ Jesus. And the things which you have heard from me in the presence of many witnesses, these entrust to faithful men, who will be able to teach others also."

Discipleship is a transferable process. The loop isn't closed until you and I teach someone else what God has worked into our lives.

PRAY ABOUT IT

As a spouse and parent, you probably already have people imitating you! Better ask God to help you make sure your example is a worthy one to follow.

GOD'S SENSE OF HUMOR

"I know the plans that I have for you," declares the LORD,
"plans . . . to give you a future and a hope."

—JEREMIAH 29:11

❦

I gladly surrendered my life to full-time ministry for the Lord when I was fifteen years old. I had always wanted to get married and share in ministry with my husband, but I had one stipulation. I told the Lord that I *never* wanted to be a pastor's wife! It just seemed to me that pastors' wives had so many expectations and demands placed on them by so many people. I decided that a life like that wasn't for me.

Well, God definitely has a sense of humor! I married Tony in 1970, we went off to seminary in Dallas a while later, and in 1976 we started the Oak Cliff Bible Fellowship with ten people in our home. I was officially a pastor's wife!

Obviously, God's plans for my life were different than my plans for my life. And I must tell you that in those early years of Tony's ministry, I struggled to accept God's will for me, going into a role where I would be expected to be all things to all people. But God proved to me that His plans were best. Because I was in God's will, He gave me the ability to get the job done without compromising my priorities of home and family.

Tony was a great help and encouragement to me in those early years of our ministry. He prayed for me and told me he didn't expect me to be whatever the people in the church wanted me to be. That really freed me up to be the *pastor's* wife, not the church's wife.

Is God unfolding a plan in your life or in your marriage right now that isn't the blueprint you had in mind? Look at today's verse again. You may not know all that God is doing, but isn't it wonderful to realize that *He* knows the plans He is bringing to pass for you?—LOIS

TALK ABOUT IT
Sit down as a couple and talk about where God seems to be taking you. Promise and encourage each other that you will stick with His plan.

HOW TO BE CONTENT

Blessed are those who hear the word of God, and observe it.

—LUKE 11:28

❦

One of the most fascinating words in the New Testament is the word *blessed.* Jesus used it to open the Sermon on the Mount when He gave us what we call the Beatitudes (see Matt. 5:1–12).

The word *beatitude* literally means "happy." But in the Greek-influenced world in which Jesus lived, it meant more than just circumstantial happiness. There was more to being blessed than just being happy because things were going well.

Jesus said we can be blessed if we will hear and heed His Word. He was saying it is our opportunity, even while we are on earth, to have the contentment of God on our lives. This is the peace and happiness that remain no matter what the world hands us. We can be as "relaxed" as God is when we are obeying Him, because He will lift us above the everyday stuff that swirls all around us.

In the Beatitudes, the Lord spelled out the ways His disciples could experience His blessedness. The beginning of Matthew 5 makes it clear that Jesus was addressing His remarks to His disciples, those who already knew Him. But Matthew 5 also indicates that there was a large crowd of people listening to Jesus as He addressed the disciples. It's as if Jesus were telling His disciples what kingdom people look and act like while the surrounding crowd "eavesdropped."

We might say that Jesus was inviting the people in the crowd to become kingdom people and enjoy His blessedness too. Luke 11:28 underscores that the blessed are people who have become obedient to God's Word.

In the same way the crowd may have observed Jesus' disciples, people around us should be able to look at us, see our divine contentment, and want it for themselves.

THINK ABOUT IT

Will unbelievers who know you be attracted to Christ or turned away from Him by your words and actions today?

WHY, DAD?

Do not work for the food which perishes, but for the food which endures to eternal life.
—JOHN 6:27

❧

Many men today are like the father who sat his son down to talk about life. "Son, I want you to go to school and get a good education," he said. "Why, Dad?"

"Because if you go to school and get a good education, then you'll get a good job. And if you get a good job, you can live where you want, wear what you want, and buy what you want."

"But why am I supposed to do all that?" the boy asked.

"So that when you have children, you can send them to school so they can get a good education and a good job so they can live where they want, wear what they want, and buy what they want."

"Let's get this straight, Dad. You want me to do all this stuff so I can help my children do all the same stuff when they grow up that you're helping me do now? But what am I doing all of this for?"

The father said, "Son, you don't understand. If you do all this, someday you'll be able to retire in comfort and enjoy your golden years."

"But Dad, you still haven't answered my question. If I achieve everything you want me to achieve, build up a good nest egg, retire in comfort, and enjoy my golden years, then what?"

By now Dad is getting a little frustrated. He says, "Boy, just go to school, get a good education, and get a good job. Work hard, get what you want, help your kids do the same, then retire in comfort and enjoy your golden years. *That way, when you die you'll have something to leave behind.*"

There are a lot of people who live like that. They get the good education and the good job, they provide for their children so their children can do the same thing; then they grow old, retire, die . . . But life doesn't have to be that way. Jesus gives you an alternative. Commit your life to Him, and you can take your life's work with you.

THINK ABOUT IT

Ask yourself, "Am I investing all my time in things that aren't going to heaven with me?" If the answer is yes, you've got some thinking to do!

NO NEED TO BLUSH

Do you not know that your bodies are members of Christ?

—I CORINTHIANS 6:15

*T*here is no issue that carries more potential for joy or disaster than the issue of our sexuality and all that it involves. Sex can foster and contribute to a wonderful intimacy in marriage, but misused, it can produce all manner of devastation in a marriage and in a family.

God's Word speaks freely and openly and fluently about the subject of sex. God does not have to blush or pull down the shades when the issue comes up. Why? Because He created us. He made us male and female. And since sex is God's idea, He reserves the right to tell us how it should function.

Paul discusses our sexuality and the proper functioning of sex in 1 Corinthians 6:15–7:9, an extended passage that introduces us to a number of key principles related to sex and marriage.

It's interesting that such an important discussion of sex should appear in Paul's first letter to the Corinthians, a partly dysfunctional church in a very pagan, sex-saturated city. Corinth was the Las Vegas of the day. It was "the Strip." When it came to sex, Corinth's motto was, "Anything goes."

For instance, Corinth was home to the temple of Aphrodite, the goddess of love. There were two sides to this temple. On one side, the "worshiper" could eat dinner. On the other side of the temple a thousand temple prostitutes were available should the person desire a sexual dessert.

Many of the Corinthian Christians came out of that background (see 1 Cor. 6:9–11), so they needed a new message concerning their bodies. As believers, the Corinthians needed to know that they belonged to Christ—body, soul, and spirit. Therefore, they could not do whatever they wanted in the area of sex.

The fact is that each member of a marriage, and every believer, belongs first to Christ. When you understand that, your commitment to marital faithfulness takes on a new dynamic.

THINK ABOUT IT

God does not wince when He discusses the subject of sex. To Him, sex within the commitment of marriage is one of the purest topics there is.

A STARTING POINT FOR BIBLICAL MANHOOD

I want you to understand that Christ is the head of every man.

—I CORINTHIANS II:3

*T*don't have to tell you that the very concept of manhood has been taking a real beating for some time now. The world has attempted to redefine manhood based on a feminist, homosexual, New Age, or other kind of agenda. And a lot of men, in an effort not to appear out of touch or behind the times, have rolled with the punches so far that they have rolled over and played dead when it comes to their manhood. The political and social climate has become an excuse for them not to take their God-given role of leadership.

But the real crisis of manhood is a theological crisis. We have misconstrued what God has said about gender, and in particular about maleness. And having misconstrued God, we have tried to make things work by our faulty system. But it *doesn't* work.

In today's verse, the apostle Paul made a foundational statement about the way God intended the world to function. Paul said that God designed creation to function by means of a hierarchy—that is, a chain of command.

Even the Trinity operates under a chain of command according to 1 Corinthians 11:3, which says that God is the head of Christ. This does not mean Christ is inferior to the Father. Instead, it's a matter of management. God the Father calls the shots, and Christ the Son is obedient to the Father.

For believers, authority flows from God the Father to Christ, and then from Christ to man. So the starting point for a biblical definition of manhood is that we as men are to function under the authority of Jesus Christ.

That means He calls the shots in our personal lives, our careers, and our families. A real man is not the mythical rugged individualist, out there on his own. Instead, a real man is one under divine authority.—TONY

PRAY ABOUT IT
My Christian brother, does Jesus Christ call the shots in your life? If not, then don't complain that your wife resents your calling the shots for her.

A SEASON FOR EVERYTHING

*There is an appointed time for everything. And there is a time
for every event under heaven.*

—ECCLESIASTES 3:1

One thing that is crucial for keeping life's priorities in their proper place is to remember that everything has a season. God doesn't want us to do it all now.

When our children were young, I would sometimes get frustrated that I wasn't using my administrative abilities outside the home. But it just wasn't my season for that work. God's first priority for me was to concentrate on my kids.

People didn't always understand that. I can remember women getting upset because I declined their invitations to speak at their churches or other events.

But as my children grew older and started going to school, God began to open up new doors and give me desires that matched those open doors. The season God had for me was changing.

God enabled me to meet the challenges of my changing seasons. As the demand for Tony's ministry began to grow, I was able to help meet the needs of the work by taking on administrative duties at The Urban Alternative, our national ministry that seeks to help churches rebuild their communities from the inside out.

In this new season, I knew that God was calling me to use my administrative gifts, skills, and training to organize, set up, and lead a ministry that He would use to bring the Word to hundreds of thousands of people.

No matter how much you may wish to change the season you are in today, it's important that you don't try to rush God's plan. If you try to change seasons on your own, you will remove yourself from God's will and lose your peace, productivity, and power. Relish the season God has you in, and wait with patient expectation for the change of situations and opportunities that will surely come.—LOIS

THINK ABOUT IT

It is so important, whatever season we are in, to love God and wait on Him as well as to seek the advice and encouragement of other believers who have traveled this way before and are overcomers.

DOING WHAT GOD DOES

God saw all that He had made, and behold, it was very good.

—GENESIS 1:31

***

God enjoyed His creation work. We know this because every time He made something, He congratulated Himself. "That's good." Then He made man and woman, His crowning achievement, and He looked over everything He had made and said, "Very good!" God definitely felt good about what He had accomplished.

You're supposed to feel good when you work too. It's the feeling an accountant gets when the numbers come out right. It's the feeling an athlete gets when he or she scores, the sense of accomplishment a business executive feels when the deal is closed. When you can say about your work, "That's good," you're imitating God. That's how it was meant to be.

You were made to be a producer like God because you were created in the image of a God who works. That's why one of the first things God did when He created Adam was to give him a job (see Gen. 2:15).

Please note that sin had not yet spoiled the scene, so Adam's job as overseer and manager of Eden had nothing to do with the curse.

God gave Adam a job, and then He gave him the authority to do something creative by naming the animals (see Gen. 2:18–19). God had given the day and the night their names, and now He allowed Adam to share in this aspect of His creative work. Adam was free to make up the names, because God said, "Whatever you want to call these creatures is cool with Me" (see v. 19).

Then God gave him a helper, Eve, to work alongside him and help him fulfill the divine mandate. As people made in His image, we were designed to enjoy the delight of creative, productive work. We were given the authority to help shape His creation. We were not put here just to watch what someone else is doing but to help cultivate, manage, and shape God's creation. What an awesome honor! We get to do what God does.

THINK ABOUT IT

If you can say of your work, "That's good," you're blessed! If you can't say that, try to find out why. Ask God what He wants you to do about it.

GOD'S GRACE PLAN

He predestined us to adoption as sons through Jesus Christ . . . to the praise of the glory of His grace, which he freely bestowed on us in the Beloved.

—EPHESIANS 1:5–6

※※※

Since everything God has done, does today, and will ever do for us is grounded in His grace, we need to grasp this tremendous concept. Let me give you a definition of grace today. Grace is the inexhaustible supply of God's goodness by which He does for us that which we could never do for ourselves.

Now, you might want to get another cup of coffee or tea and look that definition over for a minute. What could we not do for ourselves? Well, we could not save ourselves. But the death of Christ on the cross freed up the grace of God by dealing with the issue of sin. So God saved us by grace.

He also keeps us day by day in His grace. And it is grace by which God gives us the power to pull off what He wants us to do. It's all by grace.

See, God's whole plan for us from start to finish is a grace plan. And it's such a big plan that according to Ephesians 2:7, God is going to put us on display for all eternity as the prime example of what His grace can do.

Think about it for a minute. God's grace is so inexhaustible and His grace plan for us is so huge that one million years from now, the Niagara Falls of His wonderful grace will still be flowing with no letup. God will never run out of grace!

Now let me make an application to your marriage. If God's only plan for dealing with you as individual believers is to deal with you in grace, how do you suppose He wants you to treat each other? With grace!

In other words, you are never more like Jesus Christ than when you treat your mate with the same grace you have received from God.

TALK ABOUT IT

Because we are human, we will never be perfect in the way we dispense grace. But marriage gives us a built-in training ground to help us learn to respond in grace.

ARE YOU FAITHFUL WITH YOUR MONEY?

If therefore you have not been faithful in the use of unrighteous mammon, who will entrust the true riches to you?

—LUKE 16:11

᪐

*J*esus was very practical when it came to His teaching. He lived in a real world with real people. So when He wanted to make a point real, He often used real illustrations.

For instance, one of Jesus' favorite ways to illustrate spiritual truth was through the issue of money. In Luke 16:1–13, He told the story of a faithless manager to show that the way an individual, or a couple, uses money says a lot about their priorities and their ability to handle the things of God's kingdom.

Someone has calculated that of Jesus' thirty-eight parables, sixteen of them use the issue of wealth as a measure of a person's spiritual maturity. In fact, one out of every ten verses in the New Testament makes reference to material things as a reliable gauge of a person's spiritual life.

Jesus didn't talk about material things so much because He was concerned about money or property per se. But He knew that money is a very accurate measure of a believer's spiritual temperature.

Let us give you one more statistic to make our point. The Bible contains about five hundred verses on prayer, a little fewer than five hundred verses on faith, and more than a thousand verses on money and finance.

You can see that this was a big deal to Jesus and the apostles. They understood that our spiritual condition is often most clearly revealed in our attitude toward our possessions.

If we blow it in the way we use our money, we are not giving God any reason to trust us with the "true riches," which are spiritual. But if we use our money for eternal purposes, we'll have true treasure waiting for us in heaven.

TALK ABOUT IT
Is each of you happy with the shape your financial life is in? If not, share that honestly with your mate. Then get down to some solutions!

PLEASURE THAT LASTS

Thou will make known to me the path of life; in Thy presence is fulness of joy; in Thy right hand there are pleasures forever.

—PSALM 16:11

Lots of people are living for temporary pleasure today. To them, work and everything else is just filler between the parties. But today's richest pleasure-seekers would pale in comparison to King Solomon, the wealthiest and wisest man who ever lived. Later in his life, Solomon lost a sense of the meaning of life. In an attempt to recapture it, he turned first to pleasure, as he himself admitted in Ecclesiastes 2:1–11. He thought if he could "party hearty," if he could have a good time, he would find the sense of purpose he sought.

Read these verses and you will notice three key words: me, myself, and I. Solomon began living for these three people, and he said he didn't deny himself any pleasure his heart could imagine (2:10).

As we said, many people today are living for that goal, working hard for the day when they make enough money that they won't have to deny themselves anything they want. They can enjoy the good times.

Well, Solomon could probably identify with that. So let's ask him where all this leads. This guy didn't go to parties. He *was* the party. Did earthly pleasure solve Solomon's problem of purposelessness?

Here is his answer: "All was vanity and striving after wind and there was no profit under the sun" (Eccles. 2:11).

Talk about futility! Try to grab a fistful of wind, and you'll have the essence of what Solomon was saying. That's what the wrong kind of pleasure was like for Solomon. He threw the party, but the party ended. He had the good times, but the good times expired. And he was left as empty as when he started.

If you are banking on the world's pleasure to fill you up, you are going to be left empty. But once you find *real,* satisfying pleasure in a dynamic relationship with God, you'll find "the path of life"!

PRAY ABOUT IT

Since God's desire to lead you is greater than your desire to be led, ask Him to guide your footsteps—and follow where He leads.

A "THEOLOGY" OF SEX

May the God of peace Himself sanctify you entirely; and may your spirit and soul and body be preserved complete.

—I THESSALONIANS 5:23

When the apostle Paul addressed the issue of sex in 1 Corinthians 6:12–19, he essentially used a Trinitarian argument. In other words, when you read these verses you'll encounter God the Father, Jesus Christ, and the Holy Spirit. So while we may think of sex as a pretty "earthy" subject, Paul is saying that what happens on earth is not all the story. The holy, divine Trinity in heaven is intimately concerned with the issue of how you handle your sexuality and what you do with your body.

Paul's argument in 1 Corinthians 6 is that sexual purity is demanded because of God the Father (vv. 12–14), it's expected because of God the Son (vv. 15–16), and it's possible because of God the Spirit (vv. 17–19).

Many people who falter sexually do so because they lose sight of God's perspective on sex and limit themselves to the human dimension. So whenever you hear someone say, "But I'm only human," that's a human-centered argument reflecting man's way of thinking, not God's.

Paul rejected that argument when he reminded the Corinthians that even though some of them used to be "fornicators" and "adulterers" (v. 9), they were no longer like that because they had been sanctified (v. 11). Paul said, "Don't give me that 'I'm only human' argument. You may have been 'only human' at one point, but now you have God the Father, God the Son, and God the Holy Spirit to help you."

When you got saved, something divine happened to you—to *all* of you. God redeemed your body as well as your soul and spirit. And He is in the process of sanctifying your body, setting it apart for His use. If you or your spouse lose sight of the "theology of sex," then you won't have God's power to help you with the human decisions of day-to-day living.

PRAY ABOUT IT

Don't limit your prayers for sexual purity and marital faithfulness to your body. Ask God to preserve your soul and spirit too!

TOO PERFECT?

An excellent wife, who can find? For her worth is far above jewels.
—PROVERBS 31:10

W henever I wonder how a Christian wife and mother can find the time and energy to do all the things she needs to do, a biblical image comes to mind—the "excellent wife" of Proverbs 31.

I am convinced that if we women are going to see ourselves in the proper light, we must turn the searchlight of God's Word on our lives. And that light shines very brightly in Proverbs 31:10–31.

This woman demonstrated a fervent love for the Lord while loving, supporting, and serving her husband and family. And yet at the same time, she developed the abilities and gifts God gave her as an active woman in her community.

Many women today think the Proverbs 31 woman is almost too perfect. They argue that no one can match the standards portrayed by this woman.

But I don't believe God put this profile in the Bible to frustrate women because we feel like we can't measure up to the ideal. Instead I believe God is inviting us, in the power of His Holy Spirit, to strive toward this portrait of a godly woman, wife, mother, and businesswoman.

In case you are wondering where to begin today, I invite you to look at Proverbs 31:30. "A woman who fears the LORD, she shall be praised." Here is the key to this woman's life, or any woman's life. When our walk with the Lord is in its proper place of priority, He helps us balance and prioritize other responsibilities.

Proverbs 31 does *not* imply that you have to do all the things this woman did in order to emulate her example. Ask God to help you serve and love Him and your family right where you are, and He will make it clear if He has other callings for you.—LOIS

PRAY ABOUT IT
If you are feeling overwhelmed, ask God to help you identify unnecessary things that may be sapping your time and energy.

FOUR ABSOLUTE NECESSITIES (DAY 1)

All authority has been given to Me in heaven and on earth. Go therefore and make disciples of all the nations.

—MATTHEW 28:18–19

---

*I*f you want to find out what matters most to someone, one good way to learn that is to read his last words. I believe that, like Lois and me, you and your spouse want to be obedient followers of Jesus Christ, both in your individual lives and as a married couple. Since that is exactly what this devotional book is designed to help you do, for the next few days I want to discuss with you what matters most to Jesus, so that it can matter most to you too.

Thankfully, when it comes to that which is uppermost on the mind and heart of Jesus, we don't have to wonder about it. Just before His ascension into heaven, Jesus told us what was most important to Him in the well-known text that has come to be known as the Great Commission (see Matt. 28:18–20).

Christ's mandate for the church is to *make* disciples. This is the only command in the passage. Therefore, if Jesus' all-encompassing will for the church is to make disciples, it follows that His will for us as individual believers is to *become* disciples.

A disciple is a learner, a student; to become a disciple of Christ means that we become like Him (see Matt. 10:25). Working toward this goal consists of what I call the four absolute necessities of discipleship: worship, fellowship, Scripture, and evangelism.

We can see these four essentials in action in the first church ever established, the church at Jerusalem (see Acts 2). We're going to "look through the window"of this church the next few days and see what its members had going.

One reason this church was so dynamic is that it got off to a great start. Jesus had told the disciples in Acts 1:8, "Don't have church until the Holy Ghost shows up" (Evans paraphrase). They obeyed Him, and the Spirit showed up in great power at Pentecost.

Then they got moving, living out the reality of being Jesus' disciples.—TONY

TALK ABOUT IT

Take the four vital, Spirit-inspired experiences mentioned above and talk about how dynamic these things are in your lives right now.

FOUR ABSOLUTE NECESSITIES (DAY 2)

The true worshipers shall worship the Father in spirit and truth; for such people the Father seeks to be His worshipers.

—JOHN 4:23

❦

*J*ohn 4:23 is an astounding verse of Scripture. Imagine: The great God of the universe is looking for people to worship Him! No wonder one of the four necessities for discipleship is worship.

There is one key passage in the book of Acts we will come back to several times this week (Acts 2:42–47), because in it we can see all four of the necessities we want to talk about. Worship is one of those: The text says the believers devoted themselves "to the breaking of bread [celebrating the Lord's Supper] and to prayer" (v. 42). Later it says they were going to the temple every day and "praising God" continually (vv. 46–47).

Worship is the furnace of the spiritual life, the celebration of God for who He is and what He has done. The point of worship is not necessarily what you get out of it but what God gets out of it. Worship does not start with what God did for you today. It starts with what you did for Him.

You will be surprised how the Spirit of God ignites your Christian lives, both as individuals and as a couple, when worship becomes not an event but an experience, not a program but a way of life. That includes both public and private worship, because both are crucial for growing disciples of Jesus Christ.

Many of us want to quit worshiping when something goes wrong. But no matter what is wrong in our lives, there is always a reason to worship, to praise God. Praising God doesn't mean denying your problem. But what does Paul say? "Be anxious for nothing, but in everything by prayer and supplication with thanksgiving let your requests be made known to God" (Phil. 4:6). If you want God's power in your life, then worship must be part of your daily operation.—TONY

THINK ABOUT IT

Expecting worship on Sunday to roll over to worship on Monday through Saturday is like depending on a big Sunday dinner to carry you through the rest of the week nutritionally.

FOUR ABSOLUTE NECESSITIES (DAY 3)

They were continually devoting themselves . . . to fellowship.

—ACTS 2:42

⁂

ellowship is another of the necessities we must learn to practice if we are going to be Christ's disciples. Biblical fellowship is not just coffee and donuts in Sunday school or sharing a meal in the fellowship hall. Fellowship is the sharing of our lives with other believers. You cannot become a disciple of Jesus Christ independently of others.

That's why the church is so important. It is the "fireplace" where one log touches another and the fire is maintained. If you are getting dull in your spiritual life, you need to be in proximity to others who are on fire so their fire can ignite you. If you are losing your spiritual fire and you're alone, you're going to become ashes.

So the question is, are we connected with other believers who desire to be on fire too? Fellowship is designed to keep the fire burning. There was no such thing as a non-churched Christian in the New Testament. They were in dynamic fellowship with each other.

We need each other because the best of us can get spiritually dull sometimes and want to throw in the towel. The best of us sometimes fall flat on our faces. As the apostle Paul warned, "Let him who thinks he stands take heed lest he fall" (1 Cor. 10:12).

In generations past, Sunday was a much more important day. People would come together for worship and then devote a major part of the day to fellowship. People made time to be with one another. Monday was often painful, with heartaches and headaches. So the fellowship experienced on Sunday was a critical reinforcement. But as we have become more affluent and more independent, we've lost our need for one another.

Fellowship in the Bible was designed to show us that we can't make it on our own; we need other believers.—TONY

TALK ABOUT IT
One of the great things about being married is that you have built-in fellowship! Make sure the two of you are "stimulat[ing] one another to love and good deeds" (Heb. 10:24).

FOUR ABSOLUTE NECESSITIES (DAY 4)

The word of God is living and active and sharper than any two-edged sword.

—HEBREWS 4:12

We're talking about the essential components of discipleship, the ingredients that tell us what it means to be followers of Jesus Christ. Our model for these devotional studies is the church at Jerusalem as described in the early chapters of Acts. These believers were growing in their knowledge of Scripture. This is the third necessity for following Christ, because Scripture equips us to live the Christian life.

Your mind is key to becoming a disciple, because you are what you think (see Prov. 23:7). Many of us have come into the Christian life with warped minds, contaminated by an ungodly system. Only when our minds are renewed will our lives be transformed (see Rom. 12:2).

A transformed mind comes through the study and practice of the Bible. All of us know about brainwashing. It's repeating certain data over and over again until a person absorbs that data into his or her brain, believes it wholeheartedly, and begins to act on it.

That's what the Word of God is designed to do. Many of us have habits in our lives that we want to get rid of. But we say, "I can't" because we've been brainwashed by the enemy to believe we will never have victory in this area. But God's Word can change that if we will feed on it regularly.

If you are going to become a disciple, you must have a dynamic experience with the Bible. When it comes to our spiritual education, we have a divine Teacher, the Holy Spirit, who reminds us of all that Jesus taught (see John 14:26).

You say, "Sure, Tony, if Jesus would come and teach our Sunday school class next Sunday, we would get excited about the Word." You actually have something even better—the indwelling Spirit—to make God's Word come alive. He is eager to set your heart on fire!—TONY

THINK ABOUT IT

A disciple is a person for whom the Word of God is as necessary and desirable as food is for the body.

FOUR ABSOLUTE NECESSITIES (DAY 5)

He who is wise wins souls.

—PROVERBS 11:30

When the Holy Spirit came on Pentecost, the church at Jerusalem stood up in a dynamic witness for Christ (see Acts 2). The most obvious event of the church's witness was Peter's great Pentecost sermon. This is the same Peter who, just a few weeks earlier, had been too scared to admit he even knew Jesus. What made the difference? The Holy Spirit had taken control of Peter, and Peter was about to take off and soar in his spiritual life, becoming a bold and faithful witness for Jesus Christ.

Evangelism is the fourth and final necessity for being a disciple. But you may argue, "Tony, I'm not bold. I'm a private person."

Well, the fact is that most of us are only private when we want to be. For example, when something exciting happens in your life, you will undoubtedly talk about it without a whole lot of prompting. Anyone who is so private that he or she never talks about anything that matters has to be a pretty boring person!

One reason a lot of us Christians don't share Christ is that we've lost our excitement about Him. When He is exciting to you, you can't keep Him to yourself.

The enthusiastic witness of the believers who received the Spirit on Pentecost and Peter's dynamic sermon on that special day added three thousand new believers to the body of Christ. Now *that's* a witness! And please notice that these three thousand people did not come because of an evangelistic "program." They came because God's people were so overwhelmed by experiencing the presence of His Spirit that they couldn't keep the faith to themselves.

This ought to be happening in our churches and our individual lives as we scatter each week to witness for Christ wherever we go.—TONY

PRAY ABOUT IT

One thing you must ask God to do if you're going to grow as a Christian is help you open your mouth and be a witness.

DOING IT ALL

Many daughters have done nobly, but you excel them all.

—PROVERBS 31:29

he feminist movement of the last thirty years has given us a lot of angry and frustrated women who are determined to prove to themselves and everyone else—particularly to men—that they can do anything a man can do and do it better.

This movement's song of liberation seemed to boast, "I can do it all." The fact is, though, that modern-day feminists have nothing on the woman of Proverbs 31. She did all of the things modern feminists struggle to do, and she clearly did them right.

But she didn't do these things out of anger or frustration, or to prove something to herself or to someone else. And it wasn't because she was a "superwoman" who did not need anyone else. Instead, what we see in Proverbs 31 is a woman who accomplished more than most feminists will ever accomplish yet did so with unswerving devotion to the Lord in the setting of a loving home and family.

The message to women is this: We need liberation but with biblical application. God's Word gives us true liberty without causing our focus to be sidetracked onto the oppression of women and a fierce competition between the sexes.

With all of the duties and demands that wives and mothers face these days, you may not feel like a queen in your home. But the writer of Proverbs wants you to know that any woman who can meet the daily challenges while keeping her love for God strong deserves the honor paid to a queen (see Prov. 31:10).—LOIS

PRAY ABOUT IT

A Proverbs 31 woman is rare, but you can be this kind of woman in God's power. Go for it!

BLESSED POVERTY

Blessed are the poor in spirit, for theirs is the kingdom of heaven.
—MATTHEW 5:3

*J*esus began the Sermon on the Mount by pronouncing blessedness, or happiness, on those who reflect the attitude of the kingdom of God and the character of the King.

Jesus' first beatitude has nothing to do with economic poverty, of course. Jesus is not primarily concerned with how many cars you have or what kind of clothes you wear.

Neither is the Lord talking about a "poor me" syndrome showing how low you can hang your head because you feel so worthless and humble.

Instead, those who are poor in spirit are people who recognize their total dependence on God. They are husbands and wives who understand that they cannot be the marriage partner they need to be apart from God. They are fathers and mothers who understand that effective parenting is impossible unless they cry out to God for help.

Being poor in spirit has to do with true humility. The opposite attitude is to be "rich" in pride—to think you can live your life independently of God.

Now we need to ask, how poor in spirit does Jesus really expect us to be? He answers that for us in very graphic terms.

The word Jesus used for *poor* means "a beggar." Beggars were common in His day, and from what we can tell they were not necessarily ashamed to beg for their living. That is, by crying out for money or food they were making a public declaration that they were in desperate need of help. They were dependent people, relying on others for the food they needed to eat each day and survive. God wants us to make the same discovery about ourselves spiritually.

On the streets of God's kingdom, it's the beggars who are happy!

PRAY ABOUT IT
Ask God to forgive any streak of self-sufficiency He may find in you. Pray as a couple that you will help each other live in dependence on God.

CONSULT THE LIFE-MAKER

You will seek Me and find Me, when you search for Me with all your heart.
—JEREMIAH 29:13

⟞⟞⟞⟞⟞⟞⟞

*I*f you're like me, life has a lot of pieces to it. There's the spouse piece, the kids piece, the work piece, the financial piece, and so on. And as soon as you get one piece in place, another one comes loose.

Things like that happen with a purpose. God is trying to tell us, "Look, quit trying to fix everything yourself. Quit trying to put it all together on your own. You won't find the answer until you find it in Me."

But what do so many of us men do with our lives? We do like I did one year with the bicycle I bought my son for Christmas. It came with one of those thick assembly manuals written by someone for whom English was a second language.

It was going to take a long time to read that manual, and I hate taking the time to read those things anyway. So, like any intelligent, self-respecting American man, I figured, "Hey, I've got a doctoral degree. I can certainly put a bike together without any help."

Eight hours later, I had nothing but the handlebars on. Lois came to the door of the garage with a novel suggestion: "Honey, why don't you just read the directions?"

In my frustration and futility, with my pride crushed, I finally did just that. I let the creator of the bike tell me how to put it together. Forty-five minutes later, the bike was assembled.

The One who created us knows more about putting life together than you or I ever will know. We need to humble ourselves and say, "Lord, I don't know how to put life together by myself. It has too many pieces. Show me the purpose You have for me."

Life starts making sense when you begin your search for purpose in the right place—by seeking the face and the heart of God.—TONY

PRAY ABOUT IT

A great way to begin this search is by praying, "Search me, O God, and know my heart" (Ps. 139:23).

NO CHAINS

All things are lawful for me, but not all things are profitable. All things are lawful for me, but I will not be mastered by anything.

—I CORINTHIANS 6:12

You've probably heard the old story about the smoker who said, "I can quit smoking anytime I want. I know, because I've done it a hundred times." A person who says something like that is telling you that he or she is under the mastery of nicotine. Filling your body with nicotine may be lawful in our society, but it certainly isn't profitable—physically, financially, or spiritually!

Paul's classic statement gives us a timeless truth principle that we can apply to any activity we may engage in as individuals and also as married couples. This principle helps us discard and avoid that which is bad and unprofitable while choosing the better over the good and then choosing the best over what is merely better.

One reason this biblical principle is so valuable is that we have a tendency to carry even good things too far, until they can take control of us.

Even though an activity may be lawful, it should never boss us around. Even though it's legitimate, it should never become our supervisor. Even though an activity or appetite may be OK, it should never make you its slave.

In 1 Corinthians 6:13, Paul gave two such examples. The first is food. It's lawful to eat—praise God! But it's not OK to let food dominate your life until your appetite is out of control.

The second example is sex. It's lawful to say, "I have sexual desires." After all, God gave you those desires; they are healthy and normal.

But Paul said we are not to be mastered by our sexual desires. God did not give us our bodies so we could practice immorality or insist that our mates meet our sexual demands regardless of their wishes or the circumstances. Don't let something legitimate get out of hand, or it will slap chains on you.

TALK ABOUT IT

Can you and your mate say that your legitimate appetites are under control? Be honest with each other. Break the chains.

NO MORE RAMBOS

Hear, O sons, the instruction of a father, and give attention that you may gain understanding.

—PROVERBS 4:1

~~~

*P*roverbs 4:1 is a great verse for a Christian father to quote to his children, because the Bible instructs children to obey their parents. Notice, however, this verse presupposes that Dad is providing godly instruction worth listening to and obeying. Today far too many fathers are failing to live out their roles as godly leaders in the home, church, and society. The result is a culture in shambles, particularly within the next generation.

Today's children are sometimes referred to as a lost generation. But the fact is that our children, especially our boys, are the *product* of a lost generation. They are being raised in an environment that does not model biblical manhood or hold them accountable to that standard.

The new male model is the Rambo-type superman who can slay dozens and never go down, who carries out his one-man vendetta of violence and never sheds a tear.

We now have a generation of boys and young men who have this mentality. They are quick to deal out violence, and that's scary enough. But what's even more scary is that they can deal out violence and feel nothing. They seem to be beyond normal human sensitivity. That didn't just happen. These kids were nurtured on a culture of violence that has left them uninformed as to what a real man is.

The effect of this dearth of biblical manhood on young girls is just as devastating. We have a generation of girls who don't know how to identify the right kind of man because they haven't seen enough of them.

And when these boys and girls produce children of their own, another generation is born that will not get the nurture it needs.

God is using the Christian men's movement to begin reversing this trend, for which I am very grateful. We men need to recapture our homes for Christ. If you're ready, He'll help you!—TONY

PRAY ABOUT IT
Ask God to help you draw a line in the sand and declare to the enemy, "Here I stand."

FEEL THE BURN

Speak, LORD, for Thy servant is listening.

—I SAMUEL 3:9

---

*I*f you have ever tried to lift weights or exercise in any serious way, you probably experienced some pain the first time you worked out. It's called "feeling the burn."

The reason it hurts, of course, is that you are using muscles that are not used to being exercised. What you want to do at that point is quit, but the way to get over the pain is to work those muscles some more and make them ache more. Eventually, you will get used to the exercise, and the pain will be replaced by the rewarding feeling you get when your body is in good shape.

You cannot "audit" exercise. You can't just go "sit in" on an exercise class and watch everyone else work out. And you can't just go to the gym or the health club once a week and expect to come out looking like the people on television. Similarly, if you want to be an "in shape" Christian, then you have to be an effective spiritual exerciser. Obedience has to become a way of life.

Some of us want to "audit" the Christian life. We want to come to church and get all the instruction, but we don't want to do any of the hard work of obedience.

If you want an adventure, ask the Lord, "What do You want me to do with what I have learned? What do You want me to do so that You can disclose Yourself to me? What must I obey so that I will have the fruit of Your blessing in my life?"

And if you want an even bigger adventure, pray this way as a couple. But this means you must be ready to make a large spiritual investment and not waste time by hearing things you do not intend to do anything with.

THINK ABOUT IT

If you will accept the challenge of obeying Christ in everything, the payoff will be beyond your wildest dreams!

MIRROR, MIRROR ON THE WALL

Man looks at the outward appearance, but the LORD looks at the heart.

—I SAMUEL 16:7

❧

We live in a culture that worships youth, beauty, fitness, and all that goes with a woman's outward appearance. No wonder so many women feel intimidated by the subject of physical beauty! Let's face it. Even a woman who is blessed with unusual attractiveness will still fall prey to the passing of the years and the inevitable fading of her youthful good looks.

There is nothing wrong with physical attractiveness. Women do not need to apologize for their beauty. There is nothing godly about a woman neglecting her appearance. The problem comes when outward beauty ceases to be merely one aspect of a woman's life and becomes the main focus of her heart.

"Charm is deceitful and beauty is vain," said the writer of Proverbs (31:30), not because charm or beauty is inherently sinful. The deceit comes when a woman tries to capitalize on her beauty to get what she wants or allows her identity to be wrapped up in the way she looks. Beauty was never meant to be a measure of anyone's worth. The Bible assures us that what God looks at is the heart.

First Samuel 16 is the story of David's anointing as Israel's future king. Eliab was the oldest boy in the family, and a fine specimen of young manhood. But God chose David, not Eliab, because He was using a different set of criteria.

So don't let the subject of physical beauty make you feel intimidated. God is not holding a beauty contest. By depending on the power of the indwelling Holy Spirit, you can achieve the noble character that God desires.—LOIS

THINK ABOUT IT

Physical beauty eventually fades, but a godly character grows more beautiful with time.

YOUR PLANTING RESPONSIBILITIES

He who sows sparingly shall also reap sparingly; and he who sows bountifully shall also reap bountifully.

—2 CORINTHIANS 9:6

❧

*C*onsider this question: If you knew that your next-door neighbor was a thief, would you leave your windows unlocked and your garage door standing open when you left the house? Of course not. You wouldn't want the thief to have access to your goods.

Well, God says that many of His people are thieves, and He has locked the windows of heaven so they can't have access to His blessings.

You might be saying, "Excuse me. But did you say *thieves?*"

In Malachi 3:8–10, God accused the Israelites of robbing Him by withholding their tithes and offerings. "Bring Me the whole tithe," God challenged the people, "and I will take the padlock off the windows of heaven" (see v. 10).

Giving God the portion of their income that He requests is one of a couple's basic, non-negotiable "planting" responsibilities in the handling of their finances. When it comes to taxes, on the other hand, couples don't have to worry about keeping back what belongs to the government. In most cases, the government takes its share first. Those who withhold the government's share can face severe consequences enforced by law.

Even though God doesn't force us to give Him His share, the consequences are still there if we don't. I'm convinced that some Christian couples who are having financial woes and are deeply in debt are not just poor handlers of money. They are under God's curse because they are disobeying Him.

See, if a couple is not honoring God in their finances, it doesn't matter how much they have. It will never be enough, because God will punch holes in their pockets (see Hag. 1:6). On the other hand, when a husband and wife honor God with the minimum of the 10 percent tithe, He gives them access to His supply.

PRAY ABOUT IT

Ask yourselves what God would find if He "audited" you. If you aren't sure of the answer, take it to Him in prayer.

LIFE BLESSING OR LIFE SENTENCE?

Whatever you do, do your work heartily, as for the Lord rather than for men; knowing that from the Lord you will receive the reward of the inheritance. It is the Lord Christ whom you serve.

—COLOSSIANS 3:23–24

few weeks ago, when we discussed how work is a gift from God that we are meant to enjoy, your reaction may have been, "That sounds great, but my job's not like that." If that's your situation, it's because sin entered the Garden of Eden and messed everything up.

When Adam and Eve rebelled against God, one consequence of their sin was a curse on work. God told them, "Cursed is the ground because of you; in toil you shall eat of it all the days of your life. Both thorns and thistles it shall grow for you; and you shall eat the plants of the field; by the sweat of your face you shall eat bread" (Gen. 3:17–19).

From that point on, mankind definitely had a problem. In the garden, everything was perfect; Adam didn't need a Weed-Eater in Eden. But with the introduction of sin came thorns and thistles to jab and prick man's efforts. This is why so many people feel like work is a life sentence rather than a blessing. When you're in a job you don't like, when you feel your job is meaningless, what you're feeling are the thorns and thistles of the curse. It's part of mankind's fall into sin.

This also explains why people can be so creative in evil. We were born to create, but sin has distorted that ability so that now we use our creative ability to create evil. Therefore, we not only have to work against a created order that grows thorns and thistles. We also have to work against people who are themselves thorns and thistles.

That's the bad news. But here's the flip side: In Romans 8:19–25, Paul said creation is awaiting redemption, when Eden's curse will be reversed. Our final redemption is still in the future, but we don't have to wait for heaven to enjoy our work. When Christ redeemed us, He also redeemed work and filled it with new meaning. We're now working for Him!

PRAY ABOUT IT
Who are you working for today—"the man" or the Son of Man?

THE NEVER-ENDING STORY OF GRACE

Grace and peace be multiplied to you . . . seeing that [God's] divine power has granted to us everything pertaining to life and godliness.

—2 PETER 1:2–3

* * *

*T*f you two were like Lois and me when we were first married, you lacked a few of the essentials—like a house and furniture! Contrast that time in your married life with the moment when you got saved: At that instant you were a spiritual infant, but God had put within you everything you would ever need to become a fully mature, fully functioning believer. And He did it by His grace, which Peter said is so big you need a multiplication table to figure it out. What an awesome truth! You don't get saved by grace and then move on to God's really good stuff. You get saved, and everything He has for you is already yours through His grace.

For any baby to realize its full potential, it must eat and grow. In the same way, our grace potential is only realized as we grow spiritually. It is growth that brings out what's inside us. And we should be satisfied with nothing less than the multiplication of God's grace in our lives.

Do you remember when you were eight or nine years old and wanted to be a teenager? I remember when I was ten telling my father, "Daddy I'm almost a teenager!"

Then I became a teenager and got used to that, so I started looking forward to becoming a man. Then I would say to my father, "Daddy, I'm almost a man." I was always looking forward to what was next. Being able to vote. Being able to drive. Meeting the right woman and getting married.

Eventually, life runs out of new expectations, because our lives are finite and limited. But God's grace knows no limits. The story of grace never ends, so you can always look forward to the next chapter. There's no reason that you cannot grow into the fullness of everything that God by His grace has encoded in your spiritual DNA!—TONY

THINK ABOUT IT

In case you haven't figured it out yet, marriage is one of the things God gives you to help bring out your potential and allow you to grow into full maturity.

WHERE ARE YOU PUTTING IT?

Do not lay up for yourselves treasures upon earth, where moth and rust destroy, and where thieves break in and steal.

—MATTHEW 6:19

❧

*Y*ou are probably well acquainted with this familiar verse. Many of us memorized it when we were kids. Let me share a short Greek lesson to show you why this verse is so important. In the original language, the words *lay up* and *treasure* are from the same root. So Jesus was literally saying, "Do not treasure up treasure for yourselves."

In other words, if we are going to follow Jesus we cannot give our hearts to the accumulation of material wealth. Does that mean Jesus doesn't want your family to have a savings account? Does this command disqualify you from investing on Wall Street? Is it wrong to have some money put aside for tough times?

This cannot be what Jesus was saying, because the Bible applauds saving. The writer of Proverbs urged us to study the ant and the way it stores up its food and then to imitate the ant's wise preparation (see Prov. 6:6–11).

Jesus' intent was not to discourage preparation for the future. The following two verses, Matthew 6:20–21, make it clear that the Lord's concern was that we not let earthly accumulation become the focus of our lives.

Jesus wants us to examine why we are accumulating wealth. If it's to prepare for the future, fine. But if we are spending our time stockpiling for earth rather than stockpiling for heaven, we are in trouble.

So how do we make sure our money and other treasures, including our time and talents, are producing dividends in heaven? By investing them in God's work down here on earth. The question you need to ask yourselves today is, In what ways is the kingdom of God benefiting from our wealth?—TONY

TALK ABOUT IT
Do a "checkbook checkup" together today, answering the question above. If you don't like the answer, decide how you're going to fix it!

SAME OLD SAME OLD

The conclusion, when all has been heard, is: fear God and keep His commandments, because this applies to every person.

—ECCLESIASTES 12:13

⬥

*B*rother, if we were to say to you, "Tell us who you are," could you do so without giving your name, occupation, or any of the other means most men use to identify themselves?

Plenty of men know their names and their occupations but don't really know who they are at the core of their beings. Therefore, they have no sense of purpose in life.

When you have no purpose for what you're doing, all you have left is the routine of what you're doing, which becomes an escape, an excuse not to search for anything more.

Legions of modern men suffer from what we call the "same old same old" disease. You ask them how it's going, and they answer, "Oh, you know, same old same old."

What they mean is, every day they get out of that same old bed and go to that same old bathroom to stare in the mirror at that same old face. They go to that same old closet and thumb through those same old clothes to put on that same old body. They sit at that same old breakfast table and eat that same old breakfast cooked by that same old wife. (We're treading dangerous ground here, aren't we?)

Then they get in that same old car and drive down that same old road to that same old office. There they work with the same old people, doing that same old thing, receiving that same old pay.

At five o'clock, they drive that same old road back to that same old house so they can start it all over again the next day.

Are you in a rut right now? Don't look around; look up, because God wants to give you a new sense of purpose and significance.

PRAY ABOUT IT

Ask God to interrupt your routine with His renewed vision for life and living for His kingdom.

HAPPY MOURNERS

Blessed are those who mourn, for they shall be comforted.

—MATTHEW 5:4

W hat causes you to go into spiritual mourning? We don't want to cloud your day, but Jesus said if you want the happiness of His comfort, you are going to have to mourn.

The mourning Jesus was talking about in this beatitude is sorrow over our sin. It's what Paul called "the sorrow that is according to the will of God" (2 Cor. 7:10).

We don't often come to grips with how sinful and messed up we sometimes become. The problem is, we are measuring ourselves against the wrong standard.

We laugh at things we know are not right, and we think, "Well, this isn't nearly as bad as some of the stuff out there." We do things that are questionable and tell ourselves, "God understands."

But God says, "No, you ought to be crying, not laughing." When Paul saw himself he cried out, "Wretched man that I am!" (Rom. 7:24).

Paul mourned because he saw his sin. When he looked at the character of God and his own life, there was such a discrepancy that he mourned. Peter wailed bitterly after he had denied the Lord three times because he felt the pain God felt over his failure.

Mourning also includes a deep concern for souls. When we see lost people as they are, bound for an eternity without Christ, it should do something to us.

So the spiritual mourner cries about the things that make God cry, hurts where God hurts, and is impassioned about the things God is impassioned about.

The godly sorrow Paul spoke of in 2 Corinthians leads to repentance. In other words, true spiritual mourning leads to a solution. The mourner deals with sin, and in doing so experiences the comfort of God's forgiveness.

PRAY ABOUT IT

Here's a prayer for a spiritual mourner: "Lord, help me to feel about sin the way You feel about it. Help me to think as You think, to hurt as You hurt, and to hate sin as much as You hate it."

BETTER SEW UP THAT HOLE

You have sown much, but harvest little . . . and he who earns, earns wages to put into a purse with holes.

—HAGGAI 1:6

✦～✦～✦～✦

*E*ver felt like your purse or wallet had a hole in it? It's easy to feel that way as we watch our money. As one guy said, "Yeah, my money talks. It says, 'Good-bye.'"

The people of the prophet Haggai's day had that problem. But it wasn't just because they had a lot of expenses. It was because they were, in the words of Jesus, storing up for themselves instead of storing up for God (see Matt. 6:19–21).

Haggai was talking to people who had returned to Jerusalem from the Babylonian captivity. Their first priority should have been to rebuild God's temple so the worship of God could be restored. But after beginning the temple, the people let it sit unfinished while they built lavish houses for themselves.

Here was a clear case of God's people laying up treasure for themselves while God's priorities were ignored. God could not let this insult continue, so He sent a few of His "moths" (see Matt. 6:19) to eat holes in their purses.

There's a fundamental principle here we don't dare miss. If you aren't using your material possessions to further the kingdom of God and reflect His priorities, there's no place you can stash your money where He can't get at it if He chooses to do so.

Now in Jesus' day, the fear of moths was very real because people might only have three or four garments in their entire lifetime. So having your precious few garments eaten by moths was a very real possibility. When that happened, even those garments for which people spent a lot of money would have no long-term value. We also know from the story of the Good Samaritan that getting hit by thieves was as big a problem in Jesus' day as it is in ours.

So if your bank account seems to have holes, it's a good idea to check out the "eternal value" of your portfolio.

THINK ABOUT IT

Jesus said if your spending and investing can't be traced in terms of eternal value, that money is lost!

THE INCREDIBLE VALUE OF TRUST

The heart of her husband trusts in her, and he will have no lack of gain.

—PROVERBS 31:11

❦

The verse above comes from a very well-known portion of Scripture, the description of an excellent wife and mother who exhibits the character God honors.

I wanted you to notice verse 11 in particular because it states an ingredient that is foundational to a healthy and growing marriage: the quality of trust. No relationship can survive and flourish very long without trust between the members, and this is especially true of marriage.

This picture of confident trust is a sharp contrast to the "battle of the sexes" that is being promoted today in the secular culture, the battle that is shredding so many marriages.

The Bible does not say so here, since the focus is on the woman, but we can be confident that a husband who has a wife like this will not repay her trust with mistrust. In fact, this woman's husband was "known in the gates" of the city as he took his place among the elders (v. 23). Thus he occupied a trusted position of leadership, marking him as a man of excellent character as well.

Marriage is such a close relationship that a husband and wife gain intimate knowledge that needs to be held in complete trust. This is not because these things are wrong but because they are private.

A woman in particular understands the power of these things, and she can be tempted to use them against her husband when she is angry. And when a husband breaks his marital trust, it takes a woman of extraordinary character not to retaliate.

Is your marriage marked by absolute trust? I hope so. When a husband knows his wife is a trustworthy person, he can take risks and soar to greater heights in his calling. And when a wife knows her heart is safe in her husband's care, she is free to grow into the person God wants her to be.—LOIS

PRAY ABOUT IT
Pray as a couple today that God will keep you from ever using your trusted secrets against each other.

THE CENTRALITY OF THE HOLY SPIRIT

I will ask the Father, and He will give you another Helper, that He may be with you forever; that is the Spirit of truth.

—JOHN 14:16–17

he Holy Spirit is not merely a nice addendum to the Christian faith. He is at the heart and core of it. I'm convinced that if believers like you and me get a handle on who the Holy Spirit is and what He does, our individual Christian lives—to say nothing of our marriages and family lives—will never be the same. The fact is that the Holy Spirit's role in your life is the indispensable factor in determining whether you are a failure or a success as a Christian.

To understand the Person and work of the Holy Spirit, study Jesus' Upper Room discourse (John 13–17). It was here He promised His followers that God the Father would send them "another Helper."

This was not one of the greatest moments in the lives of the disciples. It was a spiritual down time. Everything was going wrong. Judas had shown himself to be a traitor. And Jesus had just told Peter that within twenty-four hours he would publicly deny Christ. Plus, the Jews wanted to get rid of Christ and all of His followers.

Then came the worst blow. Jesus told them, "I am going to go away to prepare a place for you. You can't come to Me until I come for you. I am not going to tell you when I will come for you, but trust Me" (see John 14:1–3). Thomas said, "Jesus, You have to be kidding! We put all our marbles in Your basket, and now You tell us You have to leave us? Jesus, we had enough problems trying to make it with You here. How in the world do You expect us to make it if You leave us?" (see v. 5).

This was the tension-filled environment in which Jesus introduced His disciples to the stabilizing ministry of the Spirit.

What problems and tensions are you facing today? They can't be much worse than the disciples' predicament. Today, you can draw on the same supply of power and strength Jesus promised them—the Holy Spirit.—TONY

THINK ABOUT IT
Jesus said the Spirit "will be in you" (John 14:17). That means He will never desert you!

DO YOU HAVE A KINGDOM VISION?

The LORD has sought out for Himself a man after His own heart.

—I SAMUEL 13:14

❧

et me give you some exciting news today, my Christian brother. God has a thrilling, demanding, and fulfilling kingdom agenda for you—and it starts right there in your home. Let's talk about what it will take for you to be God's kingdom man in your marriage and family.

To be a kingdom husband and father, you must seek the vision God has for you—the place He wants you to fulfill in your personal and family life, and in the church and community. A lot of Christian men are existing day to day without any kind of all-encompassing divine vision to move and motivate them. If that's true, the problem is not that God is hiding His will from men. God is always looking for men whose hearts are faithful toward Him.

In Jeremiah 4:25, the lament was that "there was no man" who could be found faithful to the Lord. Then in Jeremiah 5:1, God sent Jeremiah roaming through the streets of Jerusalem trying to find just one man "who does justice, who seeks truth."

God made an astounding promise. If Jeremiah could find even one man like that, God would pardon the people! But the prophet could not find one man of justice and truth, so God's judgment fell on the nation.

God is still hunting for faithful men, men after His heart, men who have a vision of what God can do with them.

One problem is that too many of us men have learned our manhood from the wrong sources. And we try to import the nonsense of Hollywood and sports into our marriages and families.

We Christian men need a twofold kingdom vision. First, we need to see the agenda God has laid out for men in His Word. Second, we need a clear picture of how God wants us to carry out that agenda in our lives.

God wants to give you a vision. Are you ready?—TONY

PRAY ABOUT IT
Ezekiel 22:30 says God is looking for a man to "stand in the gap." Why not tell God you want to be that man?

IT'S ALL JUST BORROWED

Not to us, O LORD, not to us, but to Thy name give glory. . . . Our God is in the heavens;
He does whatever He pleases.

—PSALM 115:1, 3

hy does God deserve all the glory? Why can He do whatever He wants?
Because everything in this world is His—including all of us. God didn't
create us for our pleasure. He created us for Himself. He's the owner, and
you and I are just the managers.

The universe is God's place; He does whatever He pleases with it.

The patriarch Joseph is a great example of someone who understood this principle.
His brothers sold him as a slave, and he wound up in Egypt under the ownership
of a man named Potiphar. According to Genesis 39:6, "[Potiphar] left everything
he owned in Joseph's charge." He made Joseph his steward, in other words.

Later, when Potiphar's wife tried to seduce Joseph, his reply showed that he
clearly understood his role (see vv. 8–9).

The Bible declares that God owns it all (Ps. 24:1–2). That's about as clear as it
gets. Now, unless you and I helped Him create the world, we don't really own a
thing. This is important for us men in particular to understand and believe,
because men are into ownership. That's where we get a big part of our masculine
identity.

It's sort of the Tarzan thing. Was there any doubt about who owned the jungle?
Tarzan was king of his domain, and we want to be king of our domains too.

But since we can't swing through trees and fight lions, we collect stuff. Then
we compare our stuff with other guys' stuff to see who has the most stuff. Like the
bumper sticker says, "He who dies with the most toys, wins."

My brother, you and I were born with nothing but our skin on. The only reason
we will be buried in a nice suit is because somebody else will dress us. And there
will be no U-Haul following the hearse, because everything we have is only bor-
rowed from God.—TONY

THINK ABOUT IT

Start living today as if everything you have is on loan from God, and you'll save
yourself a lot of worry.

LOSING OUR "LOSER'S LIMP"

Walk in the way of good men, and keep to the paths of the righteous.

—PROVERBS 2:20

❦

*Y*ou can probably tell that one of my passions is to raise up a generation of "kingdom men"—godly husbands and fathers who will reclaim their marriage, family, church, and community for Christ.

But for that to happen, we "baby boomers" and older Christian husbands and fathers must get our act together. That's one of the things I want to help you do in our devotional studies together. Wife, I encourage you to read these days with your husband so you can help him.

The problem is that many men today are suffering from what I call a "loser's limp." This is what happens when a guy is playing baseball and the ball is hit over his head. He knows he should make the play, but he misjudges the ball.

He doesn't want anyone else to know he muffed the play, however, so he falls down and gets up limping. The idea is if it weren't for whatever he tripped over he would have caught the ball. A loser's limp is a way of camouflaging failure.

Far too many Christian men are camouflaging their failure to be kingdom men. They give excuses: "If it weren't for the way I was raised." "Well, my father left my mother." "If it weren't for this woman God gave me . . ."

But excuses won't get the job done. We need to realize that just being a male isn't enough to make us faithful kingdom men who are effective for Christ in our homes.

There used to be plenty of older men whom younger men could look to—men who had been through the course and could help guide the younger men through the mazes of life. But today, mentors like that are hard to find.

A spiritual fog has descended over many Christian men. But the good news is that God is still looking for men He can trust and use. How about it, brother? Let's go for His best together!—TONY

THINK ABOUT IT
When it comes to their marriages and families, some men are like the abominable snowman—footprints everywhere, but you never see him. Don't let that describe you.

THE ABSOLUTE NECESSITY OF THE WORD

Preach the word; be ready in season and out of season; reprove, rebuke, exhort, with great patience and instruction.

—2 TIMOTHY 4:2

The core of a church service is the Word of God. When you come to church, you've got to have your Bible with you because the issue is truth. In many churches, you don't need your Bible because you are never evaluating truth. The question there is, Did the preacher sound good and did the choir jam? The question is not, Was my inner being exposed to God?

If you are going to worship God in spirit and truth you must be willing to accept the absolute authority of His Word. This makes some people uncomfortable because they don't want anybody—not even God—messing in their business.

If I came into our church in Dallas all sweaty and smelly, people would say, "How can you come in here smelling and looking like that?" Well, God looks down on our worship and says, "How can you come to church with that spiritual dirt all over you? How can you come to your private worship time smelling and looking like that?" God wants to get into your business because He's into truth. My commitment as a pastor is to tell it like it is. Sometimes the people at our church will like it and applaud. Other times, they won't like it. They may even get mad. But that's all right, because the issue is truth.

In the course of some tremendous teaching on worship in John 4, Jesus made one of the most awesome statements ever recorded. He said God is looking for worshipers (v. 23)! The great God of the universe is hunting for folks who want to worship Him. Volunteers ought to be lining up by the millions! But can you believe it? God is having a hard time finding people who really want to worship.

Are you ready to volunteer? Do you understand that the essence of worship is coming to God on the basis of His truth, with your spirit communing with His Holy Spirit (see John 4:24)? If so, you're ready for some great worship! And it doesn't have to be limited to church. You can engage in God-pleasing worship at home with your mate and family.—TONY

THINK ABOUT IT
Worship is coming before God with your inner person, not just your body, resting on His truth.

SOLID INVESTMENT ADVICE

Lay up for yourselves treasures in heaven, where neither moth nor rust destroys, and where thieves do not break in or steal.

—MATTHEW 6:20

Matthew 6:20 is the best investment advice you'll ever get! Any financial counselor would tell you to go for an investment that is protected against losses while yielding incredibly high dividends. That's what Jesus is offering you. Talk about a golden retirement plan!

Sometimes we are tempted to push statements about heaven off into the distant future—the "pie in the sky, by and by" mentality. We tend to compartmentalize life into the here and now and the hereafter . . . and seldom do the twain meet.

But Jesus doesn't operate with that dichotomy. His concern is that we live *today* with heaven in view. His intense desire for us is that we do God's will on earth just as God's will is being done in heaven.

Jesus wants His kingdom to be our primary focus now so that whether it's our savings account, our home, or whatever, we use it for eternal purposes.

It's not that you can't enjoy the house God has given you. On the contrary, when you start living with heaven in view, you begin to enjoy the good things God gives because your heart isn't all wrapped up in them.

We need to remember that heaven begins on earth. Eternal life begins the minute we accept Christ as our Savior. Heaven is not only our future, it's our present. So the issue isn't *when* we get our treasure, but *where* our treasure is located.

If you are using the time, abilities, and material things God gives you to store up treasure in heaven, there's no question that you are securing your tomorrow. But you are also securing your today. Why? Because the person who has heaven's view of earth's stuff is the person who gets the most enjoyment out of life. The person who tries to hoard it all down here is the one who loses, both now and in eternity.

TALK ABOUT IT

Sit down together and look over your checkbook for the past thirty days. Do the transactions give you clues about the location of your real treasure?

ENJOY THE GIFT

I know that there is nothing better for them than to rejoice and to do good in one's life-time; moreover, that every man who eats and drinks sees good in all his labor—it is the gift of God.

—ECCLESIASTES 3:12–13

R ight in the heart of a book written to explore the futility and meaninglessness of life, Solomon stopped and said, "Actually, life is a gift from God." That is a great perspective. It's only when we view life as the gift of God that we begin to find its purpose. It's only as we live our days with the perspective of eternity that we find life's meaning.

Now if life is God's gift to you, then the fastest way to find your purpose in life is through thanksgiving. What do you say when someone brings you a gift? You say, "Thank you," and then you enjoy the gift. You don't try to take it apart and figure it out.

In other words, if you want to find your purpose, don't go looking for your purpose. Look for the Purpose-Giver. That's why the greatest way to find out who you are is not to look in the mirror but to look to God, the One who gave you your identity. You find what you're looking for when you stop looking for it and let the Giver of life grant it to you.

You may have to think about that for a minute. But when you do, you'll realize what a freeing thing this is. Instead of looking for your purpose within yourself, locate God, and you will find yourself.

So what is the purpose of life? The discovery and the enjoyment of God. There is no greater purpose or passion in life. That's why the apostle Paul said he had one goal: "that I may know Him" (Phil. 3:10).

If you know God, you will know your purpose. Not because you went purpose-hunting but because you went God-hunting. And when you find God, you will find you.

PRAY ABOUT IT

"God, I want to know You more than anything. Reveal Yourself to me, and I'll let You reveal me to me." When you do that, you'll know why you are here and where you are going.

IT'S NOT THE SAME THING

The body is not for immorality, but for the Lord; and the Lord is for the body.

—I CORINTHIANS 6:13

---

*H*ave you ever heard this argument? "Sex is no different than eating. You get hungry, you eat. You get turned on, you have sex. It's the same thing." If you haven't heard this line of thinking yourself, we can guarantee you that your kids have, especially if they are teenagers.

But the Bible teaches that any attempt to treat our sexual drives the way we handle other natural appetites is a huge mistake, because the correlation breaks down. Just before he wrote the words quoted above, Paul said, "Food is for the stomach, and the stomach is for food." This is basic physiology. When you're driving down the road and your stomach says, "hungry," you pull into the drive-through at the nearest burger place and order a meal to go because you want to satisfy your hunger.

For many people today, indulging their sexual desires has become as ordinary as eating when they are hungry. But Paul said in no uncertain terms that while the stomach is made for food, our bodies are not made for immorality.

In other words, morality is not a "drive-through" issue. It is *not* the same as eating—or anything else, for that matter.

Why? Because our bodies were made for the Lord. That is, they are much more than a container for sexual desires. Our bodies are vehicles through which we are to honor and serve God and bring Him glory. What we do with our bodies impacts our spirits, and that impacts eternity.

God wants us to make a clear distinction between fast food and fast sex. He is honored when we exercise control over our desires and keep ourselves pure in His sight. This means that God can be honored and glorified in our physical intimacy as married couples when we give ourselves to Him and commit ourselves to our partner and no one else.

PRAY ABOUT IT

Our culture has debased sex, taking away its beauty and holiness. Pray that God will use your marriage to model His original idea!

NO SIMPLE ANSWER

She looks well to the ways of her household, and does not eat the bread of idleness.

—PROVERBS 31:27

---

*M*ost of us like questions that can be answered with a simple yes or no. But there are some questions that can't be decided so simply. Here's an example: Does the Bible permit believing wives and mothers to work outside the home? The answer depends on several factors. For instance, the noble woman of Proverbs 31 was a capable businesswoman as well as a wife and mother. This woman dealt in textiles and real estate, and she made garments. She also engaged in works of charity outside the home (v. 20). But it's obvious from this entire passage (Prov. 31:10–31) that none of her business dealings or activities caused her to neglect her family. This woman's family was well fed, well clothed, and ready for every season.

This illustrates a biblical principle that governs the choice of outside activities for a wife and mother who seeks to please God. The principle is this: These things are permissible as long as they don't take priority over a woman's primary responsibility to be a "[keeper] at home" (Titus 2:5, KJV).

The Bible is clear that a woman's primary focus is to be on her home, even though being a worker at home does not necessarily mean being a "stayer" at home.

This is where the woman of Proverbs 31 is a far cry from many of her modern sisters. A lot of working women today are stressed out, overworked, and absent from home. I don't know how things are in your home, but when I feel stressed out and harassed I know I am probably trying to handle more things than God wants me to handle.

This is where a caring husband can help his wife restore the balance in her life and free her up to accomplish the important things. He can do this by not making unrealistic demands on his wife and by helping lighten her load when things do get too hectic. His wife will benefit—and so will he!—LOIS

TALK ABOUT IT
Discuss whether you feel your home reflects biblical priorities—and if not, what you can do about it.

TOUGH TIMES, EXCITING TIMES

My God shall supply all your needs according to His riches in glory in Christ Jesus.

—PHILIPPIANS 4:19

When Tony and I moved to Dallas in the early seventies so he could enter seminary, we had one small child and no extra money. Tony was going to be a full-time student, but he still accepted his responsibility to provide for his family. This was very important to us, because we both knew that our daughter needed me at home.

Tony had to get a job that would allow him to go to school during the day. So he began working the night shift at the bus station in Dallas, loading luggage onto the buses. He brought home $350 a month.

I'm sure you can identify with our situation as you think back on the early years of your marriage. Our monthly rent was $170, and our tithe was $50. Add up those numbers and put them next to $350, and you can understand why we say those were hard times financially.

But they were also exciting times. We saw God meet our needs time and time again. I remember one day when there was no money and not much to eat in the house. I was in tears because I couldn't understand why the Lord would put us in that situation. That morning Tony did what he always did, which was to lead family devotions before he left for school. He asked me how much it would take to meet our needs, and I said five hundred dollars.

That sounded like so much money, but together we asked God to supply. Tony said if God did not give him some sign of provision, he would drop out of seminary for a year to give his family some stability.

But when Tony went to his mailbox at school that day, he found five hundred dollars! I will never forget that experience. God's supply is always more abundant than our need. The promise of His Word is one you can rely on today. The key is earlier in Philippians 4:6: "In everything by prayer and supplication with thanksgiving let your requests be made known to God."—LOIS

TALK ABOUT IT

Do you want a blessing today? Recall together some of your tough times and how God supplied—and praise Him for those precious experiences. He is a Lord who provides.

DO YOU NEED A NEW BOSS?

Slaves, be obedient to those who are your masters according to the flesh, with fear and trembling, in the sincerity of your heart, as to Christ.

***

*P*art of the "package" we received in salvation is the fact that in Christ, God offers us the redemption of work. Even though sin is a reality and the created order is messed up, if you are a Christian you have the opportunity to regain a significant measure of the meaning of work.

That happens because now that you know Christ, God can plug you back into His will. And His will for you, which is "good and acceptable and perfect" (Rom. 12:2), includes your work. This is important to understand, because apart from Christ you can have the best job in the world and still be empty inside. Work itself can't give you meaning. In fact, James 4:13–17 says work can become a source of sin when God's will is excluded.

Work apart from Christ can be a curse. Conversely, it becomes blessed when God's will is included. The Bible is very practical about this. The degree to which you integrate God into your work is the degree to which you will find meaning in what you do every day.

What we're saying is that if a couple of hours on Sunday is all that God gets from you, don't be surprised if Monday through Friday is meaningless for you.

If you don't go to work tomorrow thinking, *I'm going to work for the Lord,* then you've missed the meaning of work. The quickest way to transform a bad job is with a new attitude. And the quickest way to get a new attitude is to change bosses.

Paul says if you work for the Lord, you get your reward from Him (see Col. 3:23–24). If you're just working for the boss, the boss can give you whatever reward he or she wants. But if you're working for the Lord, the boss has to give you what the Lord decides to give you.

THINK ABOUT IT

Today's verse is written to slaves. You may be thinking, You got that right! *You may feel like a slave at work—and you are! But you are* Christ's *slave, and that makes all the difference.*

WEEK EIGHTEEN—TUESDAY

BE CAREFUL WHERE YOU PUT IT

Where your treasure is, there will your heart be also.

—MATTHEW 6:21

⬥

*I*n this encouraging and convicting statement, Jesus tells us we had better be careful where we invest our time and money and talents, because our hearts will follow along behind our investment.

You know how this principle works from your own courtship. As you started investing time and emotional energy in each other—and as the man started spending his hard-earned cash—your love started to blossom. Your hearts followed your treasure, in other words.

If you have investments in the stock market, you probably subscribe to *The Wall Street Journal* so you can track your money. There's nothing wrong with that—as long as you don't start getting more blessing and pleasure from reading the *Journal* than you do from reading your Bible.

Suppose you are sitting in my church next Sunday morning while I am preaching. An usher comes up, hands me a note, and asks me to read this urgent announcement. I read the message, which is that your house is on fire. Now I doubt that you would stay to hear the rest of my sermon. You would probably get up immediately and rush out to check on your house.

Nothing wrong with that. I would rush home too if I got a message like that. Why would we do that? Because we invest a lot of ourselves and our treasures in our homes, and a big piece of our hearts are there.

Jesus isn't forbidding us from enjoying and protecting the things He has given us. It's OK with Him if we reap a legitimate return for our work. What He's talking about here is the problem of living for ourselves.

See, when you live for yourself, your real problem isn't the love of money. That's only a symptom of the problem. The real problem is your priorities. Because we will come to love what we invest in, Jesus says to make sure that God's kingdom and His righteousness are the focus of our lives.—TONY

THINK ABOUT IT

If God is your focus, He will have your treasure. And whoever has your treasure will get your heart!

TRANSMITTING GODLY VALUES

My son, observe the commandment of your father.

—PROVERBS 6:20

T am afraid that as a society today we are trying to perpetuate a system that was unworkable from the beginning. Ever since President Lyndon Johnson instituted the "Great Society" programs in the early sixties, some five trillion dollars have been spent to address the problems that have been tearing an entire generation of families and communities apart.

Although they were well intentioned, I think most of us will agree that many of these programs have been utter failures because they did not address the core problem of values being transferred from one generation to another. One of the reasons God created the family was to give us a system for perpetuating and transferring values.

If you grew up in a home that had a system of values, even if you rebelled against those values, you had to work at it. You had to climb over your mother whispering in your ear even if you were many miles away from home at college, because that godly influence was there.

We parents love to quote Proverbs 22:6: "Train up a child in the way he should go, even when he is old he will not depart from it." This verse assumes that a body of biblical data is being transmitted to our children that God can use to quicken their spirits.

But by and large that is not happening today, and we are paying the price. Our schools have metal detectors, the media are redefining the family, and homosexuals are not only coming out of the closet, they're parading down Main Street.

Despite this, I believe the future of our children and our nation still lies primarily in the hands of men. I do not mean by this that women are not important and crucial to the process. But I am calling Christian husbands and fathers to stop making excuses and step up to the plate, ready to own and *fix* the problem of a lost, valueless society.—TONY

THINK ABOUT IT

What we need is a generation of men who have a proper—that is, a God-centered—perspective on what it means to be a real man.

A VISION WITH STAGGERING DIMENSIONS

Let Us make man in Our image, according to Our likeness; and let them rule over the fish of the sea and over the birds of the sky and over the cattle and over all the earth.

—GENESIS 1:26

❦

I want you to think about this familiar verse for a few minutes in terms of what God is calling us to do as His children. Specifically, let me address my fellow husbands and fathers today. Adam was given the headship in his relationship with Eve, so he was to take the lead in carrying out God's agenda.

And what a big vision this is. God wants man to rule and dominate the earth. The vision God gave Adam was worldwide. The dimensions were staggering. Adam, along with Eve, was not only to rule the earth, but he was to bear and reproduce the image of God. That's bigger than any man can pull off by himself.

God gave Adam a job, but He gave him a job so he could achieve a bigger goal, a kingdom agenda. If you cannot sit in your chair right now and articulate God's kingdom call on your life, then something is missing.

A vision is the ability to see beyond the immediate and the visible. A kingdom vision is a view of life that is far bigger than just getting by day after day. A kingdom vision is a calling that allows you to make an impact for eternity while you are here in history.

God has called you and me as men to something that is bigger than life. He has called us to set the pace and lead the way in our homes, in the church, and ultimately in His worldwide kingdom.

So if the sum total of your life is working, then going home to read the newspaper and watch a few TV shows before going to bed, don't be surprised if life seems boring. God has so much more for you! He wants to give you a vision so big, only He can give you the power to accomplish it!—TONY

THINK ABOUT IT

What about you, my brother? Has God called you to do something that is too big for you to accomplish apart from His power? If so, congratulations. You have been given a kingdom-sized vision!

WE BELONG TO GOD TWO WAYS

From Him and through Him and to Him are all things. To Him be the glory forever. Amen.

—ROMANS 11:36

Suppose I came over to your house today and said, "Look, I don't like your furniture. It just doesn't look right. It's got to go. All of this has to be changed." What are you likely to say to me? "Excuse me, you're in my house. I paid for this furniture, and I'm paying this house note. You haven't made one dime's worth of investment in this house. So with all due respect, mind your own business."

We haven't made one dime's worth of investment in God's creation. We haven't added one iota to what He has made, so He doesn't want us to live like we helped Him make this deal. A Christian recognizes God as the absolute owner of everything.

The sin of Satan was that he wanted to share ownership with God—only Satan wasn't after things. He wanted to be like God Himself. He said, "I will make myself like the Most High" (Isa. 14:14).

Having failed at that, he got Adam and Eve to try the same thing, telling them, "You will be like God" (Gen. 3:5). That didn't work either. God will not share His glory with anyone.

That is Paul's point in today's verse. God created this world for Himself. So He owns everything by virtue of His creative act. But if you are a Christian, you not only belong to God because He created you. You belong to Him because He redeemed you. "Do you not know that . . . you are not your own? For you have been bought with a price" (1 Cor. 6:19–20). Therefore, "Whether, then, you eat or drink or whatever you do, do all to the glory of God" (1 Cor. 10:31).

If you're the Creator, you have the right to demand that your creation fulfill your purpose and nobody else's. This is our challenge and our call as a couple: to do things God's way.

PRAY ABOUT IT
There are two approaches to any issue, God's approach and everyone else's—and everyone else is wrong!

STRENGTH UNDER CONTROL

Blessed are the gentle, for they shall inherit the earth.

—MATTHEW 5:5

*I*n the King James Version this verse begins, "Blessed are the meek." This idea of meekness or gentleness is probably one of the most misunderstood concepts in the Bible. To most people, meekness, or gentleness, is a kind of cowering timidity, a synonym for weakness.

Of course, the fact that Jesus referred to Himself as gentle (see Matt. 11:29) ought to put an end to that idea. The Savior was neither cowering nor weak. So let's talk about what gentleness involves and why we are blessed when we display this spiritual quality.

To help you understand the strength behind this term, you need to know that it was also used to describe a wild horse that had been brought under control. A wild horse doesn't do anybody any good because it will buck its rider off, refuse a bit and bridle, and fight against a saddle or harness.

But when a powerful, wild horse has been tamed by a skilled trainer, it can be ridden or harnessed to pull a chariot or whatever. The animal is still as strong as it was when it was wild, except that now that strength is under control.

Similarly, a person of gentleness is one whom God has tamed and put into His service. Gentleness is the ability to love when you feel like hating, to forgive when you feel like getting revenge. It's the ability to submit to the will of God even when that's not your natural propensity.

Why? Because you've been domesticated by heaven. God has brought you under His control.

The promise to gentle people is that they will "inherit" the earth. Because they are followers of Jesus, the gentle One, they will share in His ultimate victory someday. And in the meantime, they will see God intervene in their circumstances to bring the benefits of heaven to bear on their lives.

THINK ABOUT IT

If Jesus wasn't embarrassed to call Himself gentle, why should we be ashamed to wear the "bit and bridle" of the Holy Spirit?

THE HEART OF A SERVANT

Even the Son of Man did not come to be served, but to serve.

—MARK 10:45

❦

*I*f there is any message that the culture around us tries to drum into our heads, it is that being number one is all that matters. Winning is what counts. What a startling contrast to the attitude and the spirit of the Lord Jesus Christ! He came to be a servant. He taught His disciples that the greatest among them was the one who was willing to be their servant. And remember, Paul told us to have the same attitude as Christ (see Phil. 2:5).

And what was Christ's attitude? He left the glory of heaven, laid aside the independent exercise of His deity, and took on the form of a "bond-servant" (v. 7).

What does this mean for us as Christian women today? It means that as we are willing to exhibit a servant's attitude, we can expect God's blessing on our homes and families.

To illustrate this, I go back to one of our earlier sisters in the faith, the woman of Proverbs 31. Verse 15 of this passage says that she had servants, but she also had a servant's heart.

How do we know this? Because the Bible says she prepared breakfast for her servant girls as well as for her family.

This is not the normal procedure, is it? Servants usually do the serving with the family doing the receiving. But evidently this woman valued people so much that she invested her service in the lives of her household helpers.

The writer also notes that this woman reached out to the poor and needy in her community (see v. 20). That was definitely not a move calculated to gain power!

How can a godly woman serve her husband and family without becoming overworked and underappreciated? One key is her husband's attitude. The husband of Proverbs 31 honored his wife and praised her, and his attitude filtered down to the children. He made it easier, not harder, for his wife to fulfill her calling.—LOIS

THINK ABOUT IT

Christian husband, are you making it easier—or harder—for your wife to fulfill her calling at home? Marriage is a partnership, not a sole proprietorship.

GRACE WHEN THE PROBLEMS DON'T GO AWAY

Be strong in the grace that is in Christ Jesus.

—2 TIMOTHY 2:1

*D*id you know that the strength you need every day to live the Christian life is found in God's grace? First we are saved by God's grace (see Eph. 2:8), and grace is also what keeps us. That lesson usually comes in the midst of hardship.

Paul learned the lesson of sustaining grace through an affliction that dogged him all his life. He wrote about it in 2 Corinthians 12, where he says he asked God three times to remove this affliction. But God's answer was grace: "He has said to me, 'My grace is sufficient for you, for power is perfected in weakness'" (v. 9).

God was saying to Paul that His grace is so comprehensive it's sufficient to deal with the problems that don't go away. Paul's physical problem didn't go away, but grace covered its presence.

We all need that kind of powerful grace, because we all have to deal with things that won't budge, with problems that won't go away.

The frustration we often feel is why this is happening to us. The answer could be that your next lesson in grace is wrapped up in that hard circumstance or immovable problem. One thing God wants to teach us is that even when we are out of answers and out of strength, grace always has a fresh supply.

No wonder Peter referred to God as "the God of all grace" (1 Pet. 5:10). He has all the grace we will ever need, and His grace is totally comprehensive. It touches every area of our personal lives, our marriages, and our families.

If the two of you have not yet discovered how great God's supply of grace truly is, you have a wonderful surprise coming! God's goodness is staggering, and He's waiting to give it away to you!

THINK ABOUT IT

All you have to do is ask God for the grace you need. It's already there. It just needs to be unveiled, unloaded, and expanded in your life.

THE MODESTY OF A KINGDOM WOMAN (DAY 1)

I want women to adorn themselves with proper clothing, modestly and discreetly, not with braided hair and gold or pearls or costly garments.

—1 TIMOTHY 2:9

*I*f you have a daughter you will at some point face the issue of modesty in dress. We can almost guarantee you it will be an interesting time. In 1 Timothy 2:9–15, Paul gave detailed instruction on the kind of adornment and activities that should mark God's kingdom women, women "making a claim to godliness" (v. 10). The first item on this agenda is a godly woman's propriety when it comes to her appearance.

God understands that women will spend time arranging themselves, putting everything in order. He knows that women give special attention to what they wear and how they look. The instruction to kingdom women is not to ignore this area or pretend it doesn't matter but to dress with modesty and good decorum as the standard. We need to remember that many of the women coming into the church at places like Ephesus and Corinth were coming out of pagan backgrounds. So they were coming to church dressed like the world. They were in style with the times but not in style with the kingdom.

Paul told Timothy, "Make sure the women in God's family understand that as kingdom women, their need for modesty and propriety in dress may mean they have to take on a different look." Modesty has to do with not drawing undue attention to yourself or being ostentatious in appearance. The issue is excess.

Another problem in the early church was a disparity of wealth. Some women in Ephesus, where Timothy was pastor, could outdress other women and afford the latest fashions (see 1 Tim. 6:17–18).

The problem with this in terms of propriety is that the fashion emphasis today is heavy on immodesty, even as it was then. Too often, to dress fashionably is to dress immodestly, especially for girls and younger women. But as kingdom families, we are called to a different standard.—LOIS

TALK ABOUT IT

It may require extra time or a little extra planning to maintain a godly woman's modesty, but it can be done.

THE MODESTY OF A KINGDOM WOMAN (DAY 2)

I want women to adorn themselves . . . by means of good works, as befits women making a claim to godliness.

—TIMOTHY 2:9–10

---

*M*any of the things our two daughters wanted to wear when they were growing up never left the house until a seamstress got hold of the garments first. That was simply because the clothes were immodest, not in keeping with kingdom propriety.

On more than one occasion, I've also had to turn down a dress or a skirt I wanted to buy because the hem could not be let down, and therefore, it would have been improper.

In the little church where I grew up, the older women used to walk around with extra pieces of cloth. If a girl's or a young woman's dress came up too high when she sat down, they would spread the cloth over her knees.

Now, you may think that's extreme. But we have gone so far to the other extreme of immodesty that I say, give us some of those older ladies again!

A woman's standard of dress can either draw attention to her Lord or to her body. As a mother and wife as well as a pastor's wife, I am deeply concerned that we as kingdom people and kingdom families set a higher standard for ourselves.

Paul's point is that a kingdom woman is called of God not to dress in a way that stimulates inappropriate responses. His mention of gold and pearls and expensive clothes was a way of saying to believing women, "Don't look like the women out there on the street. Don't try to dazzle and impress others."

Just in case I'm being misunderstood, let me say that the Bible does not condemn beauty. The woman of Proverbs 31 was beautiful to behold. But her beauty was accomplished with propriety and modesty. I am not trying to lay down legalistic rules on dress for your family. I am simply saying that God calls Christian mothers and daughters to dress as women of dignity and honor.—LOIS

TALK ABOUT IT

There ought to be an air of dignity and respect about a kingdom woman—a kind of beauty that doesn't depend on anything external!

THE MODESTY OF A KINGDOM WOMAN (DAY 3)

The fruit of the Spirit is . . . self-control.

—GALATIANS 5:22–23

❦

Talking about the issue of modesty in women's apparel can sometimes be like walking through a mine field. No matter which way you step, you're likely to set something off.

My purpose here is not to create controversy. Instead, I want to help you think biblically about an issue that every Christian dad and mom must deal with, no matter the gender of your children.

For some women, setting an example of godly modesty in dress may mean a change of wardrobe. For others, it may just mean a simple alteration here and there.

The word *discreetly* refers to self-control. It has to do with making a decision of discipline. In this case it may involve a believing woman saying, "I like that dress, and it looks good on me. But I have to say no to it because it is not modest."

In Isaiah 3:16–18, the Lord addressed the immodest women of Judah. "Because the daughters of Zion are proud, and walk with heads held high and seductive eyes, and go along with mincing steps, and tinkle the bangles on their feet, therefore the LORD will afflict the scalp of the daughters of Zion with scabs, and the LORD will make their foreheads bare."

Read verses 19–24 of this chapter, and you will see that the Lord was very specific about the various adornments these women wore to attract men. They were advertising themselves as immodest and available, and the men were taking them up on their offer. But the whole thing made God sick.

The challenge to kingdom women is not to send the wrong message by the way they dress. Don't let people decide who you are by what they see, unless what they see is a woman of dignity and honor.—LOIS

THINK ABOUT IT

Mom, you can have a tremendous positive influence in this area, especially with your daughter(s). Pray that God will help you make the most of your example.

GIVE GOD SOMETHING HE CAN BLESS

The plans of the diligent lead surely to advantage, but everyone who is hasty comes surely to poverty.

—PROVERBS 21:5

God is big on financial planning. Now, don't misunderstand. We're not saying that God is a businessman in a suit who is looking to help you cut deals and make the best investments. The financial plan God is most interested in is the plan the two of you have to honor Him and help build His kingdom while taking care of your family and helping others in need.

God is interested in your financial plan because everything you have is on loan from Him, and one day He will call you to account for how you handled His resources. He wants to help you make a wise and godly plan now so that you won't have to be ashamed before Him when He returns. And He says if you don't know how to plan, you should talk to people who do: "Without consultation, plans are frustrated, but with many counselors they succeed" (Prov. 15:22).

Here is one important element of a plan that will help you be prepared to meet needs and even emergencies and avoid debt. Your plan must always include a surplus.

God expects you to plan in such a way that there is always money left over. If you never have money left over at the end of the month, you know you're not in God's plan.

The Book of Proverbs advises us, "Go to the ant, O sluggard, observe her ways and be wise. . . . [She] prepares her food in the summer, and gathers her provision in the harvest" (6:6, 8). Even an ant knows you need to lay something aside.

Planning that includes a surplus is wise because you don't want to work all your life only to give it all away to somebody else. You don't want to work all of your life so that your creditors can take everything and leave you with nothing for yourself. God has a better idea for His people.

THINK ABOUT IT

Planning to have a surplus means you must look at the future—and taking the future into account is a biblically wise way to live.

A PERSON, NOT JUST A FORCE

The Helper, the Holy Spirit, whom the Father will send in My name,
He will teach you all things.

—JOHN 14:26

❧

*A*s Jesus reclined in the Upper Room the night before His crucifixion, He faced a group of discouraged men. Jesus had just told them He would be leaving. But the Lord gave His followers a great promise that night when He said another divine Person would take His place in their midst.

This Person, the Holy Spirit, would be with them, as Jesus had been with them, for comfort, strength, and guidance. But the Spirit would also be *within* them, never to leave.

How do we know the Holy Spirit is a Person instead of just a force or an "it"? Because He has all the attributes of personality: intellect, emotion, and will.

For instance, the Holy Spirit knows certain things (see Rom. 8:27; 1 Cor. 2:10–11). He has emotions because we're told He can be grieved (see Eph. 4:30). And the Spirit's will is seen in the fact that He acts with purpose (see 1 Cor. 12:11). Only persons can do all of this.

When God saves us, then, He calls us into a relationship with the Holy Spirit. But sometimes we look for the wrong thing when it comes to the Spirit. We hear people talking about their need for Holy Spirit power. We *do* need Holy Spirit power. But only after we have met the Holy Spirit Person. When you start dealing with the Holy Spirit as a power first, you may just miss the relationship God wants you to have with the Person. The Spirit's job is not just to give you a power boost to lift you to the next spiritual level. Many people come to church on Sunday morning looking for a Holy Ghost "oomph" to get them rolling.

But if you leave with momentary Holy Ghost power without a relationship with the Holy Ghost as a Person, as *God,* you will wind up with a Holy Ghost deficit in your spiritual life. The Spirit is a Person we need to know and relate to, not just a force to be used.

PRAY ABOUT IT
Is your marriage or family life suffering from a Holy Spirit deficit? If you'll ask Him, He will help you draw closer to one another as you draw closer to the Lord.

LOOKING GOOD

She makes coverings for herself; her clothing is fine linen and purple.

—PROVERBS 31:22

᠁

*W*e've talked so much about the work of the woman of Proverbs 31 that you may be thinking by now, *Goodness! This poor woman must have looked pretty worn out and haggard.*

Not according to the verse we are considering today. This wife of noble character also took care of herself.

We modern women are often told to put ourselves first and not let a husband or a family keep us from "self-fulfillment." In fact, some would go so far as to tell women it is OK to rid themselves of people who get in the way of their self-fulfillment.

However, this "me first" mentality is a far cry from the kind of self-care that Proverbs 31 is talking about. It is obvious that this woman did not neglect her family to lavish attention on herself. But she understood that to be able to minister to others effectively, she needed to take care of the temple of her own body.

Tony often says to husbands, "It's a tragedy if your wife is less beautiful today than she was the day you married her. I don't mean she has to look as young as she did twenty or thirty years ago. But if you load your wife down with all kinds of responsibilities and demands and then talk about how bad she looks, that's your fault! It's your responsibility to make sure that your wife is so well cared for that all of the beauty she possesses is enhanced."

My sister, God does not expect you to wear yourself to a frazzle doing His will. If you are seeking Him and living for His glory, He will give you the time and energy you need to accomplish your calling. As you serve others, don't forget to keep your own body and spirit in tune.—LOIS

THINK ABOUT IT

Husband, let me ask you this question today: "What are you doing to help your wife develop and maintain her beauty?"

COMING UNDER GOD'S AUTHORITY AT CHURCH

Obey your leaders, and submit to them; for they keep watch over your souls, as those who will give an account.

—HEBREWS 13:17

B rother, let me give you a tangible way to strengthen your marriage and family: Make sure you are under the God-ordained authority of your church. A man under Christ (see 1 Cor. 11:3) is in subjection to Christ's authority in the church. The church is to exercise discipline where needed. This was evident in the case of the unrepentant, immoral man of 1 Corinthians 5, and it's true with any man in the church who refuses to work (2 Thess. 3:10–15).

I remember telling Anthony Jr. one time to empty the trash, to which he responded, "I don't feel like it, Dad."

To which I responded, "I can change the way you feel, boy!" My instruction to empty the trash had nothing to do with Anthony's feelings at that moment. It had nothing to do with whether he was into trash emptying that day.

My instruction needed to be obeyed for one reason, because Papa said so and Anthony was under the authority of my house. In the same way, Christian men are under the authority of God's house, the church, and are to submit themselves accordingly.

Many Christian men today don't want to be married anymore because they don't feel like being faithful. They don't want to work because they don't feel like working. They don't want to raise children because they don't feel like raising children.

My response is, "You felt like getting married at the time. You felt like having children at the time. So it is a moot point to say, 'I don't feel like it anymore.'" What we need is a generation of kingdom men who are responsible under God.

Any man who is not following Jesus Christ is not maximizing his manhood. Any man can follow the crowd, but only a kingdom man can follow Christ.—TONY

PRAY ABOUT IT
It takes tenacity and commitment to follow Christ and fulfill the agenda He hands you. If you need more of these commodities, ask God to supply them to you today.

THE BLESSING (DAY 1)

By faith Jacob . . . blessed each of the sons of Joseph.

—HEBREWS 11:21

✦

In the Jewish world of Bible times, every child looked forward to the blessing of parents and grandparents. Today, Orthodox Jewish families still bless their children, especially their sons at their *bar mitzvah*. The blessing we're talking about is not the quick handshake and the "God bless you" we see so often today. It was not a trite statement or greeting. It was a life blessing that every child longed for.

There are at least two reasons that the blessing was so important in Bible times. The first reason is that God participated in the blessing and honored it. When a father like Jacob or Isaac blessed his sons or grandsons, he spoke under the direction of God. The blessing was actually a prophecy of what was to come about.

The second thing that made the blessing so important is that it served as the bridge between generations to pass on the favor and blessing of God from parent to child. Where the blessing was absent, there was a generational break in God's favor that meant potential trouble for the grown child left without a blessing. We'll see that later on in the case of Isaac and his sons, Jacob and Esau.

The blessing we're talking about is first and foremost a spiritual reality. That ought to be encouraging to us, because it means that the poorest parents among us can pass on just as rich and full a blessing to their children as the wealthiest of parents. No child needs to be left out of this deal. All of us can transfer the things of God to our kids, help them absorb His truth into their lives, and pass it on to the next generation.

TALK ABOUT IT

In the biblical world, it was unthinkable that a child could look forward to a fruitful, dynamic life without the parental blessing. Are you blessing your children, verbally and often?

THE BLESSING (DAY 2)

"Let the children alone, and do not hinder them from coming to Me. . . ." And after laying His hands on them, [Jesus] departed from there.

⁂

When it comes to the ministry of blessing children, we have the perfect example in Jesus. The disciples tried to shoo away the parents who were bringing their children to Jesus for His blessing. But Jesus set the record straight on the importance of children.

What Jesus did for those children is something every Christian father needs to do with his children. The Bible has always recognized the key role of fathers and their God-given task of passing on to their children what the Bible calls the blessing.

Today I want to emphasize the value of this ritual or ceremony where a father lays his hands on his children and pronounces God's blessing on them. Unfortunately, many people in our generation have learned about the value of a parental, generational blessing the hard way. That is, they now realize as adults that they missed out on it.

Many Christians are struggling today as adults, and they think the problem is confined to their current situation. But when a counselor says, "Tell me about your childhood," that query is in part an attempt to determine if the person's problem is linked to what did or did not happen in childhood.

I'm convinced that much of the pain adults suffer is because they never received the blessing. I don't mean they just missed a little ceremony. I'm talking about the lack of a clear sense that their parents, particularly their fathers, attempted to transfer a Christian heritage and blessing to them when they were children. Some adults even recognize that their family life left them with a curse.

But even for those who are not in this extreme category, the lack of a clear sense of blessing and continuity between their past and their present is still damaging. But the good news is, it's never too late to confer a blessing on your children.—TONY

PRAY ABOUT IT

Do the two of you have a clear sense that you possess the blessing yourselves? If not, ask God to reverse any negative effects of that lack in your life, so that you can both be a blessing and pass on a blessing to your children.

THE NEW ENVIRONMENT OF GRACE

By the grace of God I am what I am, and His grace toward me did not prove vain.

—I CORINTHIANS 15:10

⟡

*I*f you have ever been to a foreign country, you know what it's like to enter a different environment and feel uncomfortably out of place. I have a good friend in the ministry who was born and raised in India then came to America for further training. In India, my friend had driven on the left side of the road. Here he had to start driving on the right side. The same kind of changes and adjustments awaited him in every area of life. Everything in America was so different.

This is how many believers feel when they enter the environment—the new country, if you will—of God's grace. Since we are saved by grace, we enter this country the moment we become a Christian.

But even though we are full citizens of our new country, we bring with us a lot of mental and spiritual baggage from the "old country." This means that living by grace will take some getting used to for many of us.

When my friend entered America, he got his passport stamped. But even though he had permission to be here, he brought his "India orientation" with him. Similarly, we got our passports stamped when we received Christ as our Savior, so we are already living in the environment of grace. But most of us brought with us the old standard of being accepted on the basis of how well *we* perform, not on the basis of how well someone else—Jesus Christ—performed. Grace says we serve and please Christ, not to earn His love and favor, but because we already have His love and favor.

There's a tremendous, liberating principle here for marriage. Sometimes one partner in a marriage will put the other on a performance basis. But God's grace extends to marriage! Spouses need to love, serve, and accept each other by grace, not because one spouse meets the other's performance criteria.

PRAY ABOUT IT

If you suspect your marriage is on a performance basis, even to a small degree, get that mess taken care of before the Lord and set each other free—today!

A NETWORK OF SUPPORT

Her children rise up and bless her; her husband also, and he praises her.

—PROVERBS 31:28

The matter of a wife and mother fulfilling her God-given roles is not a one-sided affair. No woman can do it all by herself. Neither can any man. God never asked us to do it all alone. He provides the strength we need to fulfill our calling as wives and husbands as we love and support each other.

We have talked a lot about the wife of Proverbs 31, but we also need to talk about her husband. He was so well-supported at home that he was able to take his place at the city gate among the elders of his city (see Prov. 31:23). In other words, one reason this man was able to exercise leadership was that he had the support of an excellent wife.

But the support flowed both ways. This husband let everyone know that he had an excellent wife. His praise and encouragement of her was also reflected in the love his children expressed for their mother. She was well-supported herself.

All of us need words and actions that express support. Whenever Tony preaches on Proverbs 31, some man always asks him afterward, "How can I get my wife to be a Proverbs 31 wife?"

Tony always points to verse 28 and tells him, "If you want a Proverbs 31 wife, you need to be a Proverbs 31 husband."

I don't know for sure, but I suspect that there are legions of my Christian sisters who are starving for a little attention and praise from their husbands. I hope that is not true in your marriage and home.

Wives want to hear their husbands affirm them and lift them up the way the Proverbs 31 husband affirmed his wife (see v. 29). Most women would grow and flourish under that kind of genuine praise.—LOIS

TALK ABOUT IT
Get together as a couple today and agree that for the next few days, no "discouraging word" will pass between you. Decide to affirm each other, then watch what happens.

WHAT GOD IS AFTER IN YOUR WORK

There is nothing better for a man than to eat and drink and tell himself that his labor is good.

—ECCLESIASTES 2:24

W hat a lot of Christian men and women need is a reorientation to their work. God wants you to find meaning in your work, but the thing that makes it meaningful is your relationship with God in the task, not the task itself.

Even if you're assigned to a project you're not excited about, if your attitude is that you are participating with God in the project, He can change the meaninglessness of your work into the meaningfulness of that work.

If you're struggling with your job, read the Book of Ecclesiastes. Solomon had a lot to say about finding meaning in our work even in a sinful world.

The two of you have a relatively few years to live and do productive work. Solomon advised that you make the most of your work opportunities. In other words, don't make it your goal just to warm a spot for eight hours each day. Ask God to give you the ability to enjoy your work. He wants you to have a job you enjoy doing and can do to the full for His glory.

There's nothing worse than having to get up and go to a job you hate. But a lot of people feel that way about their work because all they're doing is putting in time rather than cooperating with God to help advance His kingdom and glory. It's a perspective problem.

The goal of work is not for you to put in your forty hours a week for forty years so you can quit and retire in Florida. The goal of work is the joy and sense of achievement you get when you accomplish a God-given task. That's what God is after, so that's what you should be after.

TALK ABOUT IT

Here's a conversation starter for your next meal: Discuss this statement: It is better to make less money wanting to get up in the morning than to make more money wanting to stay in bed.

SOAP IN YOUR EYES

The lamp of the body is the eye; if therefore your eye is clear, your whole body will be full of light. But if your eye is bad, your whole body will be full of darkness.

—MATTHEW 6:22–23A

I remember one miserable occasion in the shower when I got soap in both of my eyes. I couldn't open either eye and the soap was burning, so I started fumbling around, feeling for the towel. But the towel had fallen to the floor. As I tried to reach for it, I slipped on the soap, which had fallen out of the soap dish, and bumped my forehead on the soap dish sticking out of the wall. Blood started trickling down my face.

That's what it's like when your eyes go out and your whole body is full of darkness.

Jesus used the eyes to illustrate a spiritual point. He said that when our spiritual eyes go dark, everything else goes dark too. We lose our spiritual perspective when we allow the stuff of this world to get in our eyes and block our view of God's kingdom.

The problem with getting soap in our eyes, spiritually speaking, is that everything else goes out of focus too. When we can't see God and His priorities clearly, we can't see to handle our marital relationship and marriage problems properly. The family also begins to look blurry so that family problems aren't dealt with the right way.

The same can be said for our careers or for financial or emotional problems. When your spiritual eyesight goes, the rest of you is in the dark. Many Christians are living in darkness today because they are failing to look at life from the perspective of God's kingdom.

Have things been a little blurry to you lately? For instance, are you having trouble seeing your spouse through God's eyes? There's a cure. You need to refocus. Fix your eyes on Jesus (see Heb. 12:2).—TONY

PRAY ABOUT IT

Ask the Holy Spirit to give you a spiritual vision test. Let Him search your heart and reveal anything that needs to be dealt with.

YOU DON'T GET ALL THE ANSWERS

[God] has also set eternity in their heart, yet so that man will not find out the work which God has done from the beginning even to the end.

—ECCLESIASTES 3:11

***

I was on a cruise a couple of years ago, and as I stood on that boat looking out over that vast Pacific Ocean, I was reminded of my insignificance. All around me was the largest body of water in the world. Here I was, a little speck on a huge ship that was a little speck in the middle of that huge ocean.

Then I happened to turn around and see that as the ship went through the water, it caused a lot of turbulence. But within a couple of seconds, the water closed up and everything was back to normal.

Then the thought hit me, *This is me. I'll go through this life in seventy years, Lord willing, and cause a little stir. But after I'm gone, it will all go back to normal.* Talk about a sense of insignificance!

As I reflected on that experience, I realized that the advertising folks on Madison Avenue have picked up on modern man's lack of significance. Virtually every commercial we see is designed to exploit our innate need for significance.

To attract the women, you've got to splash on a certain perfumed water. To be recognized as successful, you've got to drive that special car. Then, knowing how bored men get after a while, the manufacturers and the advertisers make everything "new and improved" to attack our sense of insignificance all over again.

Solomon said that God put eternity within the heart of man. In other words, we were made for something more than just eating, sleeping, and going to work. God wants us to look up, to seek Him. But He has not solved all of life's riddles for us.

What He *has* given us, though, is something infinitely better: a clearly marked path to real significance by inviting us to know Him intimately.—TONY

PRAY ABOUT IT
Have you ever thanked God for the things He doesn't reveal to us? This is an act of His grace too!

"LET'S GET PRACTICAL"

God has not only raised the Lord but will also raise us up through His power.

───※─────

*H*ave you ever listened to a sermon and wondered how you were supposed to do what the pastor was talking about? You say, "Come on, pastor, let's get practical. I'm just a human being. Where am I supposed to get the ability to do all the stuff the Bible says?"

The Bible provides the answer in today's verse: God has made available to us all the power we will ever need to do anything He asks us to do, because God has made available to us *His* power.

How powerful is God? God is so powerful that three days after Jesus died, God the Father said, "Get up." Through the power of God, the stone rolled away from Jesus' tomb, and He walked out on Easter morning.

But that's not all. Paul said that God is going to exercise that same resurrection power on our bodies someday. Thus even though we may die, one day God is going to say, "Get up." And we are going to come out of our graves the same way Jesus came out of His, to spend eternity with Him. That's how powerful God is.

If God can raise Jesus from the dead, and if He is going to raise you and me up to eternal life someday, giving us the power to live for Him today is no problem at all.

The issue Paul was discussing in 1 Corinthians 6 was that of sexual morality, an area where a lot of people hide behind the argument that they're only human. But Paul's point was that people's inability to control their sexuality has to do with the lack of accessing God's power, not with the level of their passions.

Do you need to be more understanding with your spouse or more patient with the children? Is your job getting to you? The answer is not to get practical. The answer is to get theological—to draw near to God and appropriate His incredible power.

THINK ABOUT IT

The problem is not that we have too much humanity working within us. It's that we have too little of God working within us.

SEEKING GOD: A WOMAN'S DEVOTIONAL LIFE

Mary . . . was listening to the Lord's word, seated at His feet.

—LUKE 10:39

ary of Bethany was one sister in the Lord who knew how to keep her life in spiritual balance. Mary was the willing worshiper, the person who would rather sit at Jesus' feet and hear from Him than eat or do anything else. She understood something that we women need to keep coming back to today: A woman's *spiritual* life is the anchor that holds all of life in place and keeps her from drifting away.

When a woman fears the Lord—when her spiritual priorities are in place and she integrates God into every area of her life—she discovers something wonderful. She discovers within herself a well of strength, joy, and peace that will never run dry. When a woman is vitally connected to Christ, He renews her strength and her spirit day by day.

So the question we need to ask is, What must we as women do to keep our "first love" (see Rev. 2:4) for the Lord fresh?

The first thing we must do to keep our love for God fresh is not let anything take the place of our daily time in His presence. A vibrant, disciplined devotional life is essential if you want to stay close to the Lord and be in a position to receive His strength each day. It's so easy for us to let life's daily demands slip in between us and the Savior. Before long, we are like Martha, sweating and fuming over our tasks while Jesus Himself is in the next room, waiting to meet with us.

If you find yourself tempted to let your time alone with God slip by because of pressing duties, hear what Jesus told Martha. It is better to do less *for* Him if that's what it takes to have more intimacy *with* Him.—LOIS

THINK ABOUT IT

If spending time with God is at the bottom of your "To Do" list today, you need to turn your list upside down!

FATTENING UP YOUR SOUL

Blessed are those who hunger and thirst for righteousness, for they shall be satisfied.
—MATTHEW 5:6

How's your spiritual appetite today? When you're really hungry and thirsty for the things of God, you don't have to worry about going away unfulfilled.

How thirsty for righteousness do you have to be to qualify for Jesus' pronouncement of happiness? As thirsty as the deer in Psalm 42:1. The psalmist wrote, "As the deer pants for the water brooks, So my soul pants for Thee, O God."

How hungry for God do you have to be to have your spiritual appetite fully satisfied? As hungry as Paul was to know God. It was the consuming passion of his soul. He counted everything else in his life as "rubbish" in order that he might know God intimately (Phil. 3:8–10).

Our society is fixated on being skinny. But many of us are too spiritually skinny. A good, stiff breeze would blow us down. A fair-sized trial would wipe us out. We're spiritually anorexic because we don't eat right.

People who are spiritually skinny are always saying, "Lord, change my circumstances."

But the Lord is saying, "No. Fatten up your soul. Develop a deeper hunger and thirst for righteousness. Seek Me with all your heart, and your circumstances will be no problem." Rather than always changing the wind of circumstance, God wants to "fatten" us up so we will be able to stand up against the wind.

The best part of this beatitude is that Jesus promises satisfaction for this hunger. One of our problems today is that we have a lot of dissatisfied people. They say, "If I only had more money or a bigger house, I'd be satisfied."

But the kind of soul hunger we're talking about can't be satisfied by things. The more we get, the more we have to be dissatisfied with. We need to learn to be satisfied with God. And once God satisfies you, you are full.

TALK ABOUT IT
One way the two of you can express your hunger for God is by skipping a meal to spend time with Him. Why not agree to do that in the next week?

A SATISFYING VIEW OF WORK

I hated all the fruit of my labor for which I had labored under the sun, for I must leave it to the man who will come after me. And who knows whether he will be a wise man or a fool?

—ECCLESIASTES 2:18–19

***

*E*cclesiastes is about a man's search for significance in life. But this man wasn't just a guy off the street. This was Solomon, *King* Solomon, the richest and wisest—and at one point the most godly—man on earth.

Now, you would think that being king would be a pretty satisfying line of work. Just like some people today think that if they could just get the right job, they would finally have a reason to look forward to getting up in the morning.

But Solomon, like many of us, found that work isn't the place where we find life's deepest meaning. It distressed him to think that when he died he would have to leave his kingdom to someone who might mess up what he had built.

Solomon lay awake at night fretting about his work (see v. 23). How many sleepless nights have you spent worrying about your work? If your whole identity and purpose in life are tied up in your job, you're probably going to spend a lot of nights fretting over it. That's not good.

Solomon said, in effect, "Look, even though life's ultimate significance isn't found in what you do for a living, that's OK, because God didn't intend for you to find all of your significance in work. But once you understand that work is meaningful because it is a gift from God, you can truly begin to enjoy what you do" (see vv. 24–26).

The problem is that we want to know all the questions and all the answers while God says we need to see life as His gift to be received and enjoyed. If God can ever get us to enjoy life as His gift without trying to take it all apart, He knows we will be set free from the futility of trying to find all our purpose in the things of this life.

In other words, we will be free to pursue Him.

TALK ABOUT IT

Ask each other this question today: "Are we depending on our jobs and hobbies and material stuff to give us joy, or are we finding our greatest pleasure in knowing God?"

THE "GUM" OF MARRIAGE

Flee immorality. Every other sin that a man commits is outside the body, but the immoral man sins against his own body.

—I CORINTHIANS 6:18

———————

Some time ago, Lois was awarded an honorary doctoral degree from Eastern College in Saint Davids, Pennsylvania. While we were in town for the graduation ceremonies, we rode in a taxicab. When we arrived at our destination, I paid the fare and we started to get out of the cab only to discover that someone had left chewing gum on the seat, and Lois had sat in it.

Now, you have to understand, Lois was really looking good! And here was someone's old chewing gum stuck to her beautiful dress.

We tried to pull and scrape it off, but of course we couldn't get it all. Lois went into the restroom to try to clean the gum off. But the more she pulled on it, the more she snagged the fabric of the dress. Finally she came out and said in frustration, "This is not working. The harder I try to remove the gum, the more I'm tearing my dress."

Let me tell you something. This is exactly what happens when a man and a woman come together in sexual intercourse. There is a joining together not only of their bodies but of their spirits too. That's the way God designed sex to work.

But when a person commits adultery and then pulls away from that temporary partner, there is a tearing that happens because the adulterer has joined with that other person's spirit. So when the adulterer pulls away, he or she leaves part of his or her soul behind in the adulterous relationship.

This is one reason the Bible warns us so strongly against committing sexual immorality! You can't play games with God and come away undamaged. Cultivate and enjoy the union He has given you.—TONY

PRAY ABOUT IT

A marriage was never meant to be torn apart. Pray that God will keep the two of you totally in love with each other!

"SPEAK, LORD . . ."

Jesus said to them, "Follow Me, and I will make you become fishers of men." And they immediately left the nets and followed Him.

—MARK 1:17–18

What is God looking for in a man? If God were to draw a picture of a real man, what would this person look like? Would he be bulging with muscles because he works out at the health club five days a week? Well, most of us better hope not, because most of our bulges aren't muscles!

Is a real man somebody who is sexually active and always on the lookout for his next conquest? No, my dog lives like that. Is a real man someone who slaps his wife and shows her who's boss? The answer to that is obvious.

That's the downside of manhood. We know what a real man *isn't*, but what *is* he? What kind of commitments characterize the man God is looking for? I want to suggest that the response of Peter, Andrew, James, and John to Jesus' call to discipleship is a great place to start in defining biblical manhood.

Today's verse tells us that Peter and Andrew immediately left their fishing business to follow Jesus. They dropped everything, even the stuff that most men consider the most important, to obey Jesus' call. Then we read in verses 19–20 that James and John did the same thing.

These four men, and later the other members of the Twelve, left their means of livelihood—their careers—to become Jesus' disciples.

Does that mean you should drop your job to follow Jesus? Not necessarily. What I want you to see is that a biblical man is one who is prepared to obey God no matter what the cost. If your heart attitude is, "Speak, Lord, for Your servant is listening," you won't have any problem providing the kind of leadership your wife, your children, your church, and your community need so badly.—TONY

PRAY ABOUT IT
God is looking for guys who are man enough to follow Him. Ask Him to help you be that kind of man.

THE INTIMATE FELLOWSHIP OF OBEDIENCE

If you love Me, you will keep My commandments.

—JOHN 14:15

❧

Obedience to Christ not only gives you a solid foundation for life, it also brings you into fellowship with God. Obedience is the result of a love relationship with Christ. Jesus said it is incongruent to say you love Him and yet disobey Him. The proof of your love is in your obedience.

Then in John 14:21 Jesus said, "He who has My commandments and keeps them, he it is who loves Me; and he who loves Me shall be loved by My Father, and I will love him, and will disclose Myself to him."

Why did Jesus say that? Because the Father responds to the Son, so if you do not love the Son, the Father can't respond to you. When you decide to obey, God moves on your behalf.

And it gets even better. You not only get God's activity in your life, you get God's presence in intimate fellowship (see John 14:23).

Many Christians say, "Oh, Jesus, come closer to me." Jesus is saying, "I will, if you will only obey Me." Jesus is not asking you to be perfect. What He wants to know is that you are moving toward radical obedience to Him.

Here's another wonderful benefit that comes when we are experiencing the fellowship of obedience with God: Jesus promises that God will send us "another Helper" (John 14:16).

This Helper is the Holy Spirit, who has come to live within us and give us the power to obey. But obedience comes before the promise. Verse 15 of John 14 comes before verse 16. Many of us get it backward. We say, "Lord help me to obey."

Instead, our prayer should be, "Lord, I am obeying You. Please help me." The Holy Spirit enables us as we obey. He is not going to pick us up off the ground and levitate us to the right place. He is going to empower our feet as they move toward the right place.

PRAY ABOUT IT

Can you honestly pray, "Lord, I am obeying You"? Then you have the right to say, "Please help me."

TAKING A SABBATH REST

By the seventh day God completed His work which He had done; and He rested on the seventh day from all His work.

—GENESIS 2:2

Sometimes when we preachers talk about not letting work consume too much of one's time and focus, the folks in the pew think, "He can say that because he doesn't have to face the deadlines I face at work."

I know people have to support their families. I know that few if any of us have work schedules we can control perfectly. But I also know that God's principles are always in force.

And trust me, pastors aren't that far removed from the pressures their people feel. We are tempted to overwork, too, and for what seems like a good reason. After all, we're doing the Lord's work!

God says there should be a day in every week when we let work go. He didn't create us as workaholics. We do that ourselves. I'm guilty here because I love what I do. So I tend to neglect adhering to Scripture that relates to this area of overworking.

But even God rested from His work of creation. To enjoy His accomplishments, He stepped back and looked at them. He was finished, so He rested. Now, God didn't rest because He was tired. His rest was the rest of accomplishment, of a job well done. It was the rest of reflection on and enjoyment of His work.

God thought it was such a good idea to rest one day in seven that He commanded His people to do the same. The seventh day became known as the Sabbath. This was a big deal with God. In the Old Testament, breaking the Sabbath carried the death penalty.

We're not under law, but as Christians we are to cease from our work and take a day to worship the God who provided for us all week long.

Taking our "Sabbath rest" is similar in spirit to giving God His tithe. It's a way of recognizing that we can do more in six days with God's blessing than we can do in seven days without it.—TONY

THINK ABOUT IT

Overwork is a form of unbelief, because it says, "God, I can't trust You to provide for me in six days."

MADE FOR NURTURE

Fathers, do not provoke your children to anger; but bring them up in the discipline and instruction of the Lord.

—EPHESIANS 6:4

Here's a common scenario. Mom says to Dad, "You need to talk to your son. He's getting sassy and giving me a hard time." But Dad doesn't want to confront Junior and have one of those emotional scenes. He figures as long as Junior's not getting suspended from school or arrested, he'll be OK. Every kid lips off to his mother once in a while.

So Dad hides behind the paper or goes back to channel surfing, and Mother is left to deal with their son. Then when the call comes that Junior is in trouble at school or with the law, Dad finally gets stirred out of his recliner. He's also very frustrated because he's wondering, *What happened?*

If that scenario sounds familiar, Dad, I want to help you get beyond the excuse that you're too busy or too tired or too whatever to keep up with what's going on in your kids' lives.

I also want to disabuse you of the notion that raising children is really kind of the woman's thing.

When God's Word addresses the issue of raising and nurturing children, the instruction is given primarily to fathers. But Christian fathers who would never harm their children physically are harming them emotionally and spiritually by being the silent partner in their nurture and training.

With this kind of fathering, what we are getting is a generation of children being raised on the world's values. Now a father may say, "Well, I tell them what to do." That's fine, but it's not enough.

Children are born in sin, just like you and I. Given the opportunity, apart from Jesus Christ they will do what they are not supposed to do. Their bent is toward sin. What children need is a father who can guide them in the way of truth and train them in the things of God.—TONY

PRAY ABOUT IT

A father's prayer: "Dear God, thank You today for my children. Help me to love and discipline them the way You love and discipline me."

GRACE IS A PERSON

Of His fulness we have all received, and grace upon grace. For the Law was given through Moses; grace and truth were realized through Jesus Christ.

—JOHN 1:16–17

❧

race is a beautiful name that many parents give to their daughters. That's very appropriate because grace—God's undeserved favor toward us—*is* a Person, Jesus Christ. The apostle John, who was as close as anyone was to Jesus while He was on earth, said that Christ is the full expression of God's grace.

But notice that God's grace does not begin and end at salvation, as wonderful as that is. Jesus keeps showering us with "grace upon grace." It just keeps on coming and coming as often as we need it. James calls it "greater grace" (James 4:6).

So how do we make sure we are tapping into the endless flow of God's grace? By drawing closer to the Person of grace. The more intimate your fellowship with Christ, the more you will grow in His grace. Notice that John contrasts grace in Christ with the Law of Moses. He's not saying there was something wrong with the Law. God's Law is perfect. The problem is with us, because we are not. That's why Paul said we could never have been saved by attempting to keep the Law.

Do you see why grace is so wonderful? It doesn't give us permission to sin, but it deals with the one issue we can't handle: our sin. Once you understand what God's grace has done for you, you can't help but want to draw closer to Christ in loving, intimate fellowship.

Now let us speak to the primary focus of this devotional, which is your life together as a Christian couple. The relationship between intimacy and a greater enjoyment of God's grace also applies to marriage. The more the two of you draw together in genuine spiritual and emotional intimacy, the more your individual spiritual lives will feel the benefit. We're convinced you can't be in intimate, growing fellowship with Christ unless your marriage is also growing in grace.

TALK ABOUT IT

Take a reading of your spiritual, emotional, and physical intimacy. Are you growing in intimacy, or have you stagnated? If you've stagnated, what can you do to start correcting it?

YOU CAN'T DO BOTH

No one can serve two masters; for either he will hate the one and love the other, or he will hold to one and despise the other. You cannot serve God and mammon.

—MATTHEW 6:24

A servant can't serve two owners. That's what Jesus said in this classic verse that helps us to get our priorities in order. The word *master* means slave owner. No owner was about to share his slave with anyone else. There can be only one master.

The word *mammon* Jesus used is from an Aramaic word that means property, and it was used generally of money or material possessions. When it comes to the material or the spiritual, you have to make a choice about which one you are going to serve. You can have material possessions, but you can't *serve* these things and still give Christ priority in your life.

"Serving" material possessions means they become your master, and when it comes to a choice between what the master wants and what anyone else wants, the master wins.

So Jesus' question to you today is, Who tells you what to do? Do you take your orders from God and His Word, or does your material well-being dictate your choices? Who wins? This is Jesus' concern. He is interested in our priorities, not the size of our bank accounts. God's complaint against Israel in Malachi 1 was that the people were giving Him the leftovers. They did not prioritize God.

It's like the farmer who had two prize calves. He told his wife, "Honey, I'm going to give one of these calves to the Lord, because I realize that both of them are gifts from Him. I'll raise one calf for us and the other for the Lord. We'll sell it and give the money to the Lord."

But a few weeks later, he came in dejected and sad. His wife asked, "Honey, what's wrong?"

"The Lord's calf just died."

It's always the Lord's calf that dies, isn't it? If we do not prioritize God's kingdom and His glory, He loses out when it comes to making our choices.

THINK ABOUT IT
Jesus didn't say it is hard to serve two masters. He said it's impossible!

PROFOUNDLY SIMPLE ADVICE

Remember also your Creator in the days of your youth, before the evil days come.

—ECCLESIASTES 12:1

❧

*T*f you're going to get advice from somebody on an important subject, you want to hear from somebody who has made it. If you are trying to grow hair, you don't go to a hair-growth expert who is bald. If you are trying to lose weight, you don't go to a three-hundred-pound nutritionist. That just doesn't compute.

So when we want the real deal on life's purpose, we need to find somebody who can speak from experience. We need to hear from somebody we can respect. We need somebody who has it together, who has what we are looking for, who is going after what we are going after. That's why Solomon is the perfect person.

One reason why we know this issue of life's purpose is so important is that God has devoted a whole book of His Word to addressing it. The Book of Ecclesiastes addresses our need to grasp a compelling reason for our existence. It was written by Solomon, a man who had everything he needed to pursue every possible avenue that might promise an answer.

Solomon had more money than most nations. He also had seven hundred wives and three hundred concubines. Solomon could soak himself in any pleasure a man could imagine.

And talk about a career! If you make it to king, you can't go any higher. And in addition to unimaginable wealth, pleasure, and power, Solomon was also given wisdom beyond what anyone before or since has possessed.

And yet Solomon's advice to us after all he possessed and all he experienced was profoundly simple: "Remember God." Don't leave God out of the picture as you plan your life.

THINK ABOUT IT

You may not consider yourself to be "in the days of your youth," but as long as you're still here you can turn it around and discover God's purpose for you.

SEEKING GOD: FOLLOWING HIS CALL

We have as our ambition . . . to be pleasing to Him.

—2 CORINTHIANS 5:9

❦

E arlier we learned that one way we women can keep our love for God strong is to make sure we are spending time with Him in prayer and study of the Word.

Today, let me suggest another way to keep God first in your life: Make sure you are following His call on your life and not simply trying to fulfill the expectations of people.

Of course, we need to be sensitive to others. Your husband and child have legitimate needs that must be attended to. And you may be active in your church and community. But remember, at the judgment seat of Christ the issue will be how well we pleased Him, not how well we pleased others.

When gaining the Lord's "well done" is the dominating concern of our lives, we will not so easily succumb to the demands and expectations that people may try to place upon us. We will simply run their demands through the grid of God's will for us.

And if the demands don't fit, then we can say no in love without feeling guilty. Too many women are living unfulfilled lives because they are doing things God never expected them to do.

Dr. Howard Hendricks, one of Tony's mentors in seminary and a wonderful Christian leader, used to tell his students they should practice saying no every day in front of a mirror so they could say no to things that would distract them from their primary goal.

It takes a person who is secure in God's will to do this. And it requires some real discipline of your time and energies. But if you don't plan your days according to what you believe is God's will and calling for you, there are plenty of people—even well-meaning people—who will plan your days for you.—LOIS

TALK ABOUT IT

A married couple can really help each other at this point. Husband, do you help guard your wife's precious time? And my sister, do you do the same for your husband?

SEEKING GOD: MAINTAINING YOUR PRIORITIES

Well done, good and faithful slave; you were faithful with a few things, I will put you in charge of many things.

—MATTHEW 25:21

One of a woman's greatest challenges and privileges is learning how to keep God first in her life. We can do that by spending daily time with Him and making sure we are pleasing Him.

Here's another way to keep God first: Maintain your biblical priorities.

For us women, this means that anything outside the home that conflicts with God's priority of our family must either be readjusted or released. It's amazing how many Christian men and women want to fix the world but aren't willing to fix their families first.

After family, our priority should be our ministry in the local church. Tony often says that there is no such thing as "Lone Ranger" Christians, and I agree. As I have said several times, we were never meant to try to make it alone.

A third priority we need to maintain is our service to others outside of the family and the church. Such service not only contributes to the well-being of the community but also gives us opportunities to share our faith.

A woman (or a man, for that matter) whose priorities are in line with God's purposes will experience His joy and empowerment. Our job is not to get God to adjust to our priorities but to adjust our lives to His will.

I believe that a woman who is walking closely with the Lord, pleasing Him in her daily life, and living according to His priorities can say to even the most rigorous feminist, "I have what you're looking for. I have a family, fulfilling work, satisfaction, and peace of heart. I have a husband who loves me and whom I love. My children are well cared for. I have confidence in the present, and I know where I'm going in the future. Now, what are *you* offering me?"—LOIS

PRAY ABOUT IT

"Dear God, help all of us who desire to be godly women to learn the joy of seeking you with all our hearts."

GET OFF YOUR DONKEY

Blessed are the merciful, for they shall receive mercy.

—MATTHEW 5:7

***

Mercy involves putting yourself in someone else's "skin" and identifying with that person to the point that you feel what he or she feels. It also means being willing to do whatever you can to alleviate the other's pain.

It is what God extended to us when He looked down from heaven and decided to extend His grace to sinful people like you and me. God acted in mercy toward us by sending His Son to die for our sins. Jesus came to earth and "mixed it up" with us in the daily grind of human life. He fully identified with our hurt and misery and reached out in mercy to save us.

Remember the story of the Good Samaritan in Luke 10? The man who was robbed and beaten and left for dead certainly needed someone to feel his pain and do something about it. He needed mercy.

The two "preachers" who passed by him first were too busy working on their sermons to stop. But the Samaritan came along, got off his donkey, treated the man's wounds, took him to an inn, and picked up the tab.

One of the first and best places to begin showing mercy is in your home. Far too many couples show more mercy to those outside the marriage than they do to their partners—regularly passing by their mates in their hurts and pains. The home should be the premiere place for giving and receiving God's mercy.

That's the idea behind Jesus' statement, which meant, "If you want to be a receiver of mercy, you must be a giver of mercy."

There is coming a time when all of us are going to need mercy. One of the best ways to prepare for your time of need is to ask that God will make you a merciful person today. Jesus says the mercy-giver is blessed, or happy. If you want a sense of joy you can't find anywhere else, get off your donkey; that is, stop to help someone who needs you, starting with your mate.

PRAY ABOUT IT

Wounded people are lying all along the road of life. Ask God to open your eyes to see them.

TEACHING YOUR CHILDREN HONOR (DAY 1)

*Children, obey your parents in the Lord, for this is right. Honor your father and mother
(which is the first commandment with a promise).*

—EPHESIANS 6:1–2

These are verses Christian parents love to quote to their children. God wants children to be obedient, of course, but notice that qualifying phrase "in the Lord." That means you have to instruct them in the things of God if they are going to know how to obey. In other words, your children need the right biblical information and the right application. You can't leave them to themselves thinking someone else is going to teach them.

Now, you can't know what is right until you know what God said about it. So you need to be hanging around where the Bible is being taught and be in the Word yourselves as parents. Dad, it is primarily your assignment to instruct your children in how they ought to live under God's authority. The best way to do that is to make sure you are submitted to the Lord's authority yourself.

That's key, because remember, even though they will move out from under your authority someday, your kids will always need to be under God's authority. So God tells children to honor their parents. Here is a great place to begin teaching your children what it means to obey you in the Lord.

Children need their parents, especially their fathers, to help them understand that we are the adults and they are the children, and children are to respect adults. In time, they are going to get that right. But in the meantime, we parents need to be consistent in teaching honor, expecting honor, and encouraging honor.

Paul said there are two good reasons for this. First, because it's right. God says, in effect, "When you teach your children according to My ways, it pleases Me. And when I am pleased, I will bless you." The second reason is that this commandment carries a blessing of long life (see v. 3). Teaching our children to obey us is the healthiest thing we can do for them!

TALK ABOUT IT
*Being under authority isn't easy for kids to learn, because no one wants to be under
anyone else's authority. How are you doing in honoring the authorities in your lives?*

TEACHING YOUR CHILDREN HONOR (DAY 2)

These words, which I am commanding you today, shall be on your heart; and you shall teach them diligently to your sons.

—DEUTERONOMY 6:6–7

❦

We learned yesterday that God makes a special promise of long life and blessing to children who obey their parents (see Deut. 5:16). God knows that the children in a home become the fiber of a society. If honor and respect for authority do not start in the home, they will never hit the street. And if they never hit the street, they will not affect the community, the state, or the nation.

We say, "Well, one kid not obeying his parents isn't going to bring down the United States of America." Maybe not, but try fifteen or twenty million children who have no idea what it means to honor or respect anyone!

The fifth commandment reminds us that honor isn't just some nice little concept we teach to help polish our kids' manners and keep them from being rude. It has the power of life and death.

Deuteronomy 6 teaches that a nation's destiny is determined in large measure by the quality of spiritual instruction in its homes. Deuteronomy 6:4, perhaps the most important statement of this truth in the entire Old Testament, declares, "The LORD is our God, the LORD is one!" Verse 5 is indispensable too, according to Jesus (see Matt. 22:37). Then notice the very next thing God said in verses 6–9. Let me summarize it:

"Now fathers, go home and train your children in My truth. Train them when they wake up. Train them when they lie down. Train them in between their waking up and lying down. Train them formally. Train them informally. I want My truth tied on their foreheads and on their wrists. I want them to bump into My truth when they come into the house and when they leave the house."

Teaching God's truth as a lifestyle is a huge responsibility for parents, but the payoff is great. What you do today to teach your children God's truth can impact your family for generations!

TALK ABOUT IT

Do you verbally bless your children, telling them how you see God at work in their lives (see Genesis 27)?

A SPECIAL WORD TO DADS (DAY 1)

Fathers, do not exasperate your children, that they may not lose heart.

—COLOSSIANS 3:21

***

Diligent fathers don't let their kids run the show. But they also understand that a dad can't exasperate and frustrate his children and still expect them to come out right.

What are some ways we dads provoke or anger our kids?

One way is by smothering them, or overparenting them. This is not a problem fathers are usually guilty of as much as mothers, but it is a possibility and needs to be mentioned. Fathers can smother their children by trying to do everything for them, never letting the children try—and sometimes fail—on their own.

Favoritism is another spirit-killer for kids: This can be a real temptation if, for example, you have one son who is athletic and another who is more artistic. Depending on your preference, you can end up frustrating the son who doesn't meet your idea of what a man should be and do.

A father can also frustrate his children by forcing his unfulfilled dreams upon them. "I didn't get to be a doctor, son, but you are going to be a doctor."

Son's reply: "But Dad, I don't like doctoring."

Discouragement, criticism, and the withholding of approval are several other prime ways we dads can exasperate our children. Be careful not to puncture your kids' hopes and ideas. Try not to focus too much on what they're *not* doing. Don't be afraid of words of approval and affirmation. You rarely hear a man say his mother never once affirmed him when he was young. But the men who say that about their fathers are legion in number.

Here's one more way fathers can exasperate their children, and it's a biggie in the nineties: failure to sacrifice. By that I mean fathers who send this message to their kids: "I need fulfillment now. You are in my way."

Are any of these on your list? All of us fathers have messed up, but when we do so we need to ask for forgiveness and move on.—TONY

PRAY ABOUT IT
Dad, ask God to help you be the number one encourager in your children's lives.

A SPECIAL WORD TO DADS (DAY 2)

Fathers . . . bring [your children] up in the discipline and instruction of the Lord.
—EPHESIANS 6:4

❦

One reason God gave His laws and commands to Israel is that He wanted His people to be different from the nations around them. Not so Israel could feel superior but as a witness to the nations of what happens when people love and serve the true God.

The same is true of us today as God's people. He wants our families to be built on His truth and righteousness. He has left us in the world to show what happens when a family worships and serves God as opposed to simply being like everyone else.

But that's not what we have today. We have too many Christian children who act like all the other kids in the neighborhood. We have Christian parents saying, "I love Johnny, so I don't spank him."

Excuse me, but if this is your attitude, you *hate* Johnny. Do you know what the Bible says about God? "Whom the Lord loveth, He skins alive." That's an Evans rendering of Hebrews 12:6. In other words, God disciplines His kids.

One way He does that is through the fathers He has appointed to lead our families. Ephesians 6:4 is a classic statement of our responsibility to train and instruct our children in godly living.

To discipline children means more than just correcting them when they mess up. It means to *train* them. Sure, it includes laying down the rules with the rewards and punishments attached to the rules. Your expectations need to be clear. But training also means you create an environment in which your children are set up for success, not failure.

How do you help set your children up to succeed? By *instructing* them in God's Word. Teaching your children the Scriptures will help them avoid a lot of pitfalls and learn to walk in the safe path of God's will.—TONY

THINK ABOUT IT

Dad, if you'll pay the price to instruct your kids in the Lord, you have the staggering promise that it will be well with them—and their children's children after them (see Exod. 20:5–6)!

RESTING ON THE SABBATH

Then God blessed the seventh day and sanctified it, because in it He rested from all His work.

—GENESIS 2:3

⬥

The issue of work and rest is important enough that we could spend many days exploring the implications of the fact that God rested and then blessed the seventh day.

The Sabbath was serious stuff in Israel because it was the day to cease from work and worship God. It was a time to enjoy the God of work rather than the work itself.

Today resting on the Sabbath also means you are working in the will of God and trusting God for the next week's work, the next week's opportunity, the next week's promotion, the next week's challenges. So instead of knocking yourself out, on the Sabbath you say, "God, this is it. I'm done. I'm going to stop working and trust You."

For the Christian, workaholism often reflects a lack of trust in God. It's the idea that we've got to do it all ourselves or it won't get done. It's too important to leave it up to anyone else, even God. Another problem with workaholism is that it kills relationships. The Sabbath was designed to reemphasize the importance of our relationships, with God and with each other. The reason so many of us men are workaholics is that we're scared of relationships. See, if we're not working on Sunday, we may have to sit down and talk with our spouses or our kids. And we may discover we have a problem or two. If we're working, we have an excuse for not talking.

One way to avoid letting work dominate us is to put limitations on it. We are not to be driven by greed. That's one limitation. And we are not to work seven days a week so that our spiritual lives dry up and die.

If you're working so hard that you never get time with God or with your loved ones, you're working too hard. Your work was never meant to replace God in your life. Work had its limits even with Him.

PRAY ABOUT IT

Do you ever wonder whether God is pleased with your work schedule? Why not ask Him about it today?

MAKING THE CHOICE OF GRACE

Mary has chosen the good part, which shall not be taken away from her.

⟨ornament⟩

When it comes to relating to God, we have two choices. We can relate to Him on the basis of our performance or on the basis of His grace. This choice also relates to marriage.

Some marriages operate by performance. The wife says, "I cook and do the laundry because that's my job description."

The husband says, "I go to work and mow the lawn and wash the car because that's what is expected of me. That's what I'm supposed to do."

Now, it's true that marriage involves responsibilities and routine. But the routine was never meant to degenerate into a rut that both spouses come to despise.

It wasn't like that when you were newlyweds because you were so-o-o much in love! Back then, the wife couldn't cook, but the husband wouldn't complain. "How's the food, darling?" she would ask. "Delicious, baby," he would coo. He was lying! But back then, the young couple encouraged each other even in the failures.

Back then, the wife hated to iron (probably still does!). But she ironed hubby's shirts with a smile. Why? Because the relationship was predicated on love and grace, not performance. The dynamic of love overruled the routine of performance.

Even though the performance was still there, it was driven by relationship, not by a sense of duty. The home is a happy place to be when the relationship is strong.

Jesus spoke to the difference between devotion and duty the day He came to the house of Mary and Martha for dinner. Mary chose the intimacy of devotion to Christ and intimate relationship with Him. Martha chose duty over devotion and wound up getting angry at Mary and fussing at Jesus.

A marriage where duty is the main emphasis has degenerated into a performance marriage, predicated on how much each partner does, not on how much the two people love each other.

TALK ABOUT IT

The good news is that a performance-based marriage can become a grace-based marriage in a short time. All it takes is a choice to forgive and to extend grace to each other.

THE DIFFERENCE BETWEEN NEEDS AND WANTS

The eye is not satisfied with seeing, nor is the ear filled with hearing.
—ECCLESIASTES 1:8

Solomon reminds us of a universal truth about human nature: Once you and I start trying to satisfy all of our wants and desires, there is no end to the process.

The people who put those slick commercials on TV understand that principle better than a lot of believers. Their ad campaigns are specifically designed to feed the sense of desire and dissatisfaction that today's verse is talking about.

One way to avoid falling into this trap is to sit down as a couple and draw up a financial plan that prioritizes your spending and saving. You need a plan that takes care of first things first—which means you must know the difference between a need and a want or desire.

First take care of your needs, the necessities without which you could not survive and function. First Timothy 6:8 lists food and clothing as needs. We could add things like shelter and, in our culture, some form of transportation.

An important principle of wise financial planning is that you never skip needs in order to satisfy wants. In Philippians 4:19 Paul wrote, "My God shall supply all your *needs* according to His riches in glory in Christ Jesus" (my emphasis). Whenever you skip needs and go to desires, you're skipping God's priority.

Once you have taken care of your needs, then you can start to consider some of your desires, those things that are not needs but are not wrong or sinful to have.

For example, your *need* may be a car that runs, but your *want* may be a new car that runs fast and looks sporty.

Don't mess with your basic plan by fulfilling your wants if you don't have enough to meet your needs.—TONY

TALK ABOUT IT
Look at the things you are doing with your money and list each purchase or activity under the category of need or desire. Now talk about what your chart reveals.

STAY IN THE VICINITY

I will never desert you, nor will I ever forsake you.

—HEBREWS 13:5

Occasionally, Tony and I visit my sister who lives outside of London. During one of these summer visits, I was exercising as I looked out through the window at a little park. A lady was walking through the park, throwing bread crumbs to a flock of pigeons as she walked.

But as the birds were eating, a boy approached. He had no crumbs to give the birds. Instead, with a wave of his hand he ran among the pigeons to frighten and scatter them. Some of the birds became confused and flew away while some lingered in the vicinity.

That scene made me think of how our heavenly Father provides for us in abundance (see Matt. 6:26). But Satan tries to scare us away from the Father while offering nothing good himself.

When Satan shows up to make you fearful, don't run too far from the source of your blessings and strength. Stay in the vicinity of your Father, and Satan will flee. Then you can return to enjoy what the Lord has freely provided for you.

Let me give you an example of how I am applying this truth to my own life. Satan knows how to "wave his hands" in my life and try to frighten me because I have a strong fear of flying. Before a flight, I am very nervous and indecisive.

But I know that my fears come because I lack faith in God and His Word. I have to learn, and He is teaching me, to trust in His promises and realize that everything He brings into my life is for my best and to bring glory to His name.

What I decided to do is make a conscious decision to yield to Christ. I claim victory every minute of the day by praising God for His promise never to leave me no matter where I am, even when I'm miles above the earth!—LOIS

THINK ABOUT IT
The will of God will never take you where the grace of God cannot keep you!

HIGH INTEREST

Instruct those who are rich in this present world not to be conceited or to fix their hope on the uncertainty of riches, but on God, who richly supplies us with all things to enjoy.

—I TIMOTHY 6:17

*I*f God were negative toward material possessions, as some assume He is, Paul would not have said what he said in today's verse. If you have nice things, it is because God has given you these things to enjoy. Has He given you a house and a wardrobe? Got some money in the bank? Rejoice in His provision, and enjoy what He has given!

But all of us who have things are prone to a two-pronged temptation. The first is to become conceited over what God has given us, as though we did it ourselves through our own wisdom and shrewd planning.

The second temptation is to start fixing our hope "on the uncertainty of riches." In other words, we start trusting the job or the bank account instead of the God who provided it.

Your orientation shows up in what you say. Are you always talking about what you want, need, and are going to do, or is your conversation sprinkled with what God wants and needs from you?

The antidote to a selfish orientation is to use your material blessings to make eternal investments, which always appreciate in value. In contrast, earthly investments can depreciate in value, and even disappear.

Here are four examples of the high interest you reap when you invest in God and His kingdom program: (1) God promises He will meet all of your needs (see Phil. 4:19), (2) God will reveal His will to you and give you direction in life (see Rom. 12:2), (3) You will have a God-given sense of contentment that no amount of money can buy (see 1 Tim. 6:6), and (4) God will give you His wisdom in making the decisions of life (see James 1:5).

That's high interest, and it only comes with investments in God's kingdom!

PRAY ABOUT IT

The prayer of Proverbs 30:8–9 is also a good antidote to greed. Make it your prayer as a couple today.

THE SPIRIT'S BENEFITS

It is to your advantage that I go away; for if I do not go away, the Helper shall not come to you.

—JOHN 16:7

❦

When Jesus says a situation is to your advantage, you're in for something special. He doesn't make promises lightly. In my wallet, I have a card from the airline I use. I'm a member of this airline's frequent flyer club, which entitles me to certain benefits the occasional traveler does not have.

You see, over the past ten years I have developed a very intimate relationship with this airline, because during that time I have flown more than a million miles. In the eyes of this airline, that gives me an advantage.

Jesus says because of your relationship to Him, He is going to give you an "advantage" and enroll you in the "Holy Ghost Club." If you will keep flying with Jesus, He will make sure you stay in the club and accrue the Spirit's benefits. Let's talk about a few of these benefits.

First, Jesus has said the Spirit will "guide you into all the truth" (John 16:13). Do you need guidance? Are there decisions you need to make that you wish somebody would advise you on? You have that Person in the Holy Spirit.

Jesus also said the Spirit would "bring to your remembrance all that I said to you" (John 14:26). Jesus had taught the disciples a lot. How were they going to remember it all? The Holy Spirit would recall these things to their minds.

Another benefit the Holy Spirit gives is peace. "Peace I leave with you; My peace I give to you; not as the world gives, do I give to you," Jesus said in John 14:27. Therefore, "Let not your heart be troubled, nor let it be fearful."

Jesus said this in the Upper Room just hours before being crucified. He was leaving the disciples, and they were distraught. Yet Jesus was telling them they would experience peace through the Holy Spirit.

What's your situation today? Whatever it is, if you have the Holy Spirit you have the advantage over any circumstance!—TONY

PRAY ABOUT IT
There are many more great benefits to being in the Holy Spirit's Advantage Club. Knowing Jesus gets you in the club; worshiping Jesus gets you spiritual miles.

BIBLICAL WORSHIP: LIVING WATER FOR THE "DRY ZONE" (DAY 1)

Whoever drinks of the water that I shall give him shall never thirst.

—JOHN 4:14

⁕

Worship is something that sincere Christians know they ought to be doing. They even want to worship. But they're not always sure how to go about it. Like the puzzled party-goer who asks, "Are we having fun yet?" Christians sometimes try hard to worship but feel like asking, "Am I worshiping yet?"

To help us get a handle on a big subject, let's turn to John 4, the familiar story of Jesus and the Samaritan woman at the well—one of the Bible's classic texts on worship.

It's appropriate that the setting for this great chapter on worship is a well, because we believe the reason many Christians run dry is that they have not learned how to worship.

Worship is the pump that keeps the water flowing so that the well of living water, which never runs dry, does not *feel* like it is running dry. Many of us go through the rhetoric of worship. We know the hymns and the right phrases to say at the right times. But far too many believers harbor a "dry zone" deep down inside.

No matter where you are on the continuum, the way to get the inner spring of your life flowing is by pursuing an intimate relationship with Jesus Christ and by learning to worship.

That's what Jesus told the Samaritan woman, who thought she was just going outside of town for a bucket of water. Jesus told the woman about a water that would quench her thirst forever, and she asked Him to give her some of this water. The fact that she thought this water would quench her physical thirst shows that the woman was not tuned in to what Jesus was saying.

Are you tuned in to what Jesus is trying to tell you? Tomorrow we'll see how Jesus helped the woman focus on the lesson in His words to her.

PRAY ABOUT IT

The woman may not have understood it all, but her openness in John 4:15 is something we can imitate. A good prayer today would be, "Lord, give me this water."

BIBLICAL WORSHIP: LIVING WATER FOR THE "DRY ZONE" (DAY 2)

Give me this water, so I will not be thirsty.

—JOHN 4:15

❧

Our subject this week is worship, and our Teacher is Jesus Christ. His discussion with the Samaritan woman at Jacob's well gives us several of the most helpful principles of true worship found anywhere in Scripture.

Jesus and the woman had been discussing water when Jesus suddenly asked the woman to go get her husband. This request uncovered the truth of the woman's five prior husbands and her adulterous living situation. Perhaps in an attempt to change the subject, the woman started talking about worship. Jesus was willing to pick up the topic, since the only way she could get things right at home was to get things right with God. That's true in our families too, by the way.

The word *worship* in one form or another is found no fewer than ten times in this short passage. The woman got the ball rolling when she brought up two places of worship: "Our fathers worshiped in this mountain, and you people say that in Jerusalem is the place where men ought to worship" (v. 20).

"Our fathers" referred to the woman's Samaritan ancestors. "You people" were the Jews. The Samaritans had developed their own system of worship because they weren't welcome at the temple in Jerusalem—and this was the key to Jesus' conversation with the woman. They had established their own temple on a mountain called Gerizim.

This woman wanted to know which "church" was the right one, and Jesus' response to her is the meat of our subject. Jesus didn't choose either of her options (see v. 21). Instead He said a new "hour" was coming.

In other words, Jesus was saying, "I am going to inaugurate a new basis for worship that's got nothing to do with either Gerizim or Jerusalem and the family heritages they represent. And woman, as far as you're concerned, this new hour has already come." Tomorrow, we'll talk about this new basis for worship.

THINK ABOUT IT
Worship isn't as much about a place as it is about a Person.

BIBLICAL WORSHIP: LIVING WATER FOR THE "DRY ZONE" (DAY 3)

God is spirit, and those who worship Him must worship in spirit and in truth.

—JOHN 4:24

When Jesus told the woman at the well that a day was coming when the issue in worship would not be the place (John 4:21), He was referring to the cancellation of the old covenant, the approach to God that He had made available to people in the Old Testament. If you wanted to worship in those days, you had to go to the tabernacle.

Jesus was telling this woman that the old system had been canceled. Under that system, worship was tied to where you were. You had to be part of Israel, gathered around the tabernacle or temple. But in the future, Jesus said, worship would not be tied to where you are but *who* you are. He was inaugurating a new means of worship called the new covenant. According to Jeremiah 31:33, under the new covenant God's relationship with His people would be internal.

Worship has less to do with where you go on Sunday morning than Whom you are in touch with all week long. What Jesus was teaching here in John 4 was what Paul later spelled out in 1 Corinthians 6:19: "Do you not know that your body is a temple of the Holy Spirit?" God's presence is no longer centered in the temple at Jerusalem or on any mountain. He now lives inside of His people.

So where can you worship? Anywhere! It's not where you are, it's who you are. You are the temple of the living God. He now lives within you. This doesn't mean we don't have to go to church anymore to worship God. Instead, individual worship should lead to corporate worship. The Bible commands us not to forsake the assembly of the church (see Heb. 10:25).

But if you go to church thinking you are now going to *the* place of worship, you've missed the message. If you limit worship to where you are, the minute you leave that place of worship you will leave your *attitude* of worship behind like a crumpled-up church bulletin.

TALK ABOUT IT

Is regular worship with the assembled church a high priority in your family? It needs to be.

BIBLICAL WORSHIP: LIVING WATER FOR THE "DRY ZONE" (DAY 4)

[Let us not] forsak[e] our own assembling together.

—HEBREWS 10:25

❦

This week we've been looking at the key elements of worship Jesus taught in John 4 as He talked with the woman at the well. Like a lot of people today, she was hung up on the place of worship. Those who think worship only happens in a place—the "worship center," for example—do not understand that they carry worship around within them. Jesus said the true worshipers are those who worship "in spirit and truth" (John 4:24).

Is the church meant to be a place of worship? Of course it is. But it's not the sole extent of our worship.

Hebrews 10 has some powerful things to say about this new way of worship Jesus inaugurated. "Since therefore, brethren, we have confidence to enter the holy place by the blood of Jesus, by a new and living way which He inaugurated for us through the veil, that is, His flesh . . . let us draw near with a sincere heart" (vv. 19–22).

Where can you go to worship today? Directly into the presence of God! You don't need a confessional booth. You don't even need a preacher to go before God for you.

But the Bible does not leave this thing on the individual level. People who ask, "Do I have to go to church to worship God?" aren't really interested in worship. Private worship always leads to corporate worship. If you are worshiping in private, you can't wait to worship in public. If you don't care about private worship, you'll debate whether you need church.

Some people will argue, "I don't have to go to church to worship God. I can worship right here in my bed."

Maybe—but the issue is, *do* they worship God when they kill the alarm and pull the covers back over their heads? I doubt it!

PRAY ABOUT IT

We hope these private devotions are deepening your hunger to worship with the body of Christ. If that's not happening, please pray that it will.

BIBLICAL WORSHIP: LIVING WATER FOR THE "DRY ZONE" (DAY 5)

Jesus cried out again . . . and yielded up His spirit. And behold, the veil of the temple was torn in two from top to bottom.

—MATTHEW 27:50–51

*Y*esterday we said that people who don't believe they have to worship publicly are serving notice that they probably don't worship at all. People like this have not learned that worship is a way of life for Christians. We do not go to church just to get our hour of worship in but because we have been worshiping all week and we can't help but join with others who have been doing the same.

A great event happened when Jesus died. They killed Jesus on the cross, then they went back to the temple, and guess what they found: The huge, heavy veil covering the holy place had been torn completely in two.

This veil, which separated the people from the very presence of God, was ripped in half at the moment of Christ's death because His sacrifice on the cross gave His people permission to walk right on inside.

For true worshipers that torn curtain means the focus of worship is God: not just His name but His Person.

It also means you cannot worship properly with your body only. If all God has of you on Sunday morning is your body, you are not worshiping. If you get up to have your private worship and your body is the only part of you present, that's not worship. If you don't want to be there, if you're thinking about work, if you're in a hurry, you have wasted your time, because you cannot worship a Spirit in body only.

Jesus said those who worship the Father must worship Him "in spirit" (John 4:24). Fellowship with God occurs when God's invisible Spirit and your invisible spirit get together with one another, when they commune and communicate.

You can clap to the songs. You can sing with the choir. You can say "Amen" to the words, but unless the Spirit has kicked into gear, you cannot worship.

THINK ABOUT IT

What is the attitude of your mind and spirit when you enter the presence of God? Are you distracted or focused?

BIBLICAL WORSHIP: LIVING WATER FOR THE "DRY ZONE" (DAY 6)

The Spirit searches all things, even the depths of God. . . . The thoughts of God no one knows except the Spirit of God.

—I CORINTHIANS 2:10–11

*T*f worship is primarily a matter of the spirit, how do we kick our spirits into gear so that we are truly worshiping? One way is through the Holy Spirit, who acts as liaison. The Spirit knows the mind of God, so His work is to link your human spirit with God, who is spirit.

Therefore, if you want to worship God you must be yielded to His Spirit. You must come to worship collectively or privately with the attitude, "Lord, I am depending on the Holy Spirit to bring me in contact with You."

In addition, your mind must be centered on God. If you sit in church worrying about your problems or even counting your blessings, you are not worshiping. If you stay up late every Saturday night and go to church so tired you wish you were home, you are in no condition to worship God.

And in your devotion time, if all you do is read a passage of Scripture and rattle off a few prayer items, that is not worship. Worship includes yieldedness to the Holy Spirit and a fixation on God. That means you cannot worship and watch television at the same time because the goal of worship is total fixation on God.

I realize that what I have just said means that many people who call themselves Christians are going to church but are not worshiping.

The key to true worship is "spirit and truth" (John 4:24). It's not either/or but both. Some groups really get high on spirited worship. They shout praises and sing and clap and feel good. There's nothing wrong with spirited worship. But it is not true worship unless it is combined with truth. The people may be shouting, but what is the truth God wants you to learn? True worship is when our innermost beings, having received the proper information about God, explode with joy at the very thought of such a great God being ours!—TONY

THINK ABOUT IT

Don't let your worship become unbalanced by focusing only on the style or only on the content. Both are crucial to true worship.

DEALING WITH FEAR

God has not given us a spirit of timidity, but of power and love and discipline.

—2 TIMOTHY 1:7

Flying is not one of my favorite things to do. But as I travel with Tony more and more these days, I have had to deal head-on with my fear of flying. Fear, what the Bible calls "a spirit of timidity," can manifest itself in many ways. And if left unattended and unchecked, it can grab hold of you and destroy you.

For us women, fear can be destructive to both inner and outer beauty, generating tensions that keep us uptight and irritable. It can produce mistrust, causing us to question everything and everyone. And it can definitely produce unhappiness when we are always waiting to see what is going to go wrong next.

This kind of fear is not from God but directly from Satan. And since Satan comes at us from many directions, his fear hits us in different ways too.

For a woman, the fear can attack in her family. Suddenly, she may find herself asking questions such as, Is my husband being faithful to me? Are my children involved in something they shouldn't be in? Will they accept Christ as their Savior and live for Him?

Satan-inspired fear can attack both men and women at work. It can come in the form of questions such as, Will I ever be promoted? What does the boss really think of my work? Am I going to be part of the next downsizing?"

Whatever form your particular fear may take, remember that in Jesus Christ there is a solution. I use some very basic biblical principles to overcome my fears when they surface. One of them is the principle that fear is an issue of the will, not just the emotions. Fear arises from a lack of faith in God. We must make a decision of the will to accept God at His Word.—LOIS

THINK ABOUT IT

The Lord has given us the power to overcome fear because we have the Holy Spirit within us (see Romans 8:9). Fear and faith cannot occupy the same ground.

ENTERING INTO GOD'S REST

It is vain for you to rise up early, to retire late, to eat the bread of painful labors; for He gives to His beloved even in his sleep.

—PSALM 127:2

L et me show you something about Sabbath rest and what it means for you and your work. Hebrews 4:3 says, "For we who have believed enter that rest, just as He has said." Verse 10 says, "For the one who has entered His rest has himself also rested from his works, as God did from His." The author of Hebrews was talking about a rest that awaits the people of God.

In the Old Testament, the Israelites entered into God's rest in Canaan, a land flowing with milk and honey, a land that God had already stocked with everything they needed. All they had to do was trust Him and enter into His rest.

Now, this doesn't mean that the people didn't have to work or cultivate the land. Don't mistake this *rest* for the "little folding of the hands to rest" that marks the lazy person (Prov. 6:10).

God didn't tell the Israelites just to sling hammocks and kick back when they entered Canaan. Entering into His rest was an acknowledgment that God was their provider and they could trust Him for their needs.

Today's verse speaks of how endless work and worry are futile because "unless the LORD builds the house, they labor in vain who build it; unless the LORD guards the city, the watchman keeps awake in vain" (Ps. 127:1).

These verses mean that while you're sleeping, God is cutting a deal. He's arranging things. He's fixing the system. In other words, when you place limitations on your work by entering into God's day of rest, you put yourself in line for His supernatural provision.

As you already know, a big part of work is attitude. I like the attitude expressed in Proverbs 30:8–9, where the writer asks God not to give him too much for fear that he will forget God or too little for fear that he will be tempted to steal. He asks that God meet his needs so he can keep his focus where it ought to be.—TONY

PRAY ABOUT IT

The writer of Proverbs is on to something here. Why not ask God for the same thing he asked for?

GOING FOR THE CROWNS

We must all appear before the judgment seat of Christ, that each one may be recompensed for his deeds in the body.

—2 CORINTHIANS 5:10

⁕

The Bible says a day is coming when the children of God will be judged. You may be thinking, *But I thought when we accepted Christ we moved out from under God's judgment.*

Yes, that's true in relation to your eternal status. If your sins have been forgiven and you are under the blood of Christ, your home in heaven is secure. The judgment we are talking about is not to determine whether you will make it to heaven but to evaluate your *service* as a child of God.

The Bible calls this evaluation Christ's "judgment seat," and Paul said we must all appear there to be either rewarded or reprimanded based on the quality of our service to Christ. Talk about motivation! The prospect of Jesus Christ Himself saying to us, "Well done, good and faithful servant," and bestowing honor on us ought to spur us on every day to be our best and do our best for Him.

And the thought of our works not standing up to the fire of Christ's judgment (1 Cor. 3:12–15) should make us determined to serve Him with full sincerity.

Paul was certainly motivated by the thought of Christ's judgment seat. The apostle said he was training like an athlete and disciplining himself so that he might win the prize the way the athletes in his day competed for the winner's wreath in the games (1 Cor. 9:24–27).

This wreath was the prize given at the Isthmian Games, something of a forerunner to the Olympic Games. Athletes in Paul's day competed in these games for an oak wreath placed on their heads at the *bema,* or judge's seat. This is the same word Paul used in 2 Corinthians 5:10 to refer to Christ's judgment seat. That's the imagery we want you to see here.

The New Testament says we are competing for the rewards Christ will give out—not wreaths made of perishable leaves but an "imperishable" reward that will be ours for eternity. It calls these rewards crowns and urges us to seek them.

PRAY ABOUT IT

"O God, purify my heart before You so that my service for You will be acceptable to You."

READ THIS WITH YOUR EYES OPEN

"Vanity of vanities," says the Preacher, "vanity of vanities! All is vanity."
—ECCLESIASTES 1:2

〜❦〜

*I*magine your pastor getting up one Sunday morning and announcing, "The topic of my sermon today is the nothingness of everything." That was the topic of Solomon's great "sermon" we know as the Book of Ecclesiastes.

We say, "Wait a minute, Solomon. You're the guy with all the wealth and power and wisdom. You're the king. What's this vanity stuff?"

Most people think if they had all the stuff Solomon had they wouldn't have his problem. But that simply isn't true.

Solomon's dilemma reminds us of little children at Christmas. Our kids used to wake us up at three or four in the morning, asking if they could start opening their presents. We had to keep shooing them back to bed until finally they could get up and excitedly rip open their gifts.

But a week later, a lot of the toys had been discarded. In the vanity of youth, what had been so exciting had lost its meaning a week or so later.

Some of us adults are like that. We get our new toy—maybe that new car we wanted. We drive it, and we're so excited. We look good, we feel powerful, we have a sense of significance as we drive it. But as the months go by, it becomes just a car. We have to find another toy.

This was Solomon's situation as he wrote the Book of Ecclesiastes. He had started off close to God but had lost his way. He found it again but not until he had taken a long detour.

God wants us to avoid Solomon's detour. That's why He inspired the king to write this book of the Bible. Spend time reading and absorbing the message of Ecclesiastes, and you'll avoid a lot of pitfalls.

PRAY ABOUT IT

Here's a good prayer to pray each time you turn to Ecclesiastes: "Dear God, I pray that You will enlighten the eyes of my heart" (see Eph. 1:18).

A HOLY GHOST THING

Do you not know that your body is a temple of the Holy Spirit who is in you?
—I CORINTHIANS 6:19

❦

Your body is a Holy Ghost thing! This is what the apostle Paul told the believers at Corinth as he instructed them about how to live in moral purity before God.

Paul chose his words carefully under the Holy Spirit's inspiration. The temple, the place of worship and the place where God's presence resided, was the equivalent of church for us today.

In the Old Testament, God's Spirit inhabited the temple. That was what made it a holy place. Today, if you know Jesus Christ as your Savior, your body is the dwelling place of the Holy Spirit.

This means that what you do with your body has holy implications. So, for instance, every time you engage in sex, you go to church. For us as Christians, the act of physical intimacy is a worship service because our bodies are temples of the Holy Spirit. They are God's church houses. And since sex is a holy matter to God, the question I want to ask you and your spouse today is this: Is God being glorified in the worship you are offering Him through your bodies?

In case you haven't realized it by now, God is intensely interested in what goes on in your marriage—even in the bedroom. He wants to be honored and worshiped in every aspect of your marriage. This includes your physical relationship because, as Paul goes on to say, "You are not your own[.] . . . You have been bought with a price; therefore glorify God in your body" (1 Cor. 6:19–20).

Is it possible for a married couple to glorify God in their sexual relationship? Absolutely! "*Whatever* you do," Paul said, "do all to the glory of God" (1 Cor. 10:31).

Therefore, the way you honor your marriage vows and the way you honor your mate by seeking to meet his or her needs instead of just seeking your own satisfaction are acts of worship to God. Marital intimacy is a holy thing because your body is a Holy Ghost thing!

TALK ABOUT IT
Are the two of you treating your sex life as something holy or as just a physical thing?

CHECK YOUR OBEDIENCE LEVEL

He who has My commandments and keeps them, he it is who loves Me; and he who loves
Me shall be loved by My Father, and I will love him, and will disclose Myself to him.

—JOHN 14:21

*P*eople often say, "I want to know God better. How can I draw closer to Him and come to know Him in a deeper way?" The answer is, check your obedience level. Just like you keep your car filled up with gasoline, obedience is the fuel that powers your relationship with God. Jesus said the person who keeps His commandments is the one who truly loves Him and desires fellowship with Him.

There are believers who say, "I love the Lord with all my heart, mind, soul, and strength." But obeying Him is not the passion of their lives. There's something wrong somewhere when Christians profess to know and love God and yet don't seek to obey Him. These Christians have to be jerked and pulled along to get them to obey God while other believers seem to obey Him with joy and eagerness. What's the difference? God has revealed Himself to the obedient Christians at a deeper level. Because they obey His commandments, God is free to disclose Himself to them and to unleash His Word in them.

These are the Christians who are able to experience God at a more intimate level of fellowship and intimacy because they are experiencing the fellowship of obedience. They started with the foundation of obedience, and now they have entered into the intimacy of obedience.

Besides intimacy, obedience also brings the blessing of fruitfulness. When it is God's proper time for blessing, based on your consistent obedience, you will be blessed and the hand of God will be on you. You will see Him at work in your life. You will see Him do a new work of power and blessing in your marriage and in your family. You will see Him answer your prayers, dealing with problems or changing people in your life. You will see the hand of God move in your life when you become a consistently obedient believer.

TALK ABOUT IT
What are some things you can do as a couple to help each other become more obedient to God?

STOP WORRYING!

Do not be anxious for your life, as to what you shall eat, or what you shall drink; nor for your body, as to what you shall put on.

—MATTHEW 6:25

C hristians who make God's kingdom their priority no longer need to be controlled by anxiety. Is either one of you a chronic worrier? Not worrying was so important to Jesus that He repeated His admonition three times in Matthew 6 (see vv. 25, 31, 34).

In the Greek language, there are two kinds of negative commands. One means, "Don't start doing this." The other means, "Stop doing this." The command in Matthew 6:25 is the latter type. Jesus was saying, "Stop worrying!"

You can call it whatever you want: a concern, a burden, a weight on your shoulders. But the fact is that worry is a sin for a child of God. If you are a worrying Christian, you are a sinning Christian.

When Jesus said not to worry, He meant not to worry about *anything*. The Bible makes no allowance for worry at all. It is the absence of a kingdom mentality that produces anxiety or worry.

Jesus' instructions not to worry came right after He had talked about the importance of laying up treasure in heaven and keeping our spiritual focus clear. He told His disciples they could not serve two masters. They had to choose between God and money.

When you serve money you do a lot of worrying. Once you decide to let money be your god, you have to get out there and fight for it harder than everyone else is fighting for it. But when you commit your life to God, He takes the responsibility for your welfare.

A lot of people have the idea that when you give your all to the Lord, you're taking this big risk. After all, everyone knows you have to work hard to get ahead in this dog-eat-dog world. But Jesus turned that kind of confused thinking upside-down.

THINK ABOUT IT
It's the pagans who worry about what they're going to eat and drink and wear (see Matt. 6:31–32). For believers the only issue is, Are we putting God first?

DEALING WITH FEAR

I sought the LORD, and He answered me, and delivered me from all my fears.

—PSALM 34:4

*J*ust like our other human emotions, fear is a gift of God to be used for His purposes. For example, the fear of God is a holy reverence for Him that leads us to obey Him because we realize His power and His love for us. This is a healthy form of fear. The Scripture says, "In the fear of the LORD there is strong confidence" (Prov. 14:26), and, "The fear of the LORD leads to life, so that one may sleep satisfied, untouched by evil" (Prov. 19:23).

The devil knows our weaknesses and fears and preys on us where we are weak. But we have all the power of God available to us.

So what are some practical steps you can take to overcome fear? First, you can begin to overcome fear by yielding yourself to the power of the indwelling Holy Spirit, knowing that He who is in you is greater than he who is in the world (see 1 John 4:4).

Second, believe that Jesus Christ can solve your problem, and live like it! Claim victory every minute of every day. Every time you feel you are about to succumb to your fear, remind God of His promise "I will never desert you, nor will I ever forsake you" (Heb. 13:5).

If we are not careful, we can deny with our lives what we say with our lips. Since I have been seeking the Lord to help me with my fear of flying, I can't tell you how much more relaxed my life has become. In fact, I am writing these lines in an airplane, waiting to take off from New Mexico to Los Angeles!

Fear activates the devil. Faith activates the Lord. Which do you want to be active in your life?—LOIS

PRAY ABOUT IT

Satan wants to keep you in bondage to fear. Read Romans 8:15 together and thank God that as His children, you are free!

AN EVER-PRESENT HELPER

The Spirit also helps our weakness; for we do not know how to pray as we should, but the Spirit Himself intercedes for us with groanings too deep for words.

ren't you thankful the Holy Spirit is always with us to help us when we pray? The Spirit is our *ever-present* Helper. Jesus told His disciples just before His crucifixion that it was better for them if He went away so that the Spirit could come (see John 16:7).

Now, this might not seem better at first glance. After all, the disciples must have wondered what could be better than having Jesus with them. But the truth is that if Jesus Christ were on earth today in His bodily presence, we would be a defeated, decimated people.

Why? Because when Jesus was here on earth, He encased His deity in His humanity. The result was that even though Jesus is God, as a human He was in only one place at a time. But because the Holy Spirit indwells each member of the body of Christ, we can all draw on the power of deity wherever we go.

Here's the illustration I use with our church: After I give the benediction on Sunday morning, the people at Oak Cliff Bible Fellowship get in their cars and go home to North Dallas, South Dallas, Oak Cliff, De Soto, Lancaster, Duncanville, and other surrounding communities.

Now, suppose Jesus came to our church some Sunday morning and announced that He wanted to go home with one of us. Well, since Jesus in His humanity could be in only one place at a time and since I am the pastor, He would be going home with me!

Now, if you're in Duncanville and you need Jesus, you don't want to hear that He is tied up with me in Oak Cliff. When you need Jesus in your home, you want Him accessible to you.

So in order for Jesus to meet the needs of all saints everywhere, He had to leave the earth so the Holy Spirit could come to be present with us everywhere.—TONY

PRAY ABOUT IT
The Holy Spirit is also the ever-present Helper in your marriage and family relationships. What is the greatest need you face at home today? Talk to your Helper about it.

BUILDING ON THE ROCK (DAY 1)

Everyone who hears these words of Mine, and acts upon them, may be compared to a wise man, who built his house upon the rock.

—MATTHEW 7:24

✦

*W*hat is the best possible thing you can do to make this day or this week the best it can possibly be? This is not a great mystery. In fact, I can give you the answer in three simple words: *Obey Jesus Christ.* It's that simple.

In Matthew 7:24–29, Jesus told the familiar story of two men who built houses in the same neighborhood. It is a story that has a lot to say, especially to us husbands and fathers.

I'm sure these two men pulled out all the stops and built their dream houses. There was only one difference between the houses these men built—but it was a very big difference. Jesus said that deep down, under the surface, these two houses were built on dramatically different foundations. One man was wise and built his house "upon the rock" (Matt. 7:24). The other man was foolish and built his house on sand.

The Greek word for *rock* here means a large expanse of bedrock. The wise man dug down deep while the second man built in loose, unstable sand. The difference in these two houses wasn't apparent as long as the weather was nice. It wasn't until the heavy rain and floods came that the problem with the second house was exposed.

So what was the rock that held the first house firm? Jesus said the difference was between those who hear *and act* upon His words and those who hear them but don't do anything about them.

In other words, the difference between your house—your family—standing or collapsing is your obedience to Jesus Christ in the way you build.—TONY

PRAY ABOUT IT

Here's a prayer that's appropriate for any day of the year: "Lord, help me to obey You the first time I hear You."

BUILDING ON THE ROCK (DAY 2)

The rain descended, and the floods came, and the winds blew, and burst against that house; and yet it did not fall, for it had been founded upon the rock.

—MATTHEW 7:25

❧

e learned yesterday that there's more to spiritual obedience than just hearing Christ. The key is what you do with what you hear. The power to live an obedient life is not in the Word of God you *amen* with your lips. It's in the Word you *amen* with your feet. You have to lay a foundation of obedience to Christ if you expect the building you erect to withstand the storms.

Now, obeying Christ does not mean you will not get rained on. In Jesus' story, both houses got hit by the storm. But the one built on the foundation of obedience *withstood* the storm.

In 1 Corinthians 3:10–11 Paul said he was like a wise master builder who laid out the truth for God's people. The foundation Paul laid was Jesus Christ.

So the question for today is, What are you going to do with the Word of Christ? Is there something you need to start doing or something you need to leave alone, in light of what God has revealed to you in His Word?

When you start acting on the Word, you begin to dig a foundation for your life and your family that hits solid rock. And the higher you hope to build your building, the deeper the foundation has to go down. If you want a "skyscraper" kind of family, don't build it on the foundation of a chicken coop.

Let us tell you one other thing about the foundation of obedience: It is hard to lay a foundation when it's raining. Workers have to stop pouring concrete when it rains. So before the next storm hits, get your foundation in. Make sure your life is anchored on the rock of Christ.

The classic example of obedience is Abraham's offering of his son Isaac. The Bible says in Genesis 22 that when God told Abraham to take Isaac to Mount Moriah and sacrifice him, Abraham got up *early the next morning* and did what God told him to do.

THINK ABOUT IT

Nike has nothing on Abraham! When it came to obeying God, He just did it. What about you?

MAKING THE TRANSFER

Who has known the mind of the Lord, that he should instruct Him? But we have the mind of Christ.

—I CORINTHIANS 2:16

Our families, our churches, and our communities are in dire need of Christian men who think "Christianly." I'm talking about thinking with the mind of Christ, as Paul said. Since we have the full revelation of Christ's mind in the Bible, for us this means thinking biblically.

There's a good example of this in Matthew 19 describing Jesus' controversy with the Pharisees over divorce. The Pharisees wanted to trap Jesus in a no-win situation, so they asked Him what they thought was a trick question about divorce. But the first thing Jesus said was, "Have you not read?" (v. 4). And then He quoted the relevant Scripture to them.

Jesus was saying to the Pharisees, "You're not thinking correctly. You, of all people, should know that there is a higher authority here than your sinful desires to get rid of your wives. God has given you His mind on this question."

God has given us His mind too. God wants us to think like He thinks as a way of life so we can transfer biblical values to our wives and children.

That's why Paul said that if a woman has a question in the church, she should ask her husband first (see 1 Cor. 14:34–35). And he should have some answers because he is a man of the Word.

That's the ideal—but I'm afraid it's not often the reality. Look around you. We have a generation of boys who think that being a male makes them a man, boys who don't care about themselves or anyone else. They have no values, mostly because they have no kingdom men around to pass on values to them. Instead the wrong males are doing the job.

The transfer of biblical values from Dad to Junior is missing in much of American culture today. My brother, you and I have to change that if our families are going to survive, much less advance God's kingdom agenda.—TONY

THINK ABOUT IT
If your wife or child had a question about God's Word, could you handle it?

SMILING THROUGH YOUR TEARS

Weeping may last for the night, but a shout of joy comes in the morning.
—PSALM 30:5

My sister in Christ, I want to share a special word of hope and encouragement with you today. God can enable you to smile in spite of your tears. To carry on when you feel like giving up. To pray when you're at a loss for words. To love even though your heart has been broken time and time again.

God can enable you to sit calmly when you feel like throwing up your hands in frustration. To be understanding when nothing seems to make sense. To listen when you'd really rather not hear it again. To share your feelings with others when sharing is necessary to help ease the load. Anything is possible when God is at the center of your life.

God brings trials into our lives as women to show us whether we really believe what we say we believe. It is so important that we learn the lesson of obedience in the trials God sends. We are like students in school; we must pass a test on the information given before going on to the next level.

The Christian life is a growth process. Salvation is free, but sanctification—steady growth in Christ—is expensive. It requires human effort and responsibility.

When a trial comes and you are in your night of weeping, it is natural to ask God *why?* It might be that God wants you to have a share in the "fellowship" of Christ's sufferings (see Phil. 3:10).

While we do not ordinarily think of trials and fellowship in the same breath, for the Christian suffering is linked to the joy awaiting us in Christ's presence. So when we ask God the why of suffering, His answer is that He is testing and perfecting our faith, and through suffering preparing us for indescribable joy.—LOIS

THINK ABOUT IT

There's an old hymn that reminds us of an important truth. Even though we can't see what tomorrow may bring, we have something better. We know the One who holds tomorrow—and He is holding our hand! Jesus is our hope and peace in trials.

TRAITS OF A GODLY MAN (DAY 1)

A good man leaves an inheritance to his children's children.

—PROVERBS 13:22

⁂

When the Bible describes a real man, it doesn't say anything about how big or how tough he is, how much he makes, or what title he carries at his job. Instead, the Bible talks about a man's spiritual qualities. And that makes Job a prime candidate for the Bible's definition of a real man. In Job 29, we find five qualities, or traits, from his life that help us define a real man.

The first trait of a real man is that he has a spiritual legacy to leave behind. That's what Job saw when he looked back to the days before his awful trials, the days when he was in his spiritual "prime" (see Job 29:1–5). Because God had illumined Job's way in days past, he had a history, a legacy, of God's presence to help him when his world collapsed.

Notice also that Job had shared his spiritual pilgrimage with his children when they were still alive (v. 5). Even though they were now dead, Job's children had been given a spiritual legacy.

If you don't have a history with God, if you can't see the footsteps of grace in your life, a slice of your life is missing. If God didn't do anything for you yesterday, you won't have what you need to hang in there today so that you can make it to tomorrow. And you won't have a spiritual legacy to pass on to your children.

What if our sons or daughters said to us, "Dad, has God ever done anything really special in your life?" Would we be able to recount stories of God's grace in our lives? Let's make sure the answer is yes.—TONY

THINK ABOUT IT
The Israelites often built a memorial of stones to mark the place where God had done something great. I hope you can look back and see piles of "memorial stones" you have built for your children.

TRAITS OF A GODLY MAN (DAY 2)

I have been young, and now I am old; yet I have not seen the righteous forsaken or his descendants begging bread.

—PSALM 37:25

❦

*M*any of our grandparents and great-grandparents could give a testimony like the one David gave. Because they were faithful, they have left us with a rich spiritual legacy.

We're talking about the traits of a godly man, looking at the life of Job. We learned yesterday that even in the midst of his suffering, Job could look back on a legacy he had left for his children. To get a sense of that legacy, you need to see Job 1:5, before all the calamities hit. This verse reveals Job acting as the family priest in the days before God's priesthood and sacrificial system was established on earth.

Dad, when was the last time you knelt by your child's bed and said, "I want to talk to God about you"? That kind of statement leaves a lasting impression.

I'll never forget opening my father's bedroom door one night because I heard a noise coming out from the room. It was my father wailing in prayer for his children. Just wailing in utter spiritual anguish.

It wasn't easy for my father to do that. He was a longshoreman on the Baltimore waterfront for thirty-five years. My father would come home dragging, but he was never too tired to pray for his kids. I'll never forget that.

One Sunday I asked the people in our church in Dallas how many were made to go to church as children by their parents. The majority of hands went up. I'm sure if I had asked them how many were glad for that training, the same hands would have gone up.

But that legacy is quickly fading among the generation below us. And it will probably be even more diminished in the following generation. If you aren't building a spiritual legacy, you can fret about it, or you can start building one. Bring God to bear on your circumstances now. Begin the legacy today.—TONY

PRAY ABOUT IT

Mom, you're a vital part of building that legacy too. Pray as a couple that God will establish a strong witness in your home.

TRAITS OF A GODLY MAN (DAY 3)

He who pursues righteousness and loyalty finds life, righteousness and honor.

—PROVERBS 21:21

Today we look at a second trait of a godly man as seen in the life of Job. According to Job 29:7–8, a godly man earns respect or honor. Job said, "When I went out to the gate of the city . . . the young men saw me and hid themselves" (v. 8).

That's respect! When Job showed up, they said, "Job's here, let's go. We can't be doing this out here when he's around."

One of our church members was at a bowling alley when some teenagers started misbehaving and messing up everybody else's game, using all manner of profanity. They didn't seem to care that they were surrounded on all sides by adults.

One person said, "Why don't we go over there and tell them they have to cut this out?"

The answer came back, "You're crazy!" The adults were afraid of what those kids might do.

Someone says, "Well, kids today don't have any respect for anyone." But why not? Could it be that we haven't earned it, haven't insisted on it, so they don't have it? Job said, "When I showed up, the kids scattered because Mr. Job was there."

There also used to be a time when the preacher would get a little respect. You'd show up and the men would say, "Rev's here. We can't cuss anymore."

But what happened? The men saw too many TV preachers get caught with their hands in someone else's pockets or sleeping in someone else's bed. So why should they run and hide when the preacher shows up?

Now don't misunderstand. I'm not talking about a man strutting around acting tough or throwing his influence around, demanding that people bow to him. I'm talking about a man who earns the respect of those around him because of his sterling spiritual character.—TONY

THINK ABOUT IT

You don't have to be wealthy, powerful, or famous to earn this kind of respect. You just have to be a man of real spiritual depth.

TRAITS OF A GODLY MAN (DAY 4)

Those who honor Me I will honor.

—I SAMUEL 2:30

***

A true man of God earns respect. The patriarch Job said that when he went to the city gate and took his place among the leaders, "The old men arose and stood. The princes stopped talking, and put their hands on their mouths" (Job 29:8–9). The "princes" who stopped talking when Job sat down at the city gate were the adolescents budding into manhood.

Now, Job didn't get this kind of respect by chance or by accident. He lived in a pagan world just as we do today, but he lived in an environment that had been influenced by his character.

You can earn respect for yourself by being a real man, and you can also teach others, especially boys, the same kind of respect. My son used to get ticked off at me because we would be ready to go through a door and I would say, "Just a minute. Back up and let your mother and your sisters in first."

He would give me the old line, "But, Dad, they're just my mother and my sisters." But if our boys never see us insisting on these kind of things, then they're not going to do them. Now we often forget to show respect ourselves, and when you don't show respect, you don't earn respect.

In some countries, a budding young man has to earn his manhood status. For example, in some African cultures, an adolescent boy has to go on the hunt and bring back meat to demonstrate that he is now a man.

In other words, he has to prove himself. The same is true for us spiritually. Just as a person can't say that just because of his size, age, and overactive libido he is now a man, neither can a person say that just because he goes to church and carries a Bible he is now a godly man. He has to demonstrate his claim to spiritual manhood. We all do.—TONY

PRAY ABOUT IT

Job earned respect because when he showed up, a higher spiritual standard entered the scene. Do you want to have that kind of impact? Pray that God will make you that kind of man!

TRAITS OF A GODLY MAN (DAY 5)

I delivered the poor who cried for help, and the orphan who had no helper.

—JOB 29:12

Today let's wrap up this study of what it means to be a godly man by noting three more traits from the life of Job. First, a godly man is a person of mercy and justice. Job said in 29:13–14, "The blessing of the one ready to perish came upon me, and I made the widow's heart sing for joy. . . . My justice was like a robe and a turban." A godly man hurts with people who hurt. He helps people who need help. A real man isn't cold, hard, and insensitive. He investigates things (v. 16) to get at the truth and brings justice to bear on a situation.

A godly man is also a man of stability. "I shall die in my nest, and I shall multiply my days as the sand. My root is spread out to the waters, and dew lies all night on my branch" (vv. 18–19). Job was talking about stability. When the world shook around him, he was rock-solid.

My parents live in the heart of the ghetto in Baltimore. It's bad. Recently I said, "Dad, aren't you going to move?"

"No."

"Dad, they're shooting out here in the daytime. Why don't you move?"

He said, "Because God kept me here this long, I believe He can keep me until He's ready to call me home. And whenever you want to come home, as long as I live, I want this to be the home you come back to." That's stability.

Finally, a real man is a man of wisdom. "To me they listened and waited, and kept silent for my counsel. After my words they did not speak again, and my speech dropped on them" (vv. 21–22). A wise man is a man who has been with God and who knows His Word. Wisdom is the ability to apply truth to the issues of practical, day-to-day life.

Are you frustrated because it seems that the world has robbed you of your biblical manhood? Then take your role back, not by acting tough or strutting around talking about, "I'm the man around here" but by displaying a godly life.—TONY

THINK ABOUT IT

Determine to be the man God wants you to be, and your wife and children will follow your leadership gladly.

GET A JOB!

A little sleep, a little slumber, a little folding of the hands to rest—and your poverty will come in like a vagabond, and your need like an armed man.

—PROVERBS 6:10–11

One of the benefits of work is that it teaches responsibility. When a person has a job, he has to get up. But when a guy doesn't have to go to work, he doesn't have to get up—and chances are he won't get up! That's why you have to keep fighting the good fight with your kids to teach them responsibility.

What father hasn't wondered if his teenagers—boys in particular—will ever learn responsibility and the value of work? A couple of years ago, I told my younger son, Jonathan, "It's time for you to go to work at the church. On Saturdays you're going to give the church a few hours of your time."

He said, "You mean like a janitor's job, Dad?"

I said, "Yes, like a janitor's job."

"I don't want to be a janitor."

"Well, you're going to be a janitor. You're going to set up chairs and break down chairs. [This was back when we used to worship in our church gymnasium.] You're going to work."

My point with Jonathan was that if he didn't learn to work while he was young, he might get the idea, "I don't have to work." And when a person gets the idea that he doesn't have to work, he begins to rip off other people. I don't mean necessarily hitting them over the head and taking their wallets, although that's one way to steal.

There are other ways to rip people off, like sitting home collecting a check without working, living off the tax dollars you and I have to pay. Worse yet is a man who lets a woman support him because he doesn't want to work.

These guys think they're something, bragging, "I don't have to do anything. My lady takes care of me." Well, she's a fool to do that, and he's a fool to let her.

A generation of people are growing up irresponsible. It's up to you and me to make sure our children are not among that number.—TONY

TALK ABOUT IT
How are your kids doing when it comes to learning a work ethic?

GOING FOR THE CROWN OF MASTERY

Everyone who competes in the games exercises self-control in all things. They then do it to receive a perishable wreath, but we an imperishable.

—I CORINTHIANS 9:25

The New Testament speaks often about the rewards that believers can expect for their faithful service to Jesus Christ. As a matter of fact, God's Word not only talks freely about our Christian rewards but urges us to seek them.

In 1 Corinthians 9:24–27, Paul made it clear that he was running to win a prize. The wreath he referred to was a halo of leaves given to the winners in the Isthmian games, a popular competition in his day.

Just like the athletes who disciplined themselves for competition, Christians discipline themselves to win God's prize, His reward that I call the crown of mastery. It took months of training for the Isthmian athletes to get ready for the games. If they wanted to win the prize, they had to say yes to the things that made them better athletes and no to the things that hindered their performance.

It's the same with us. The crown of mastery is for those believers who make it a pattern of life to discipline themselves for godliness, as Paul told Timothy (1 Tim. 4:7).

You may think you're too old for this kind of training. But remember: The Christian life is like a basketball game. You may be behind at halftime. The score may not look good, and the game is already half over.

But there's another half to play. And just as in a game you can't declare a winner until the final buzzer sounds, so in life you can't determine faithfulness until it's over.

So no matter where you are in the game, as long as you're still alive it's not too late for a comeback. God can give you the ability to make a comeback with Him and with your family.—TONY

PRAY ABOUT IT
Ask God today to help you get in the game so that at the final buzzer, Jesus Christ will say, "Well done, good and faithful servant. Here are the rewards you have earned."

FAILURE IS NEVER FINAL

Why are you in despair, O my soul? And why have you become disturbed within me?
Hope in God, for I shall yet praise Him.

—PSALM 42:11

Kay James, a wonderful Christian woman who was once a member of President George Bush's administration, said that the only difference between people who succeed and people who fail is that the ones who succeed get up again after they fail.

For most of us, the feeling of failure and discouragement is at its strongest when we are in the middle of a difficult trial. As a mother, my times of trial are often related to the challenges of child-rearing. Surely every mother has experienced those times when the only thing that keeps you going is knowing that you have to keep going. Children can make decisions that are hard to accept, especially after you have invested your all in them.

But whether your area of struggle today is your children, your marriage, your work, or any one of a hundred other things, let the psalmist's question and ringing affirmation remind you that discouragement never has to be final for the Christian. Even when all you can do is cry out to the Lord for the grace to continue in spite of your feelings, He will answer your cry.

And because He who is in us is greater than he who is in the world (see 1 John 4:4), you can get up from any failure or discouragement and live a victorious life—even today!

Let me share with you a passage of Scripture that has kept me strong on many occasions: "I love Thee, O LORD, my strength. The LORD is my rock and my fortress and my deliverer, my God, my strength, in whom I take refuge; my shield and the horn of my salvation, my stronghold. I call upon the LORD, who is worthy to be praised, and I am saved from my enemies" (Psalm 18:1–3).—LOIS

PRAY ABOUT IT

God often has to work in us before He can work through us. Ask Him to help you turn your weaknesses and failures into strength.

DESTINY, DISCIPLINE, DIGNITY, DOMINION

I have chosen him, in order that he may command his children and his household after him to keep the way of the LORD by doing righteousness and justice.

—GENESIS 18:19

T oday's verse, which God spoke concerning the patriarch Abraham, tells us the transfer of godly values from one generation to the next is not automatic. Our children are born in sin. They are not going to raise themselves and pick up the right values on their own. Someone has to pass them on.

That's what God called Abraham to do in his generation. Look how God equipped Abraham for his task.

First, God chose Abraham and gave him a *destiny.* Abraham knew that God's hand was on his life. You need to know that God's hand is on your life too, if you want to be a kingdom husband and father who has something to pass on. That means you need to get close to God and keep that lifeline going.

Abraham also committed himself to *discipline* so that he could "command his children and his household after him to keep the way of the LORD."

My father never asked me, "Son, do you feel like going to church today?" He got me up and took me to church, no matter how dog-tired he was. There was no negotiation. Now we have a generation of kids who tell their parents what *they* are going to do. Abraham was to "command" his children, that is, transmit standards that were nonnegotiable. A kingdom man says to his family, "We do things God's way in our home because this is a kingdom home. The King rules here, and I am the leader under the King."

Besides a destiny and discipline, Abraham also had *dignity*—the result of a life of righteousness and justice.

Finally, God gave Abraham *dominion.* Because Abraham was faithful in his own house, God expanded his sphere of influence.—TONY

TALK ABOUT IT

The last part of Genesis 18:19 says God would fulfill His promises to Abraham because he was faithful. Talk about what the fulfillment of God's promises would mean in your home.

A GODLY WOMAN'S PRIORITY

Women shall be preserved through the bearing of children if they continue in faith and love and sanctity with self-restraint.

—I TIMOTHY 2:15

When Paul said a woman is "preserved through the bearing of children" he was not talking about salvation but about a godly woman's devotion to her primary calling, the guiding and management of her home. The reference is to a believing wife and mother fulfilling her kingdom agenda.

What do children have to do with a woman's kingdom agenda? Everything! God is asking His women to reverse the damage Satan did to them and erase the stigma he laid upon them. Satan induced Eve to act independently of Adam, and as a result the whole world was plunged into sin. Ever since then, woman has borne the stigma of her contribution to the fall of mankind.

But a woman can be preserved or delivered from that stigma by bearing children and raising them in the discipline and instruction of the Lord so that they go out and wreak havoc on Satan's kingdom.

The entrance of sin allowed Satan to corrupt the human race through every child who would ever be born. What God is looking for is a righteous seed that will react differently than the seed of Eve. God wants women to bear children who have His mark on them rather than the mark of Cain. So whenever a kingdom woman produces a righteous child, she is, in a sense, getting back at Satan for what he did in the garden.

By producing godly children, a godly woman serves notice on hell that although Satan may have won the first round with Eve and her kids, he is not going to take this child. A godly seed is a woman's way of saying to Satan, "You may have beaten us the first time, but you are not going to beat us this time."

THINK ABOUT IT

Some people in the world actually believe the state can do a better job of raising children than a family can. However, when it comes to raising your kids, what matters most is what's happening in your house, not what's happening in the White House.

FIGHT FOR YOUR FAMILY

Remember the Lord who is great and awesome, and fight for your brothers, your sons,
your daughters, your wives, and your houses.

—NEHEMIAH 4:14

❧

Nehemiah has a great word of encouragement and challenge for us as Christian parents. When they were threatened by their enemies while rebuilding Jerusalem, Nehemiah called upon his fellow Israelites to remember the Lord and fight for their families.

That's what we have been talking about this week. We're in a spiritual war, although some of us haven't started fighting with God's weapons yet. When you're at war, you can't afford to let the enemy build strongholds right in your backyard.

In the Garden of Eden, Satan won the first round in this warfare. But Genesis 3:15 predicted that Jesus Christ would give Satan a blow to his head, and Satan would never be the same again. That blow was delivered on the cross of Calvary, so keep on fighting for your family. Satan cannot build his strongholds in your family if you are under the blood of Jesus Christ.

God didn't want Adam and Eve to eat of the tree of life and live forever in their sinful state with no hope of redemption. So He evicted them from Eden, but they left with the promise of a coming Redeemer ringing in their ears. That Redeemer came and died on another tree, the cross of Calvary.

That's good news for you and your family. It means that no matter how deeply Satan has infiltrated your family, because of that other tree, the cross, you have hope in God's salvation.

There is another tree. And although Adam and Eve didn't get to taste the fruit of the tree of life because of sin, we who know Jesus Christ have savored the fruit of the tree called the cross.

THINK ABOUT IT

If you will establish this other tree, the cross of Christ, in your home, there will be no room left for Satan's strongholds!

LOOKING AND ACTING LIKE OUR FATHER

Blessed are the peacemakers, for they shall be called sons of God.

—MATTHEW 5:9

⁓⁂⁓

The Bible speaks of several kinds of peace. The first and most important is peace *with* God, the peace that comes when we are forgiven of our sins and reconciled with Him through the Lord Jesus Christ. Only Jesus can provide that kind of peace. But we are called to be His ambassadors and announce that peace to others; this is one way we can become God's peacemakers.

The Bible also says we can have the peace *of* God, which is the internal calm that comes when we are walking in fellowship and obedience with the Lord.

God's Word also tells us to promote peace and unity among our fellow believers. This means we are not on the telephone or in a group stirring up disunity by passing on gossip.

Jesus values biblical peacemaking because the unity of His people is such a high priority with Him. In His last night on earth, Jesus prayed that His disciples might be one, as He and His Father are one (see John 17:21). He then went out from that Upper Room to make peace possible by His death on the cross. So don't get the idea that biblical peacemaking is easy. It's not easy; it's costly.

It's costly because in order to maintain the unity of the Spirit, we have to give something up. It may be something of value to us, like our ideas or our plans. But if we pay the price, we'll reap the reward of peace. And we'll hear people saying, "You act like the Father. You remind me of Jesus."

TALK ABOUT IT

Jesus paid the ultimate price to bring us peace. What price are you willing to pay for peace in your heart, in your marriage, in your family?

DON'T CHOKE

Be anxious for nothing.

—PHILIPPIANS 4:6

───※───

When Paul commanded us not to be "anxious" about anything, he used the same word for *worry* that Jesus used in Matthew 6:25. The word means literally "to strangle or choke." Does that sound like something God wants for His children? Of course not! In fact, worry is a sin to God, for a very good reason. It's an indictment against His character and His ability to care for us.

If my children had worried every day about whether I was going to feed and clothe them, I would have felt pretty bad as a father. They never had that worry, because they knew I would do whatever it took to feed and clothe them.

When you worry, you are really saying, "God, I don't really know about You. I'm not sure You are a caring God, a providing God. And since I'm not sure about You, I'm worried about all this stuff. I've got to take care of this myself."

Jesus asked an important question in Matthew 6:25: "Is not life more than food, and the body more than clothing?" I think Jesus was telling us that if we are going to worry, we should worry about something big, not something small, such as food. We shouldn't worry about whether we are going to have enough food to eat tomorrow when the bigger issue is whether we are going to be alive tomorrow to chew it.

Just as our love for our children motivates us to care for them, so our Father's love for us is our assurance that He will meet our needs. The great thing about God is that our need will never be greater than His ability to supply.—TONY

PRAY ABOUT IT

Have you thanked God for His faithfulness in meeting your needs and for the confidence you have that He will continue doing so?

GIVE HIM SOMETHING TO STUDY

You husbands likewise, live with your wives in an understanding way . . . so that your prayers may not be hindered.

—I PETER 3:7

The apostle Peter gave us a wonderful insight into the process of marital communication. When he said that a husband needs to live with his wife in an "understanding way," he was saying that a man should study his wife and know her well.

Tony often says that every man should study two things: his Bible and his wife. Now, that is a great assignment for our husbands. But what about us as wives? We have a responsibility here too. Anyone who wants to study has to have a body of information to study from. This is where you can help your husband. Feel free to tell him how you are feeling and what your needs are. He needs that information so he can live with you in a knowledgeable way.

In the first two years of our ministry, I struggled with being the pastor's wife, especially since, at the age of fifteen, I had told the Lord I would serve Him in any capacity—except that of a pastor's wife! Our God has a great sense of humor! During those early years, Tony and I spent a lot of time communicating and praying about my insecurities. I could not assume he would automatically know how I felt, so I tried to make my fears and feelings clear so he would understand. Our lives are busier than ever, so Tony and I have to *plan* to communicate. It will not happen by osmosis.

Remember, you are raising your children to leave, but as long as God gives the two of you life, you will be with each other. So plan to communicate. Sure, it is a lot of work. But remember what you promised at your wedding. You said, "I do!" And *do* is a verb, an action word. Good communication demands constant action, but it pays wonderful dividends.—LOIS

TALK ABOUT IT

Are you at a point in your marriage where you can simply look at each other and know what the other person is thinking? If not, that is a great goal to work toward.

THE SOLUTION TO VANITY

Wisdom excels folly as light excels darkness. The wise man's eyes are in his head, but the fool walks in darkness. And yet I know that one fate befalls them both.

—ECCLESIASTES 2:13–14

One day, Solomon, the wisest man of all time, looked out his palace window and saw the local kindergarten dropout. This guy had nothing going for himself, but it dawned on Solomon that one day both he and the dropout were going to die. And at the grave, wisdom and foolishness wouldn't matter. The wise person and the fool would be equally dead. Solomon considered this and said, "There's got to be more to life than this."

Do you ever lie in bed at night, thinking about your life and the prospect of death, and say, "There's got to be more to life than this"? Trying to use human wisdom to come up with a satisfying purpose for life will leave you just where it left Solomon: in vanity.

What's the solution to the seeming vanity of life? Let me try to answer that with an illustration about my favorite board game, Monopoly.

I show no mercy in Monopoly; I play to win. And if I'm fortunate enough to buy Boardwalk and Park Place, the most expensive properties on the board, I really take over. I raise the rent by adding houses and then raise it again by trading them for a luxurious hotel. My philosophy is simple: no loans, no mercy, no prisoners.

But I always feel let down when the game is over, even when I win. Why? Because once I put the lid on the box, I must return to the real world, leaving behind the power, wealth, and real estate of Monopoly.

Well, one day they are going to close the box on us, and you and I will go from time to eternity. That's the *real* world. The question then won't be what we left behind but what we sent on ahead. The solution to vanity is to live in time with the perspective of eternity (see Matt. 6:19–21).—TONY

THINK ABOUT IT
We must not allow the illusion of time to replace the reality of eternity.

THE ULTIMATE IN UNSELFISHNESS

Let the husband fulfill his duty to his wife, and likewise also the wife to her husband.

—I CORINTHIANS 7:3

When it comes to sex the world asks, "What can you do for me? How can you make me feel good?" The Christian marriage partner should ask, "What can I do for you? How can I make you feel good?" True sexual satisfaction in marriage comes when we say to our mates, "I want to fulfill my duty to you."

Sometimes men will say to me, "Tony, I want to fulfill my duty to my wife, but she won't let me." What we often discover is that the reason the wife feels this way is because she knows her husband isn't really interested in meeting her deepest needs. He only wants to fulfill himself.

Fulfilling your duty to your mate means more than sexual performance. Sex is just part of a larger package. For example, one indication that a husband is not fulfilling his duty to his wife is when he stops romancing her and making her feel special.

My brother, when you stop romancing your mate, you can pretty much forget about having a passionate wife. The only reason she got excited about you in the first place was because you romanced her! When was the last time you told her how pretty she was, how her eyes looked in the moonlight, pulled out her chair for her when you went out to dinner, opened the door for her, paid her a compliment, wrote her a love note? If you're not doing those kinds of things, you're not fulfilling your duty. When you romance your wife and make her feel special, she feels the desire to respond.

Christian wives, remember this principle works both ways. If your husband is making a sincere effort to do the right stuff, you need to respond by fulfilling your duty to him.—TONY

PRAY ABOUT IT

Loving, committed sex between a husband and wife is the ultimate act of unselfishness—and the more unselfish you are about it, the bigger the benefit to you!

TOO MANY "FEMINIZED" MALES

The man is the head of a woman.

—I CORINTHIANS 11:3

The statement above, which is just one part of 1 Corinthians 11:3, gives the New Testament equivalent of Genesis 2, where God created the man and then, from the man's side, created the woman. The order of creation established what I call God's covenantal chain of authority. This concept has huge implications for how we do everything, including marriage.

What has happened to God's established chain of authority is the equivalent of the old chain letter deal. Chain letters always carried the threat that if you broke the chain, something bad would happen to you. Well, that's the idea here. When you break God's chain, you lose His blessing.

Many of us have already done that. On the whole, we men have done it passively by becoming "feminized" men, abdicating our role of spiritual and marital leadership. In our place, a whole generation of women has been taught to seize that role aggressively. The result is that today's men know little of biblical leadership. So we are not giving our boys an example to follow. At home, Dad is missing in action. At school, boys are in a system dominated mostly by women. At church, the pulpit may be filled by a man, but the rest of the church programs, especially Sunday school, are largely under female leadership. And now that homosexuals have come out of the closet, boys are getting an even fuzzier picture of what it means to be male.

Now, don't misunderstand. I am grateful for every godly, gifted woman God is using in the home, at church, and at school. But over the last thirty years or so, this role reversal has given rise to a women's liberation movement that preaches a dominant role for women. I believe that if a woman were receiving the right kind of love and leadership, she would not want to be liberated from that.—TONY

TALK ABOUT IT
If Jesus Christ is a man's model for leadership, his wife won't have to worry about having to "knuckle under" to a heavy-handed husband.

IT'S WORTH THE EFFORT!

Like apples of gold in settings of silver is a word spoken in right circumstances.

—PROVERBS 25:11

<hr/>

God's Word is filled with principles to enhance our communication in marriage. One example is the fourth chapter of Ephesians, which teaches us to put away lying because, as believers, "we are members of one another" (v. 25). If this is true for the body of Christ as a whole, think how much more important honesty is in a relationship as intimate as marriage.

Paul went on to say in Ephesians 4:26–27 that we must not let the sun go down on our anger, because when we do, we give the devil an opportunity to wreak havoc in our lives.

And Ephesians 4:29 urges us to replace our unwholesome communication with words that edify or build up others so that our speech might "give grace to those who hear."

We read this verse and see it as being for our fellow believers, but sometimes we fail to remember that our mate is one of our fellow believers to whom this truth applies. In other words, we need to walk in the Spirit at home too. Our mates are a part of the body of Christ whom God calls us to serve by the way we communicate with them.

This great chapter closes with a verse for married couples to apply to each other: "Be kind to one another, tender-hearted, forgiving each other" (Eph. 4:32). Forgiving means that you do not bring up an incident again after it has been resolved.

Developing good marital communication is much like having a baby. There is pain at first, but as time goes on, your focus is more on the new life that has been produced and less on the pain involved in bringing it into the world. Similarly, it's worth all the effort to communicate!—LOIS

TALK ABOUT IT

Evaluate the communication in your marriage, noting its strengths and weaknesses. Choose one thing you can do today to enhance and affirm your partner.

A HELPER OF THE SAME KIND AS JESUS

[The Holy Spirit] shall glorify Me; for He shall take of Mine, and shall disclose it to you.

—JOHN 16:14

O ne reason many Christians don't get the help they need when they are hurting is that they go to the wrong person first. A pastor is not the Holy Spirit; neither is a Christian counselor or therapist. If you are more dependent on these people than you are on the Spirit, you are settling for second-class help.

The first Person we should go to when we are in need is the Holy Spirit, because His job is to take the things of Christ and make them real in our lives. That's what Jesus said in John 16:14.

The Holy Spirit can minister the things of Jesus to you because the Spirit is "another Helper" of the exact same kind as Jesus (see John 14:16). That's the full meaning of the word *another* in this verse. Jesus told the disciples, "The Holy Spirit will be all to you that I was to you. You are not getting any less of Me." To appeal to the indwelling Spirit is to appeal to the same level of help you would get if you were standing before Jesus Christ in the flesh.

Because many of us have not cultivated a relationship with the Holy Spirit, we are not finding the power to do what God has commanded us to do.

Cultivate your relationship with the Spirit, and you will find all the power you need to deal with any problem you or your marriage may face.

TALK ABOUT IT

Without the Holy Spirit, trying to solve problems is like rubbing ointment on a broken leg. Are you struggling with a marital need or with family issues? Make sure you haven't overlooked the one Person who can help you most.

GET IT TOGETHER AT HOME

[An overseer] must be one who manages his own household well, keeping his children under control with all dignity.

—I TIMOTHY 3:4

⌘

The Bible leaves no doubt that men are responsible to take the lead in the management of God's kingdom. His plan is that you and I practice good leadership at home so we can bring it to church. That's the idea in 1 Timothy 3:4–5, where Paul told Timothy that a candidate for church leadership must be a man who has it together at home.

Do you know why God wants a kingdom man to practice good leadership at home? One reason is to raise a godly seed, of course. But another reason is that God is preparing men for a bigger agenda than just their families.

Jesus said there is no marriage in heaven (see Matt. 22:30). The reason is that once the reality has come, we don't need the picture anymore. We are not going to heaven as family units but as individual believers. So a man needs to look at his family as his training ground for kingdom leadership and management.

Take the example of prayer. As a man becomes comfortable and capable in leading his family in prayer, he is better equipped to assume a role of prayer leadership at church. And that is God's express will, because back in 1 Timothy 2:8, Paul wrote concerning men in the church at Ephesus, "I want the men in every place to pray, lifting up holy hands, without wrath and dissension." The word for *men* here was the specific term describing males. God wants men to step forward and set the pace, to take the leadership, both at home and in the church. But it starts at home.

I don't apologize for teaching that men need to be the heads of their homes. I often say to the men at our church in Dallas, "If your wife is the head of your home, you are out of line. Your wife is only taking the leadership you relinquished." A leader leads by calling and conviction, not by permission.—TONY

THINK ABOUT IT
A kingdom man leads by loving and serving. Let's get at it, brother!

A GUIDING PRINCIPLE FOR GODLY WOMEN

Give her the product of her hands, and let her works praise her in the gates.

—PROVERBS 31:31

❦

This closing verse from the description of the "excellent wife" (see Prov. 31:10–31) illustrates a basic principle that should guide the decisions of a Christian wife and mother concerning work outside the home. The principle is this: Whenever a woman's work outside the home compromises her ministry inside the home, she is in the wrong job. It's time for her and her husband to sit down, examine their priorities, and do whatever is necessary.

The woman of Proverbs 31 received the "product," or reward, for her labor. But her "works"—the things she did to care for her family and those in need— brought her praise as well.

This is critical, because there's more at stake here than just our own generation. Of course, there are single parents who have to work and have no family to help them. But even in this case, a single mother can still make her home a priority, knowing that God gives grace to each of us to deal with our daily circumstances.

A person's role and calling in the kingdom of God is a spiritual issue. For a woman, putting her home and family first is not just a matter of economics or scheduling. It's a matter of obeying God and saying no to the devil.

A woman may say, "But we need the money I bring home." Obviously, no one can judge to what extent that statement may be true in every home. There are certainly homes in which the mother has to work to make ends meet. The woman in that situation may be able to find creative ways to produce income from within the home. But either way, she can still order her priorities in a way that God can smile on and bless.—LOIS

TALK ABOUT IT

For a woman who wants to accomplish her God-given kingdom agenda, work outside the home should complement, not compete with, the primacy of the home.

THE THEME OF THE '90S

The rich rules over the poor, and the borrower becomes the lender's slave.

—PROVERBS 22:7

*T*his could be the "theme verse" of the nineties! Biblical financial counselors warn young couples against the trap of developing a lifestyle that demands two paychecks just to make ends meet. When that happens and children come along, Mom is trapped into working just to keep the house and cars.

Too often, the need for a wife's income is the result of the pressure couples put on themselves to acquire stuff. But God did not call Christian husbands and wives to keep up with the Joneses. He called them to save the Joneses.

It's all right to get what money can buy as long as you don't lose what money cannot buy in the process! Nothing can replace the value of a strong Christian heritage.

A woman is given the primary assignment of being the manager of the home. In Proverbs 31:11, the Bible says that the husband of a faithful woman can trust in her. This refers to more than just home management, although that is included.

I don't write the checks in our house. I don't need to, because Lois does a great job of managing our home. That doesn't mean I am oblivious to what happens. I'm still responsible to be the leader at home, but I am blessed with a wife who fulfills her role very capably.

The blessing that a woman creates when she fulfills God's agenda reaches not only into the next generation through the children she bears and raises. When her children are grown and gone, she can share the blessing with still another generation—younger wives and mothers who are coming along behind her (see Titus 2:3–5).

Titus 2:4 says biblical love can be learned because it is a decision of the will and not simply a product of the emotions. We know love can be learned, because, as believers, we are still learning what it means to love God.—TONY

PRAY ABOUT IT
If two incomes are necessary to keep your home running, perhaps you and your mate don't need more money but new priorities. Ask God to guide you in developing financial priorities that are in keeping with His will for your family.

PRAYERS THAT GET DELIVERED

He who searches the hearts knows what the mind of the Spirit is, because He intercedes for the saints according to the will of God.

—ROMANS 8:27

❧

There's something you need to know about prayer that will cancel out many of the prayers you offer to God every day. Many prayers hit the ceiling because they are not from the heart. The only prayers the Holy Spirit delivers to the Father are heart prayers, not just word prayers.

We're not saying our prayers have to be complicated or sophisticated to move the heart of God. But if we are just repeating words we learned or just mouthing words without engaging our spirit, there's no heart in that. And if there is nothing in the heart when we pray, the Holy Spirit has nothing to deliver to the Father, because the Father searches the heart.

Since this is true, it follows that God will respond even to a confused, inarticulate prayer when it comes from the heart. Sometimes we are in such need that all we can do is call out like Peter did when he began to sink in the water, "Save me, Lord!"

That was not much of a prayer, but it definitely came from Peter's heart! And the Lord reached out and rescued Peter.

As is true with so many things in the Christian life, prayer has a direct application to marriage. Most married people can tell when their spouse is merely mouthing words instead of communicating from the heart. So if you want to deepen and enrich your marriage even as you deepen your prayer life, learn to speak from your heart.

You may say, "But that's going to cut way down on my conversation." That's OK—at least at the beginning. Remember, it's the heart that counts, not the word count.

THINK ABOUT IT
Just as God knows whether our words match our hearts, our mates do too.

A "THEOLOGICAL" DRIVE

Look at the birds of the air, that they do not sow, neither do they reap, nor gather into barns, and yet our heavenly Father feeds them. Are you not worth much more than they?

—MATTHEW 6:26

I love to take long drives. I can drive twelve to sixteen hours without stopping because I just love driving. You may not enjoy driving as much as I do, but let me recommend that you take a "theological" drive out into nature someday. What I mean by theological is a drive in which you take Jesus' advice and look at life from God's perspective. Go out and observe nature, and you will gain an important lesson about the futility of worry.

On your theological drive—or walk, if you're into exercise—take a look at the birds. Birds never worry about how or what they are going to eat tomorrow because God has built into their system a simple assumption that when they go out looking for food each day, it will be there. And the food *is* there because *your* heavenly Father cares enough about the birds He made to feed them (notice that Jesus didn't call God the birds' heavenly Father).

Jesus' question drives the point home. If God will stop to put a worm in the ground for a bird, what do you think He will do for you? That's like my children worrying about whether I'm going to feed them while they watch me feed the dog. If I'm feeding the dog, I'm going to at least give them some Cheerios!

Quit worrying! If you want to do something productive, follow Paul's "anti-worry" formula in Philippians 4:6: "Be anxious for nothing, but in everything by prayer and supplication with thanksgiving let your requests be made known to God."

One of the best things you can do for your children is teach them to be "thankers" instead of worriers. In fact, why not take them along on that theological drive!—TONY

TALK ABOUT IT

As a couple, be honest as you ask each other, "How am I doing in the area of worry?"

A WOMAN'S PRIORITIES

You shall love the Lord your God with all your heart, and with all your soul, and with all your mind.

—MATTHEW 22:37

Christian women are being pressed on every side to conform to the standards of this world as new opportunities open doors to career fields that were previously not available to us. While on the one hand Christian women should enjoy the benefits of these opportunities, we must be careful not to let this world system rearrange our biblical priorities.

Our first priority is to maintain a vital personal relationship with God. Proverbs 31:30 reminds us, "Charm is deceitful and beauty is vain, but a women who fears the LORD, she shall be praised." Our degrees and careers must never overrule our daily intimacy and interaction with the Savior. Daily devotions give us stability, confidence, and direction as we pursue various ministries God calls us to do.

A second priority for the Christian woman is her obligation to her family. The Bible clearly states that a woman is to make sure her home is properly taken care of (Titus 2:5). Whether you choose to stay home full time or pursue a career, make sure you are a good manager of your home and family.

Finally, we, as Christian women, should seek to be the best in whatever field of service God calls us to. Then people will "see [our] good works, and glorify [our] Father who is in heaven" (Matt. 5:16). We should also use the privileged positions our changing society has given us as a means of furthering the cause of Christ. Esther was a good example of this. God gave her a position as queen, and she chose to use it to bring deliverance to the Jews.

In this quickly changing world, there is a need for strong, stable Christian women who demonstrate a divine orientation to life.—LOIS

PRAY ABOUT IT
Tell God you want to be this kind of woman, and ask Him to help you make Him the most important Person in your life.

STEWARDSHIP: THE ONLY WAY TO FLY (DAY I)

The earth is the LORD'S, and all it contains, the world, and those who dwell in it.

—PSALM 24:I

❦

The story is told of a dying man who wanted to take his money—thirty thousand dollars—with him when he died. He called his pastor, his doctor, and his lawyer to his deathbed and gave each man an envelope with ten thousand dollars in it, directing them to put the envelope in his coffin at the funeral.

The man died, and each of the three did his job. Later, they met to talk about it. The preacher said, "I'm sure Brother Smith would have wanted to help out with the new church organ, so I took out two thousand and put eight thousand dollars in the coffin."

The doctor said, "Well, he appreciated how well I treated him, and I know he would have wanted to help build my new clinic. So I took out five thousand dollars and put five thousand in the coffin."

The lawyer said, "I did better than both of you. I took out the eight thousand you left, preacher, and I took out the five thousand you left, doctor. I kept my ten thousand and left a check in his coffin for thirty thousand dollars."

That's one way to look at life! Take the cash and leave a check. But God has a better plan for us. It's called stewardship, and it beats ownership every time.

A steward in Bible times was someone who administered or managed another person's property. I contend that an attitude of stewardship is the best way to order your financial life together as a couple.

Stewardship is God's will, His plan for His people. In fact, God set up His creation to operate as a stewardship. So when you and your spouse decide to operate your household as a stewardship under God, you are aligning yourselves with God's will. That's a decision He can bless.—TONY

PRAY ABOUT IT

What is the hardest financial struggle the two of you face? Ask God to intervene and show you the biblical way to address it.

STEWARDSHIP: THE ONLY WAY TO FLY (DAY 2)

The heavens are thine, the earth also is thine.

—PSALM 89:11

I've said that biblical stewardship, in which we function as God's managers, beats ownership every time. To illustrate why this is so, consider what would happen if Congress eliminated the income tax deduction for the taxes and mortgage interest that homeowners pay on their property. It might change your mind about being a homeowner, because one of the big advantages of owning over renting is the big deduction off your income taxes.

If that deduction were gone, you might be better off renting. Why? Because when someone else owns the house, he or she is responsible for it, not you. If the water heater goes out, you just call the owner. If the roof leaks, it's the landlord's job to get it fixed. All you have to do is live there and keep the yard mowed.

In the same way, stewardship has real advantages. It's the way to live in obedience to God while, as the Owner, He takes the responsibility.

During my student days at Dallas Seminary, Lois and I used to do house-sitting for people while they were out of town. It was a great way to make extra money for school. Since a lot of the people lived in the elite areas of Dallas, we sometimes felt like we were king and queen of the castle—at least for the weekend. Now, I'm a casual kind of guy. I make myself at home anywhere. So when I would start acting like it was my home, Lois would have to remind me that we were just visiting. She had the right idea. We were just the stewards of that house, caring for it in the owners' absence.

The nature of Christian stewardship is very easy to grasp. As stewards we own nothing but manage everything under God's ownership.—TONY

THINK ABOUT IT

I don't know about you, but I can't think of anyone I'd rather have as the Owner of my life than Jesus Christ!

DON'T JUST SPRINKLE A LITTLE JESUS ON TOP

Pray without ceasing.

—I THESSALONIANS 5:17

———

*M*any people think praying is like singing the national anthem before a ball game. It gets things started but has nothing to do with the game itself. Most Christians wouldn't start a church service or a meal without prayer. But when the amen is said, the feeling is, "There, that's over. Now let's get on with it."

I get a lot of invitations to pray at this or that function. I turn most of them down, because in most of these situations the people just want a little Jesus sprinkled on top of their secularism. The rest of the program has nothing to do with God. His ideas are the last thing that will be considered at the meeting or event.

Obviously, the Bible takes a radically different view of prayer. In today's verse, Paul was stressing the importance of developing a habit and an attitude of prayer, a state of heart and mind in which we are constantly aware of being in the Father's presence—listening, waiting for direction, seeking His will in everything. The idea is to develop a lifestyle of humility and dependence on God.

A lifestyle of prayer is also crucial because God has decided that there are some things He will not do until we pray. It's like the way the mother of a newborn lies awake in bed at two in the morning. She knows it will soon be time to feed her baby. She is ready, willing, and able, and she fully plans to get up. But she waits to hear the baby's cry to signal the need.

When God hears our cry, the response comes!—TONY

PRAY ABOUT IT

Marriage is a lot like prayer. It's a way of life, a habit of the heart. Pray that God will help you keep your marriage on a high level of spiritual and emotional intimacy.

HELPER OR COMPETITOR?

Her husband is known in the gates, when he sits among the elders of the land.

—PROVERBS 31:23

One reason marriages fail is that the wife is not out to help her husband; she's using the marriage to help herself. Instead of coming alongside her husband to help him, a wife who thinks like this has become his competitor. She is not cooperating with God's kingdom agenda for the family.

Now, if God expects a wife to help her husband, the assumption is that he needs help. I'll be the first to admit it. We men are not complete in and of ourselves. That's the reason God created woman.

So wives, when the faults of your husband show up, they are opportunities for you to fulfill your biblical job description. If you are the complete opposite of your husband, that's wonderful. That means you can fill in all the blank spots where your husband needs help. You can cooperate with God in molding and shaping him into what God wants him to be.

In Proverbs 31:12, this kind of wife is described as someone who "does [her husband] good and not evil all the days of her life." Here is a woman who is perpetually, ferociously, and determinedly looking out for the good of her man.

This idea is fleshed out a little more in today's verse. The reason this husband was able to take his place among the leaders of his city was that he had a wife, friend, businesswoman—a helper—at home.

A Christian wife seeks the good of her husband all the days of his life.

THINK ABOUT IT
Just as a husband needs to wake up and seek how to love, honor, and cherish his wife, she needs to wake up and ask, "How can I do my husband good today?"

WATCH WHERE YOU'RE WALKING

I, therefore . . . entreat you to walk in a manner worthy of the calling with which you have been called.

—EPHESIANS 4:1

*W*alking is one of the Bible's favorite metaphors for the Christian life. In the Bible, to walk means to follow a certain course of life, to conduct yourself in a certain way. Today, let's examine our walk before the Lord together and see whether we are walking in straight paths.

Walk Worthily (Eph. 4:1–2)

These verses from Ephesians tell us to make sure our conduct fits our calling. It's like the story of the queen who saw her daughter sitting sloppily in her chair and said, "Sit up! Don't you know who you are?" As a believer, you too are a child of royalty (see Eph. 2:6). Walk worthy of your call.

Walk Differently (Eph. 4:17–18)

This is another way of saying, "Do not be conformed to this world" (Rom. 12:2). Our thinking should be shaped by spiritual and not by secular values (1 John 2:15–17). By their example, my parents taught their eight children to march to a different drumbeat early in our Christian lives.

Walk Lovingly (Eph. 5:1–2)

Love is truth in action—that is, it's applying God's truth to others in such a way that it builds them up and helps them to experience God's will for their lives. Christ loved us in this sacrificial way, and we are to walk in that love.

Walk Wisely (Eph. 5:15–17)

Wisdom means simply skillful living, which can only be accomplished when we understand God's will for us. We need the daily filling of the Holy Spirit to accomplish this goal (v. 18).

Based on these guidelines, how is your walk today? God has a plan for your life if you'll walk in His footsteps.—LOIS

PRAY ABOUT IT

If necessary, ask God to do some "spiritual orthopedics" today so you can walk in a manner that honors and pleases Him.

GOING FOR THE CROWN OF LIFE

Be faithful until death, and I will give you the crown of life.

—REVELATION 2:10

❧

The New Testament uses the imagery of crowns to describe the rewards Jesus Christ will present someday when He returns and evaluates believers for their service (see 2 Cor. 5:10).

One of the crowns the Bible tells us to strive for was mentioned by the risen Jesus Christ in His message to the church in Smyrna. His message had to do with what this church was about to undergo: "Do not fear what you are about to suffer. Behold, the devil is going to cast some of you into prison, that you may be tested, and you will have tribulation ten days" (Rev. 2:10). Then Jesus stated the promise quoted at the top of this page.

The crown of life has to do with faithfulness in suffering. God always permits suffering for a purpose, and there is a crown waiting for those who hang in there and suffer by faith. It's hard to suffer, especially when you don't know all the reasons for your pain. But the Bible makes it clear that the Christian life involves hardship as well as glory. And if you are faithful in the hard times, at the judgment seat of Christ you will be rewarded with a crown that represents a higher quality of life in His kingdom. The Bible does not specify what the crown of life consists of, but that only makes the anticipation of it more intense.

If you run from trials, this crown is not for you. If you don't seek the wisdom of God to deal with your suffering (see James 1:5), this is not your crown. This reward is for those who suffer abuse for the sake of Christ. It is for the person who stays right there in a tough situation for the sake of his or her testimony for Christ.

God wants to use trials in your marriage and family life to prepare you for greater usefulness for Him.

THINK ABOUT IT

We are never told to seek suffering or persecution—but to expect it and be faithful when it comes, knowing the Lord will use it for our growth.

IRON ON IRON

Iron sharpens iron, so one man sharpens another.

—PROVERBS 27:17

<hr>

$\mathscr{E}$very Christian man who has a godly wife beside him ought to be on his knees every day, thanking God for the gift of a woman who is committed. But, my brother, unless you have some vital connections with a few other men of God, you may wind up putting too much of a load on your wife as your spiritual partner and encourager.

In Exodus 17:8–16, the well-known account of Israel's battle against the Amalekites, Moses sent Joshua out to lead Israel's army into battle while he, Aaron, and Hur went to the top of a nearby hill to oversee the battle. When Moses raised his hands, Israel prevailed. But when Moses tired, his arms drooped, and the Amalekites began winning. So Aaron and Hur held up Moses' hands, and Israel won!

Israel was able to win the fight because even though Moses got tired, he had some brothers around him to hold him up. One problem we men have today is that too many of us are "Lone Ranger" Christians. We're trying to make it all by ourselves. But even the Lone Ranger had a partner.

When you feel like you aren't going to make it as a dad or as a husband, or when the job is dragging you down, you need some friends to come alongside, hold up your hands, and say, "We're going to make it together, brother. We're going to hang in there with you. We're going to prevail for God."

Then, as you grow in the Lord, you will also be able to hold up another man's hands when he is tired. That's the ministry of the body of Christ in action. That's why we need men's ministry in the church that will go beyond playing games and talking about work, the weather, and sports.—TONY

PRAY ABOUT IT

Solomon wrote, "If one can overpower him who is alone, two can resist him. A cord of three strands is not quickly torn apart" (Eccles. 4:12). Ask God for friends who can hold up your hands and whose hands you can hold up.

HOUSEHOLD SALVATION

Believe in the Lord Jesus, and you shall be saved, you and your household.
—ACTS 16:31

When I was ten years old, my father, Arthur Evans, came to Jesus Christ. Dad was gloriously saved when he was thirty years old, and he said, "By God's grace, I am going to win my family to Christ." However, Mom didn't want his religion, and she made life very hard for him. My father, a longshoreman, would get up at 3 A.M., when the house was quiet, and pray for God to save his family. A year after Dad was saved, he was up at 3 A.M. praying and reading his Bible as usual when he heard the steps creak and knew my mother was coming downstairs. He bowed his head and thought, *Oh no, here we go again.*

But this morning was different. My mother said, "I have been doing everything I know how to discourage you. I have tried to make your life as miserable as I could. Yet you haven't budged, so whatever this thing is in your life must be real, and I want it right now."

My father got on his knees with my mother and led her to Jesus Christ right there. Then they called us kids around the table and told us that salvation had entered our home. My father led me to Christ and took the family to a church where I grew up in the Word.

My father was a high school dropout, but under his influence, I went to college. There I developed a passion for God and for ministry, and I wound up at Dallas Theological Seminary. Then we began a church with ten people in a living room, and the Oak Cliff Bible Fellowship was born. Humanly speaking, I'm where I am because one man became a faithful man of the kingdom and wouldn't give up on his family. I pray you will leave your family that kind of heritage.—TONY

THINK ABOUT IT

Because my father wouldn't quit, I am resolved not to quit either. That's what it takes to be a man of the kingdom.

A WIFE'S KINGDOM AGENDA

An excellent wife, who can find? For her worth is far above jewels.

—PROVERBS 31:10

❧

O ne of the worst statements a wife can make is, "My mama told me." Now, I don't have anything against your mama, but you need to know that her opinion is no longer the reigning voice in your life. When you got married, you broke ranks with your mama.

Other women may have taken their definition of a wife's role not from Mama but from the soap operas or from the feminist movement rather than from God's Word. They got their information from the wrong source.

Some women grew up in homes where the mother ran the show. Perhaps she had to, given the nature of the father. But still, that dominant attitude may have gotten transferred to her daughter, who then brings that domineering spirit into her own marriage.

A wife may say, "Yes, but you don't know my husband." Well, your husband can't be that bad. He chose you. He had enough sense to know whom to marry. He was smart enough to see that you would be the woman for him. He was sharp enough to woo you and win you.

If something has gone wrong, a lot of the problem could be on his side. But in these devotions, my burden, and Lois's too, is to help you be the wife God wants you to be.

There are plenty of things a husband needs to do to accomplish a kingdom agenda in his marriage. But as I examine the biblical data, I think we can narrow the wife's primary tasks down to two areas. She needs to *help* her husband (see Gen. 2:18) and *reverence,* or respect, her husband (see Eph. 5:33 and 1 Pet. 3:2).

Wife, if these two qualities mark your life, you are in line for blessing from God.—TONY

PRAY ABOUT IT
A lot of men have difficulty fulfilling God's kingdom calling in their marriages because their wives aren't fulfilling the other half of the agenda. Pray that this not be the case with you two.

IT GOES WITHOUT SAYING—OR DOES IT?

[Love] does not act unbecomingly; it does not seek its own.

—I CORINTHIANS 13:5

❧

A preacher in the middle of the wedding ceremony asked, "Is there anyone here who knows any reason these two should not be joined in holy matrimony?"

A voice rang out, "I do!"

The preacher said, "Hush, son, you're the groom."

That's the way some guys feel about marriage. But there's another way. The Bible has some powerful and beneficial things to say to Christian husbands.

People used to say a man's home was his castle. That meant he was king of his domain. By living for your heavenly King as a husband, you can bring a royal presence to your home—not because you sit on your throne and bark out orders to the wife and kids but because you reflect King Jesus.

While I don't want to dump a load of criticism on anyone, it is true that some of the things Christian husbands need to hear may seem hard. But husbands need to hear them because most husbands aren't going to get this stuff at work or on television or with their friends. So let's get it from the Word of God.

One way a husband can reflect a kingdom agenda in his marriage is to love his wife.

I can hear some husband saying, "Come on, Tony, that goes without saying. Give me something else." Sorry, but we need to spend some time on this because a lot of what goes on today under the name of love has little to do with true, biblical love.

The word *love* has become devalued today. People say, "I love my job. I love my home. I love chocolate cake." What they are saying is that these things make them feel good.

That's fine, but that's not love. Biblical love, God's *agape* love, involves sacrifice you make for the one loved. You can measure your love for your wife by the degree of your sacrifice for her.—TONY

THINK ABOUT IT

Human love is usually conditional on that love being returned. But biblical love expresses itself even when it is not being reciprocated.

WHAT'S MY PART?

Honor the LORD from your wealth, and from the first of all your produce.
—PROVERBS 3:9

❦

*D*o you like everything your boss tells you to do? Probably not. So why do you do things at work you don't like? One reason is that the boss controls your paycheck. When you can start your own business, then you get to call your own shots.

The same is true with God. When we can create our own world, then we can call the shots. But as long as we live in God's world, we need to recognize that He owns it. If God owns it all, how does that relate to the concept of tithing, giving God 10 percent of what we make? God established the tithe with Israel in the Old Testament. And the tithe was not established so that the Israelite could say, "OK, God, here's Your 10 percent. The other 90 percent is mine." No, the tithe was a way of saying, "God, this tithe is my way of acknowledging that You own it all and gave it all to me. I realize the 90 percent is Yours too."

See, we get it all mixed up. We figure if we give God ten dollars out of our one hundred dollars, the other ninety belongs to us. But giving is designed to remind us that the whole hundred bucks belongs to God. He graciously allows us to keep ninety dollars for our needs, but it's *all* His. The tithe was also to be given *first* to remind the Israelites that God would meet their needs if they honored Him.

This is a view of stewardship a lot of Christians aren't used to. They're used to digging around in their pockets when the collection plate comes around, finding something that jingles, and dropping it in. But God says, "I want you to let Me know that *you* know that I own all of it."—LOIS

THINK ABOUT IT
Giving God's portion back to Him before you pay any bills is a way of saying you know who the real Owner is!

THE PERSISTENCE OF PRAYER

[Jesus] was telling them a parable to show that at all times they ought to pray and not to lose heart.

—LUKE 18:1

⁂

One of the lessons Jesus taught repeatedly about prayer is that we need to stay at it, to hang in there when we pray. In Luke 18:1–8, Jesus taught this truth through the parable of an uncaring, unfeeling judge and a widow who was being harassed by someone. Now, even though widows were the most powerless people in Jesus' day, this widow was so persistent in appealing to the judge that she finally wore him down, and he granted her request.

Jesus was saying that if persistent asking can wear down an uncaring judge and make him act on a person's behalf, how much more quickly will our loving, caring God respond to the heartfelt cries of His people?

The original language here helps explain why God is so ready to respond to persistent prayer. The judge in Jesus' story was not worried that this widow was going to punch him in the eye but that his reputation would be harmed if he didn't help her. We use the same term today when we talk about someone giving us a black eye. We mean that the person has harmed our reputation.

Now, if an unrighteous judge is careful about his reputation, which can't be that good, how much more is the righteous Judge of all the earth concerned for His reputation and His glory? So, Jesus says, be persistent in prayer because God will act out of regard for His own glory as well as His concern for His elect.

The point of the parable, then, is persistence. Notice that Jesus only gave us two options in prayer: praying faithfully or losing heart. When you are tempted to lose heart or become discouraged in prayer, that's your signal that it's time to pray all the harder!

TALK ABOUT IT

Is there a tough circumstance you are praying for as a couple—maybe a wayward child, a family illness, or financial setbacks? Jesus' word to you today is, Don't lose heart. Keep praying. Encourage each other to stay the course in prayer.

ENJOYING THE FRUIT OF PARENTHOOD

Let us not lose heart in doing good, for in due time we shall reap if we do not grow weary.

—GALATIANS 6:9

*T*ony and I have been parents long enough to enjoy some of the harvest Paul was talking about in today's verse. Allow me to share two special "slices" from the fruit of parenthood that we have been privileged to enjoy. The first is a note Tony received from our oldest son, Anthony Tyrone Jr. He wrote:

"Dear Dad, I am writing this letter to say thank you even though sometimes I don't show it or act like it. I can't wait to come home and spend the week of my birthday with you and the rest of the family.

"Oh, and by the way, Happy Father's Day. I love you and I always will, even though I don't show it sometimes. I have always been proud when people say, 'You are Tony Evans's son.' I sometimes don't act like it, but I really feel good inside. I am so excited and proud to have your last and first name."

The second piece of parenting "fruit" I want to share with you today came in a card our oldest daughter, Chrystal, sent to me. After the card's beautiful poem about the extent of a mother's love, Chrystal added this postscript: "Know that I truly appreciate you being my mother, and believe that I think you have done an excellent job in raising all of us. As I realize how deeply and how much you love your children through my own maturing experiences, I love you more. Much love, Chrystal."

Needless to say, receiving notes and cards like these from your children do make all the times of weariness, sacrifice, and pain that parents endure for their children more than worthwhile.

Are you growing weary in the parenting struggle today? Try stepping back from the intensity of the moment and looking ahead to the harvest you will enjoy!—LOIS

PRAY ABOUT IT

Isaiah 40:30–31 is a great encouragement for those who are losing heart. Make these wonderful verses your prayer today.

BEING A SAVIOR TO YOUR WIFE

Walk in love, just as Christ also loved you, and gave Himself up for us.
—EPHESIANS 5:2

What does it mean for a husband to love his wife the way Christ loved the church? One thing it means is for the husband to be a savior for his wife. Let me show you what I mean. In Ephesians 5:25, the apostle Paul said, "Husbands, love your wives, just as Christ also loved the church and gave Himself for her."

As far as God is concerned, to talk about marital love is to talk about a cross, about Calvary, about a Savior. We have a Savior in Christ. And our wives ought to have a savior in us. Loving your wife means carrying a cross. So if you feel like your wife is crucifying you, you have the perfect opportunity to look like Jesus.

You may know that nowhere in Scripture is a wife commanded to love her husband. She is commanded to respect him (see Eph. 5:33). It's not that a woman shouldn't love her husband. But her love is a response to his salvation. Being a savior means loving as Christ loves. So a husband is called to love his wife no matter what.

This gets very practical. A husband's love cannot say, "She's meeting my needs. Therefore, I will love her." No, you love her even when she's not meeting your needs. You love her until she learns how to meet your needs.

Most men date in order to marry, but the biblical principle is marry in order to date. Most men shower a woman with love to get her to say, "I do." But the biblical ideal is have her say, "I do," so we can spend the rest of our lives showering her with love.—TONY

THINK ABOUT IT
Every man likes to think of himself as a lover. But the measuring rod for a biblical lover is the size of the cross he is carrying. Christ loved the church to death.

GOT TO HAVE THE LINES

Let your fountain be blessed, and rejoice in the wife of your youth.
—PROVERBS 5:18

⟡

S ome years ago I took Lois to play tennis. I will never do that again! I explained the game to her. I said, "Get over there, and I will hit the ball to you." I threw the ball up and hit it. Lois just stood there with one hand on her hip as if to say, "You don't expect me to hit *that* ball, do you?"

I hit the ball over the net again, and she just watched it. I told her she had to run to the ball and hit it. She said, "I am not going to get all sweaty out here running after a little ball. If you want me to hit the ball back, you hit the ball *to* me." I was getting a little evangelically ticked off at this point.

So I hit the ball right to her, and she took a Hank Aaron swing at it. *Bam!* She hit the ball way over the fence then looked at me and told me to go get it. I said, "Let's go home, because you can't play tennis outside the lines."

That little episode was a humorous illustration of a very serious truth far from the tennis court: People can't enjoy sex the way God intended them to enjoy it if they insist on playing by their rules, not God's, and if they refuse to stay within the lines He has drawn.

Today unrestricted sex is being touted as a shortcut to personal fulfillment and satisfaction. People have given up their virtue for sex, traded their families for it— and now they're getting sick and dying because of it. A lot of people are trying to make sex outside of marriage seem normal and right. But the best counter-argument to that is couples like you—married men and woman committed to a lifelong love relationship. Is your marriage a clear witness to the joy and fulfillment God intended for marriage?—TONY

PRAY ABOUT IT
Sex is a beautiful gift from God. Are you still treating it as a gift in your relationship—or as a right or obligation?

A SOLID STRATEGY AGAINST TEMPTATION

I have made a covenant with my eyes; how then could I gaze at a virgin?

—JOB 31:1

⸙

*D*on't you sometimes wish you could just shut down all temptation for a few days or so? I do. Any believer, man or woman, who is committed to please the Lord knows the reality of temptation. It's all around us, because this world temporarily belongs to Satan.

But here's a simple, biblically solid plan of attack you can use today to deal with temptation:

1. Make the same decision Job made. He said he would not allow himself to give in to the lust of his eyes. That's a great place to start. Watch what you watch, so that what you watch does not start watching you back!
2. We learn a very practical truth concerning sexual temptation in 1 Corinthians 6:18. Run! Get out of there! If you have to, start running now.
3. Proverbs 5:15–19 urges married people to look for and find their sexual fulfillment at home. Put forth the effort to build intimacy with your mate, and the result will be more than satisfying. God will reward your commitment with satisfaction you never imagined possible.
4. Colossians 3:5 says to resist the flesh because your flesh is pulling at you all day long. You need to watch the environments you place yourself in. You need to examine your spirit to make sure that you are not putting yourself in compromising situations and settings, whether knowingly or unknowingly.
5. Romans 12:1 says to present your body as a living sacrifice to God. Present yourself fully to God. Get busy for the kingdom, and you'll help to squeeze Satan out of your life.—TONY

PRAY ABOUT IT
Temptation is sort of like a plant. Deprive it of the stuff it needs to grow, and it will begin to wither and waste away.

THE GIFTS OF A LIFETIME

Children are a gift of the LORD; the fruit of the womb is a reward.

—PSALM 127:3

❧

Truly, there is no challenge quite like parenting. But it is equally true that our children are special gifts to be valued and treasured. During the early years of a child's life, parenting, particularly for a mother, requires a lot of physical energy. During a child's teenage years, parenting requires huge amounts of physical *and* emotional energy. You need kneepads during those teenage years!

Children are a gift of the Lord, loaned to us for a short time. But they belong to Him, just as we do. That's why it is important for us to give our children back to the Lord before they are ever born.

Recognizing that our children are "on loan" to us from the Lord helps us as we do the best we can and leave the rest to Him. This is not a cop-out or a lack of responsibility but a matter of relying on His all-sufficiency.

It is also wonderful to know that we are not alone in this process. Our extended families can be a big help in raising our children to know and love the Lord. Relish the help and counsel of family and close friends. What you may spend years trying to instill into your children another person may be able to accomplish in much less time because that person holds a unique place of authority or respect in your child's life.

I remember how Tony's father shared with our kids where God had brought the family from and what God had done along the way after Grandfather Evans accepted Christ. That has had a lasting impact. My sister also pours her life into the lives of my children and has helped us build a foundation that we trust will stand the test of time.—LOIS

PRAY ABOUT IT

We teach our children to say thank you for a gift. Why not thank God together today for the gift of your children?

THE DIGNITY OF WORK

I glorified Thee on the earth, having accomplished the work which Thou hast given me to do.

—JOHN 17:4

⬥

*O*ne of the rewards that honest, productive work brings us is the reward of dignity. The person who works gains a sense of dignity that nothing else can bring.

We know there is inherent dignity to work because God Himself worked at creation, and He continues to work. Jesus had important work to do also. On the cross He said, "It is finished" (John 19:30). In other words, "I have accomplished what I came to accomplish."

The word Jesus used means "paid in full." His work of redemption paid off the sin debt that hung over all of us. There's nothing like the feeling of being able to make the last payment on a bill because you worked hard and earned the money to make it. In a much greater sense, Jesus had that feeling of accomplishment. In fact, Jesus spent His whole earthly life working. We can assume He worked hard in Joseph's carpenter shop. And He spent His entire ministry working out the will of His Father. He said on one occasion, "My Father is working until now, and I Myself am working" (John 5:17).

If you take away a man's ability to work, you damage his sense of dignity and worth. Work gives a sense of worth. Obviously it doesn't determine our ultimate worth in God's sight, but it fulfills our built-in need for a sense of dignity.

Sometimes my father would take me out to the Baltimore waterfront when he picked up his paycheck on his day off, and he'd show me the other longshoremen at work. They didn't have all the fancy equipment they have today for loading and unloading ships. I remember watching them and thinking of my father, *This man really works.*

That did something for me. I saw my father work, as you probably saw your father work, and it helped to teach me the dignity of honest, hard work.—TONY

PRAY ABOUT IT

If your work entails more drudgery than dignity, ask God to give you a new sense of the dignity of work.

THE REVEALER

Things which eye has not seen and ear has not heard, and which have not entered the heart of man . . . to us God revealed them through the Spirit.

—1 CORINTHIANS 2:9–10

*O*ne thing I've always been able to do is talk. There've been a lot of things I've said that I could not back up, but the person I was talking to never knew it because I camouflaged it with so much rap. One of the things I said to Lois when I was younger, when I was trying to win her heart, was that if she had me she did not need her father anymore. Basically, I told Lois that everything provided to her by her father would be obsolete when she came to me. The best he could provide for her belonged to the Ice Age compared to what I would provide for her.

Lois came over to me, so to some degree my rap worked. Now, after more than twenty-eight years of marriage, I have fallen short of my guarantees from time to time, but that's not part of this discussion!

God has made a lot of promises and guarantees, too, and He will *never* fail to deliver on even one of them. In fact, the apostle Paul wrote that the good things God has prepared "for those who love Him" (1 Cor. 2:9) are so awesome that, left to ourselves, we could not even begin to imagine what they are.

But if the things of God are so wonderful that we can't even start to grasp them, how do we even know anything about them? Enter the Holy Spirit. One of the Spirit's ministries is as the Revealer of the things of God.

Have you ever had the experience of learning something new about the Lord and then just basking in your new understanding of His grace or wisdom or goodness? That's the Holy Spirit doing His job as the Revealer. Without the Spirit, we would be like blind people in a dark room.—TONY

PRAY ABOUT IT

Do you ever wonder if God has something more for your marriage than you are experiencing—something greater than you could imagine? Then why not get on your knees together and ask the Spirit to reveal it to you?

ROLL OUT THE RED CARPET

A gracious woman attains honor.

—PROVERBS 11:16

*f you want to be a true "kingdom" king, treat your wife like your queen, not like just another woman. Husband, does your wife feel special? Do you do things for her that let her know she is different from every other woman? Many men do little courtesies for other women they don't do anymore for their wives. But when chivalry dies, a marriage starts to die. Husband, you need to make a commitment that other women may have to get in the car by themselves, but not your wife. Other women may have to open the door for themselves, but not your wife. She is your queen, so roll out the red carpet and pull out the chair and open the door and escort her.

There are so many other ways we can make our wives feel special. A gift for no particular reason is a great way to tell your wife she's special to you. Your time is also a gift to your wife. You don't have to give her a new car. Just the fact that you want to take her somewhere in the old car will do.

Have you ever written your wife a note and put it under her pillow? Talk about how great it is to sleep next to her and wake up to sunshine even when the drapes are closed. Let her know you wouldn't have it any other way.

A lot of husbands do something special for their wives on her birthday or their anniversary. But if that's the only time we do something, we become too predictable. The key is to be consistent and creative in communicating to your wife how much you love her.

THINK ABOUT IT

It takes very little time and effort to pick up the phone, call your wife in the middle of the day, and tell her she's on your mind and you can't wait to see her when you get home.

A SACRED COVENANT

*God created man in His own image, in the image of God He created him; male and
female He created them.*

—GENESIS 1:27

❦

hy did God create sex? Well, the most obvious reason is for procreation. And another reason, a deeper purpose for sex, is to inaugurate or initiate the covenant of marriage. Whenever God made a covenant, He inaugurated it in blood. The sign of the covenant God made with Abraham was circumcision. All of the males born in Israel were to have the foreskin of their sexual organs removed to signify that they were part of God's covenant people.

Why was circumcision chosen as the sign of the Abrahamic covenant, which established Israel as God's special people and through which Abraham would become the father of many nations? Because this covenant was fulfilled and expanded as Abraham and his male descendants produced children. Therefore, their sexual organs would bear the mark of the covenant as a special sign that they and the children they fathered were set apart to the Lord. The rite of circumcision involved blood, which was part of the covenant.

So it is in marriage. According to Deuteronomy 22:13–15, if a new husband in Israel felt he had reason to suspect his wife was not a virgin when he married her, the woman's parents were to produce the evidence of their daughter's virginity and show it to the elders of the city at the city gate. The evidence was the blood-stained sheet from the bed on which the couple consummated their marriage on the wedding night. If the parents could thus prove their daughter's virginity, she was acquitted, and the husband was fined.

But if there was no blood, meaning the woman was not a virgin before marriage, she could be put to death (see v. 21). Why? Because the marriage covenant was to be inaugurated by blood—and God takes His covenants very seriously.

Isn't it great to know that marriage was not some afterthought on God's part, but an integral part of His plan for the human race?

THINK ABOUT IT

God considers marriage—your marriage—to be a sacred covenant worth cherishing and protecting.

THE VALUE OF A WOMAN

Older women likewise are to be reverent in their behavior . . . that they may encourage the young women to love their husbands, to love their children, to be sensible, pure, workers at home.

—TITUS 2:3–5

⁂

The Bible makes a woman's role clear. She is to be a worker or a "keeper" at home. This does not mean a woman has to be a "stayer" at home only. The idea is that she is to be a good manager of her domain.

A woman who understands her value in God's eyes can fulfill her role by looking at herself through the lens of Scripture. For example, Genesis 1:26–28 tells us that the woman bears equality of essence with the man as a co-recipient of God's image. Then the Gospels reveal the great value our Lord gave to women during His earthly ministry. And as Paul traveled throughout the Mediterranean, many of the believers who labored with him to spread the message of Christ were women. In fact, Paul literally owed his life to some of these female coworkers. In several of his letters, he named them and expressed his gratitude to them.

Here are some of the women the New Testament mentions: Apphia (Philem. 2), Euodia (Phil. 4:2–3), Mary of Rome (Rom. 16:6), Phoebe (Rom. 16:1–2), Priscilla (Acts 18:1–3, Rom. 16:3, and 1 Cor. 16:19), Syntyche (Phil. 4:2–3), Tryphena (Rom. 16:12), and Tryphosa (Rom. 16:12).

God's Word leaves no doubt that there is positional equality between men and women in terms of their creation and value to God. But the Bible is also clear that there is a differentiation of roles between the sexes (see Eph. 5:22–23).

Many women don't care for the command "Be subject to your own husbands." However, that is what God requires of us. It is the responsibility of women to place themselves under the biblical leadership of their husbands, using all of their gifts and abilities to further the family and the testimony of Christ.

You might not agree with everything your husband does and asks you to do, but you must respect his position. When you do that, God will honor you.—LOIS

PRAY ABOUT IT

"Dear God, help me to submit to my husband's authority the same way I submit to Your authority."

A PROMISE FOR A LIFETIME

Love never fails.

—I CORINTHIANS 13:8

※※※

I can remember my son's question as if it were yesterday. It happened many years ago, during one of our trips back home to Dallas after picking up our children from summer camp. Anthony Jr., who was quite young at the time, looked up at me and asked, "Mom, are you going to stay married to Dad?"

When I asked him why he was asking me that question, he replied that most of the kids in his cabin had parents who were either separated or divorced. I told Anthony to look me in the eyes, and right then and there I promised my son that I was never going to leave his father.

If your neighborhood and your children's school are normal, a majority of the children on any given street or in any classroom live in families that have been broken either by divorce or by the desertion of one marriage partner. In the black community, it is estimated that 70 percent of all children will be living in single-parent homes by the year 2000.

Where do we break this destructive cycle of broken homes and failed marriages?

A great place to begin is within our own marriages. I was able to promise Anthony Jr. that his mother would never leave his father because of a commitment I made to God and to Tony on June 27, 1970, and also because I loved Tony. Today, I would gladly repeat that promise to any of my four children who might ask me.

Your children need the security that comes from knowing their parents are in love with each other and are committed to each other for life.—LOIS

TALK ABOUT IT

Reaffirm your love for each other today—and if you can do so, remind your children that you are committed to one another for life.

SUFFERING FOR THE RIGHT REASONS

Blessed are those who have been persecuted for the sake of righteousness, for theirs is the kingdom of heaven.

—MATTHEW 5:10

I don't know any well-balanced Christians who go looking for persecution. Jesus didn't say we had to sport a bumper sticker that says, "I'm a Christian; thank you for persecuting me." But He knows that when we are serious about our commitment to Him, someone isn't going to like it.

This is the longest of the beatitudes, because Jesus went on to explain what it means to be persecuted for the sake of righteousness and why the person who endures persecution is blessed. First, He said, the persecution and insults must be "on account of Me" (see Matt. 5:11), that is, as a result of our ministry and witness for Christ, not because we are hard to get along with. He also said the believer who suffers in this way can be considered blessed or happy because suffering for Christ brings a great reward in heaven.

Do you want to lay up some treasure in heaven, where nothing can touch your investment? Jesus said if you encounter persecution just because you remind people of Him, He will credit that to your heavenly account. So whenever someone puts you down for your faith, the heavenly bank logs another reward in your account.

A third reason to count yourself blessed in persecution is that it puts you in great company. The prophets—and we can add the apostles—who went before us were treated this way. The apostles of Christ had it right. After being flogged for preaching Jesus, Peter and his pals went on their way, "rejoicing that they had been considered worthy to suffer shame for His name" (Acts 5:41). That's counting yourself blessed in persecution!—TONY

PRAY ABOUT IT

Where are you most likely to encounter opposition for your faith? Pray that God will prepare you to stand for Him in that place.

GOING FOR THE CROWN OF RIGHTEOUSNESS

I have fought the good fight, I have finished the course, I have kept the faith; in the future there is laid up for me the crown of righteousness.

—2 TIMOTHY 4:7–8

*T*he crown of righteousness is one of the rewards the New Testament urges us to seek through faithful service to Christ. The rest of this very familiar passage, written by the apostle Paul near the end of his life, tells us that Paul expected to be given this reward by Jesus Christ Himself, the "righteous Judge."

And the prize wasn't just for Paul. Jesus will award it "to all who have loved His appearing." That includes the two of you and your kids, we pray.

Besides the awarding of crowns, something else is going to happen when Jesus sits as the righteous Judge. In 1 Corinthians 3:10–15, Paul said that if anyone builds on the foundation of Jesus Christ, that person's work will be tested by fire someday. That day is the judgment seat of Christ (see 2 Cor. 5:10). So what you and I are going to do is present to Christ everything we have done since we became Christians.

Then He will put the fire of His judgment to our works, and at that point all the stuff we did for our own glory or simply because we felt like we had to or for any reason other than to bring glory to God will go up in smoke. When that happens, there will be a loss of rewards for those lost works.

But when we are faithful in our service for Christ, when our works consist of "gold, silver, [and] precious stones" (see 1 Cor. 3:12), those works will stand the test of fire, and we will receive a reward, the crown of righteousness. Those good works include a faithful, committed marriage and a family raised for God's glory.

I don't know about you, but I'm going for the crown of righteousness! I want to hear Jesus say, "Well done, good and faithful servant. Enter into the joy of your Lord."—TONY

THINK ABOUT IT

How do you live in such a way that you gain the crowns Jesus wants to give you? By living each day on earth in the light of eternity.

PADLOCK THE CHURCH

If I am a father, where is My honor? And if I am a master, where is My respect?

—MALACHI 1:6

❦

The proof of our stewardship is whether God winds up with our leftover time, energy, and resources, or whether we give Him our first and best. To put it another way, Jesus is either Lord of all, or He is not Lord at all.

God asked the people of Israel the pointed questions above when they were dishonoring Him by giving Him the worst of their flock for sacrifice rather than the best, as the Mosaic Law prescribed (see Mal. 1:7–8). The people would look among their sheep, see a nice fat one, and say, "We can't give *that* one to the Lord. It's worth too much." Then they would find a sheep that was born with defects or was lame or diseased and offer it to the Lord, hoping He would accept their sacrifice.

They were giving God their leftovers, the junk they didn't want, and saying, "Lord, You ought to be happy we're giving You something."

But God said, "Oh really? If you think that kind of offering is acceptable, try giving it to your governor. Go to your earthly ruler and offer him what you are offering Me, and see whether he will take it."

The point is unmistakable. If an earthly ruler would be insulted by an offering of our leftover junk, how much more would the Ruler of heaven and earth be insulted by such an offering?

Look how seriously God took this insult. "'Oh that there were one among you who would shut the gates, that you might not uselessly kindle fire on My altar! I am not pleased with you,' says the LORD of hosts, 'nor will I accept an offering from you'" (v. 10).

One reason many of us are not seeing God actively at work in our lives is that we are still giving Him our leftovers and expecting Him to be satisfied. What He wants is to be first in everything.

PRAY ABOUT IT

Where does God rate in your family's financial priorities? Do a "checkbook checkup" today.

YOUR DIVINE PRAYER HELPER

You have not received a spirit of slavery to fear again, but you have received a spirit of adoption as sons by which we cry out, "Abba! Father!"

—ROMANS 8:15

ois and I pray that the two of you are intimate prayer partners as well as life partners. This is one of the great blessings that a husband and wife can confer on each other.

But there's an even greater prayer partner that each believer has—our prayer Helper, the Holy Spirit. It is the Spirit who makes the Fatherhood of God real to your heart so that when you pray, you can say, "Daddy!" That's exactly what the word *Abba* means. It's a term of endearment, of intimacy.

But the Spirit's prayer help doesn't stop there. He also comes alongside you in those prayer times when your heart is so heavy or distressed you don't even know what to say (see Rom. 8:26). You've been there, haven't you? Lois and I have. At some point, all of us reach that place where we are too broken in our weakness to communicate with the Father in intelligible words.

The Holy Spirit helps you when all you can do is groan. He takes that non-communicative groan, that heart cry, and here's what he does. He decodes it, puts heaven's dictionary to it, and by the time it reaches the Father, that prayer you couldn't put in words is four paragraphs long!

So don't worry about it when you reach a place in prayer where language fails you. Don't feel that your prayers always have to be well spoken, flavored with the right theological language. Just say, "Holy Spirit, I don't even know what I'm thinking right now. I need You to make sense of this and to talk to Daddy for me, because I don't know how to put my feelings into words." He will do it!—TONY

PRAY ABOUT IT
The "cord of three strands" (Eccles. 4:12) consisting of you, your mate, and the Holy Spirit, makes for an unbeatable prayer team!

DON'T CHECK YOUR BRAINS

She looks for wool and flax, and works with her hands in delight. She is like merchant ships; she brings her food from afar.

—PROVERBS 31:13–14

❦

There's a warped view out there that says to be a godly woman, a wife has to check her brains at the door, throw her education and skills in the garbage, and give up opportunities to be productive. That's hardly the picture of the godly woman described in Proverbs 31. This woman earns, saves, invests, and spends money wisely. But she's doing it to the good of her husband and her household.

A lot of modern women build their own careers in relative isolation from their husbands. They have their own money in their own bank accounts on which they write their own checks. But the godly woman uses her skills and gifts for the embellishment of her home and the enhancement of her husband, because she is kingdom-oriented, not self-oriented. Her husband knows that every dollar she makes and every dime she spends will make their home a better place to live.

If a wife loves her career so much that her husband is never benefited from the career she enjoys, then she is not being a godly wife. She has bought the lie that she's her own woman doing her own thing and that her man is an inconvenience. This is hell's agenda for a home.

God did not give a woman a husband so she could continue living as an independent, single woman. He gave her a husband so she can partner with him, using her gifts, skills, and abilities to the full, so that the home is thrust forward and her husband is better off. Because he needs that help.

Don't get us wrong. We're not saying a wife is supposed to help and better her husband while she suffers. No, when a wife enhances her husband, she reaps the benefit too.

PRAY ABOUT IT

It takes the power of the Holy Spirit to go God's way when God's way is opposite of the culture. Today, pray together that God will give both of you the courage to live according to the truth.

DON'T SWEAT IT

Which of you by being anxious can add a single cubit to his life's span?

—MATTHEW 6:27

Here's a medical flash: Worrying won't help you live one day longer! It might shorten your life, but it won't lengthen it. No matter how much—or how little—you worry, when God's appointed day comes for you, you are exiting this place. It won't matter whether you are up to running ten miles a day or have given up eating meat, your life's span has been determined by God.

You may be thinking, *Thanks a lot, Tony. That's a cheerful thought for the day.* Actually, it is. What it means, first of all, is that your times are on God's hands. Is there anyone else into whose hands you would rather commit your days and years?

But this truth ought to be comforting to a believer for another reason. As long as you're here, God has promised to take care of your needs. He knows the length of your days, and He has the provisions necessary to fill those days. In other words, the person who understands the sovereignty and sufficiency of God can pray, "Lord, there may be a downturn in the economy. I may get 'downsized' by my company. I may have a health setback. But whatever happens, I remember that You are my heavenly Father. You hold my life in Your hands. And You told me in Your Word that as long as You want me around here, You are going to provide for me. So I may not know how You are going to do it, but I thank You in advance for the provision I am going to receive."

I don't know about you, but knowing I have a heavenly Father like that is a cheerful thought. It sure beats worrying myself into an early grave.

And just in case we need further testimony of God's care, Jesus advises us to go out and observe a field of beautiful flowers (see Matt. 6:28–30). If God can fill a field with lilies, don't worry about whether He can fill your table.—TONY

PRAY ABOUT IT

Spend five minutes worrying about all your problems then spend ten minutes praying about them. See which makes things better.

MY WONDERFUL ROLE MODEL

Train up a child in the way he should go, even when he is old he will not depart from it.
—PROVERBS 22:6

⁓✦⁓

As I said earlier, my role model is my mother. She has the kind of dedication, tenacity, and strong love for the Lord needed to raise eight children to know and love the Lord, and she is a wonderful example of the truth of today's familiar verse. Mother stuck it out when life wasn't fun or easy because she loved God, loved her husband, and loved her children.

Someone might say that in my mother's era, child-rearing was easier because mothers did not face all the pressures and distractions that mothers have to deal with today. I have a feeling my mother, and other women who raised large families in her day, could tell us something about pressure and the difficulties of raising children without a lot of the modern conveniences we enjoy. However, my mother is not my role model because of what she didn't have or did without but because of what she did with what she had. Mother drew her strength daily from the Lord. Although she did not have all the modern conveniences to help her, she stayed focused and relied on the God who is all-sufficient for any need we may have.

He is the same God who is available to sustain you and me today. Every mother needs a source of strength outside of herself. Have you discovered the day-by-day strength God provides to those who will call on Him?—LOIS

THINK ABOUT IT
Whose role model are you? Someone is watching your life!

SOMEONE HAS TO BLEED

The LORD God caused a deep sleep to fall upon the man, and he slept; then He took one of his ribs, and closed up the flesh at that place.

—GENESIS 2:21

husband is called to give himself up for his wife. That's first on God's agenda for us husbands. Husband, you need to decide, "I am willing to pay whatever price it takes to bring my wife to fulfillment. I am willing to go the distance to bring her from where she is to where she ought to be spiritually and every other way."

When a man comes home, he must say, "Things may not be right. I may not like what is happening, but a savior is in the house. I am your deliverer. Whatever is wrong, I am Mr. Fix-it. Whatever price has to be paid, I will pay it."

At the heart of a husband's love is sacrifice. If there is no sacrifice, there is no love. So my question to husbands is, "Do you really love your wife? If I asked her what price you are paying to love her, could she tell me? Could *you* tell me what price you are paying for her?"

When you got married, the preacher asked you up front, "Will you love this woman in sickness and in health, for richer or poorer, as long as you both shall live?" We preachers ask that because we know something. We know you haven't seen the whole deal in marriage yet, so we want an up-front commitment that you're going to stick it out.

A husband who truly loves his wife says, "If this marriage ends, you're going to have to leave me, because I'm not going anywhere. No matter how you treat me or what happens, I want you to know that I will be here."—TONY

PRAY ABOUT IT

Only a man who has abandoned himself to a kingdom agenda rather than a personal one can make this level of commitment. Pray that God will help you be a kingdom kind of husband.

A QUIET PLACE

Come away by yourselves to a lonely place and rest a while.

—MARK 6:31

I hope you have a quiet place where you can be alone with the Lord each day, a place where you can shut out the world for a few minutes and develop the quietness of heart that pleases God.

Another thing you need if you are going to meet with the Lord each day and develop the healthy habit of daily devotions is the right attitude of soul. The psalmist wrote, "Be still, and know that I am God" (Ps. 46:10, KJV).

But sometimes finding a quiet place and developing a quietness of heart is easier said than done! And we're not the only ones who have encountered this problem. In Mark 6, Jesus' disciples were in the midst of a hectic time of ministry. They were trying to tell Him the exciting results they had experienced as they ministered in His name, and yet the Bible says there were so many people milling around them that they did not even have time to eat.

Does this sound familiar? When our four children were young, our home was often a place of controlled chaos. Sometimes I had several "false starts" before I could find a quiet moment to be alone with the Lord. But the very busyness of our days and the responsibilities that fall upon us are all the more reason that we need a daily time with Him.

Morning is the best time for many people because it gives them the right start on the day. But it doesn't work for everyone, especially a mother trying to get her children fed and off to school before her own day begins. Your devotional time should be at the point when you have the best chance for maximum quiet and minimum distractions. The important thing is to fix a daily time.—LOIS

THINK ABOUT IT

We schedule other things like meals, appointments, sleep, and recreation, yet all too often we leave the needs of our souls to take care of themselves. Make a daily appointment with the Lord.

LEAVING YOUR STUFF BEHIND

We have brought nothing into the world, so we cannot take anything out of it either.

—1 TIMOTHY 6:7

❦

I love the practicality of the Bible. In our verse for today, Paul doesn't give us any lofty, closely argued theological reason for being content with the material stuff we have. He simply tells us a truth about life that is easily observable: We came into this world materially naked, and we're going out the same way.

The verses that "bookend" this wisdom (vv. 6, 8) both mention contentment, so we know that's what Paul is talking about.

You say, "But wait a minute. We don't have a house yet. We only have one car. Does God want us to be content where we are right now and not work to earn those things?"

I can't answer that for you. But let me say that I don't believe 1 Timothy 6:7 is saying you should never try to own a house if you don't have one or that you should never seek to better yourself in your work.

God is saying you should be content until He pleases to give them to you. But don't let them become your obsessions, because you will leave them behind someday, and in the meantime they can divert your spiritual focus.

Take a pair of newlyweds. They are deeply in love. Yes, they want a house, and they hope to get better jobs. But they are content in their love. They enjoy just being together. Ten years later, this husband and wife are looking good in their designer clothes. Both of them have a car and a career. The home is nice. But in all they've gained, they've lost each other. They are living like two strangers in the same house.

That happens when people fall into the trap that Paul calls "want[ing] to get rich" (1 Tim. 6:9). All your stuff is staying behind when you leave, so don't get your heart set on it.—TONY

TALK ABOUT IT

Try this little experiment together. Write down your three most valuable possessions. Then talk about how your relationship with God would be impacted if He decided to take them.

SHE MARRIED YOU FOR YOU

If a man were to give all the riches of his house for love, it would be utterly despised.

—SONG OF SOLOMON 8:7

❧

oday's verse reminds us of another timeless truth: Biblical love cannot be bought. For us as husbands, this means that no amount of financial provision on our part can substitute for our responsibility to give ourselves to our wives.

One way we, as husbands, can fulfill our calling in marriage is to follow the instruction of Peter, who told us to "live with your wives in an understanding way" (1 Pet. 3:7). The Greek word *live* means to dwell in close harmony, to be closely aligned with someone, to live together with intimacy. It's part of what I call loving your wife according to a kingdom agenda.

Many men have the idea, "I'm the husband; I go out and work. You're the wife; you stay home. I do my job; you do your job." But that's where the problem is. The home is the husband's job too. The wife is to help her husband do his job at home well, but she is not designed to replace him in the home.

It is part of a husband's kingdom agenda to make sure, as much as possible, that his home is a place of peace. That means he has to be present to be the leader. Your wife didn't just marry you for a paycheck, a car, or a job title. She married *you.*

If your marriage is typical, your wife loved you when you didn't have a dime. She married you when you were just out of college, when nobody knew your name. That's the man she wants to live with. She doesn't want to trade the relationship for a nice car or a big house.

I know we men have the responsibility to provide for our families. My plea to you is, don't let the things you do *for* your wife replace your presence *with* her. She married you to share life with you.—TONY

THINK ABOUT IT

A husband needs to create an atmosphere of intimacy in his home—and he can do it with his wife's help. But he has to try!

TEARING DOWN FAMILY STRONGHOLDS (DAY 1)

The weapons of our warfare are not of the flesh, but divinely powerful for the destruction of fortresses.

—2 CORINTHIANS 10:4

~~~~~~~~~~

*Y*ou may not know it, but Satan wants to start a "building boom" today by erecting his fortresses or strongholds in your family. If this is a new concept to you, let me explain that a fortress ("strong hold," KJV) is a way of thinking that Satan seeks to erect in our minds. This gives the devil a tremendous advantage in spiritual warfare, although we don't have to let him have the ground he needs to build his strongholds.

A stronghold is a mind-set that accepts as inevitable what we know is contrary to the will of God. Examples of these strongholds are addiction, a defeatist attitude that says "I can't" do something when God says "You can," a false view of ourselves, or a belief that our marriage or family is so far gone that even God can't save it. Satan uses these strongholds and others to get a grip on a family and keep it from being everything God intended it to be.

The devil has been at this stuff for a long time, and he knows what he is doing. He built his first stronghold right in the middle of the first family—and he did it right in the middle of the Garden of Eden.

The fall of Adam and Eve and the subsequent problems in their family were caused by an attack from the fallen spirit world. Satan infiltrated the first home and disrupted it. His attack caused spiritual deterioration in the lives of Adam and Eve, which led to relational deterioration in their family.

We know that this sin resulted in a family stronghold because it carried over to the next generation when Cain killed Abel. Satan's infiltration of Adam's family became the foundation for family murder.

PRAY ABOUT IT

This is serious stuff, but read today's verse again. We have powerful weapons to tear down strongholds. Pray that God will show you how to use the spiritual authority you already have in Him.

TEARING DOWN FAMILY STRONGHOLDS (DAY 2)

The serpent was more crafty than any beast of the field which the LORD God had made.

—GENESIS 3:1

***

It should not surprise us that the first family stronghold in history was the work of Satan. He has always sought to infiltrate the family, and his methodology is simple. He got our first parents to reverse their biblical roles and responsibilities, a trick he's still using today. We could summarize what Satan told Eve in Genesis 3:1–5 with two statements: "You don't need God. And you don't need Adam."

Satan got Eve to act independently of God. He tempted her to use her own reasoning and her own logic to reverse God's established order. Satan then influenced Adam to become a passive male and stand on the sidelines. And when that happened, Satan had an open door to infiltrate the home.

The result was a staggering curse pronounced by God in Genesis 3:14–19. Now there would be conflict in the home where at first there had been peace. God said to Eve, "Your husband . . . shall rule over you" (v. 16).

In other words, men would seek to control women by domination. As evil as it is, as wrong as it is, men would seek to dominate women. And the desire of the woman for relationship and for partnership would become a battle rather than a blessing.

God cursed the ground so that from now on, the man would become tired from a day of trying to wrestle a living out of a stubborn earth. So instead of coming home to serve his wife, he would come home expecting to be served by her, and that would produce conflict. And after all this, Adam and Eve had to endure the murder of one son by another son.

Obviously, Satan's stronghold in Adam's family was passed on to the next generation. Exodus 20:5 says that can happen. But look at the promise of the very next verse. God says He will "[show] lovingkindness to thousands, to those who love Me and keep My commandments" (v. 6).

PRAY ABOUT IT

Prayer is our most effective weapon in demolishing Satan's strongholds. Give yourselves, your marriage, and your kids to God in prayer today.

TEARING DOWN FAMILY STRONGHOLDS (DAY 3)

Let all bitterness and wrath and anger and clamor and slander be put away from you, along with all malice.

—EPHESIANS 4:31

Satan uses a handful of favorite methods to wedge his way into a family and build his strongholds. Over the next few days, we want to give you a few of the most important and common ways Satan works in our families so we can learn how to tear down what he tries to construct. The first of these methods is unresolved anger.

We're not just talking about parents having an occasional argument or about parents and kids butting heads a few times. We're talking about a situation in which a family is imprisoned by a problem of anger they can't break free of.

If a wrong has been committed against you, you have a right to be angry. Anger at sin is valid. But prolonged anger violates the scriptural command to resolve it quickly and provides the ground Satan needs to build that unresolved anger into a stronghold. Paul says it very clearly in Ephesians 4:27: Lingering anger becomes an opportunity for Satan. It gives the enemy the unlocked door he needs to break into your home and do his destructive work.

This kind of situation makes everyone else in the family pay for what one or two people have done. Suppose you were eating with your family at a restaurant, and when you were finished the waiter brought you your bill—along with all the bills for everyone else who was eating in the restaurant.

Your argument would be, "It's not fair to make me pay for what everybody else ate." In the same way, it's not fair for your family members to pay for what someone else did. Don't let anger rob your family of the joy and peace God wants to reign in your home.

PRAY ABOUT IT

Since a stronghold can involve more than one generation, begin praying that any unresolved anger in your extended family will be healed so that you might be set free.

Husbands, love your wives, and do not be embittered against them.

—COLOSSIANS 3:19

ᴛ᷊᷊ᴛᴛᴛᴛ

Today's verse suggests one way that simmering anger or bitterness can affect a family and give Satan a chance to build his strongholds. It's easy to say that we need to resolve our anger quickly, but it's another thing to do it. How can we put a stop to the cycle of destructive family anger?

One useful analogy compares unresolved anger with a videotape in a VCR. A videocassette recorder will play the same tape over and over again, as many times as you want. When the tape has finished playing, you push the eject button and take it out. Before you can play a new tape, you must first eject the old tape.

Unresolved anger is like that old videotape. As long as you keep playing it you relive what made you angry. Instead of ejecting the tape when it's done, you keep rewinding it and playing it again. You have to quit playing that anger tape! And the only way to do that is by hitting the eject button of forgiveness and releasing the offender. Otherwise, Satan will continue using your anger to defeat you in spiritual warfare and infect your family with his poison.

Releasing the offender and dealing with sin may require that you sit down and write or call a family member to say that you forgive that person and release him or her from any emotional obligation to you.

Another way to tear down an anger stronghold in your family is to seek forgiveness from others if you are the offender and to forgive yourself as well. Then when Satan tries to get you to play that old anger videotape, serve notice on him that in the name of Jesus Christ, that tape has been ejected!

PRAY ABOUT IT

God's Word (1 John 1:9) gives us the formula for dealing with any sin. Confess it, claim the cleansing of Christ's blood, and begin enjoying your newfound freedom!

TEARING DOWN FAMILY STRONGHOLDS (DAY 5)

Rebellion is as the sin of divination, and insubordination is as iniquity and idolatry.

—1 SAMUEL 15:23

*R*ebellion is another powerful weapon Satan uses to disrupt families and build strongholds. Rebellion simply means to go against God's established order of authority.

Satan was the original rebel, so it's not surprising that he would attempt to foment rebellion in the family. Rebellious children can tear a family apart as quickly as anything. So can adults who refuse to submit themselves to God's legitimate chain of command.

One of the most common examples of family rebellion that can lead to a stronghold is the rebellion of children. God takes this sin so seriously that the Mosaic Law provided for the stoning of an older child who refused to obey his parents (see Deut. 21:18–21). There is no record that this was ever carried out, but it was on Israel's statute books, reinforcing the warning that rebellious children had to be brought under authority or they would shred family life.

But spiritually, rebellion goes far beyond unruly children. If a husband and father is rebelling against the authority of Christ in his life and home, he can't blame God if his family is falling apart. To get things back on track, he must align himself under God's established chain of authority.

A woman who has bought into the lie of radical feminism and refuses to respect her husband's position of authority is allowing Satan to build a stronghold of rebellion in her family. She too must begin to operate according to God's chain if she wants God's help to break this stronghold.

This issue of obedience to proper authority even applies to Jesus Christ, because He is under the authority of His Father. Every Christian man is under the authority of Christ, and every wife is under the authority of her husband.

Rebellion is a serious sin in God's sight. The only way to deal with it is to remove it, no matter how radical the procedure required to get it out.

PRAY ABOUT IT

Mom and Dad, search your lives today and make sure there is no rebellion in your hearts. If you two get on track, the kids will be no problem.

TEARING DOWN FAMILY STRONGHOLDS (DAY 6)

Have this attitude in yourselves which was also in Christ Jesus, who, although He existed in the form of God . . . emptied Himself, taking the form of a bond-servant.

—PHILIPPIANS 2:5–7

We've been talking about tearing down the strongholds that Satan builds in our families. But to do that, we need to know the sins he capitalizes on to infiltrate a family and do his work. We have mentioned unresolved anger and rebellion as two of the most common "open doors" for Satan. A third one is selfishness.

This is a big one in our day because so many people are after "personal fulfill-ment," no matter what the cost to their marriages or families. Displaying this kind of selfishness is like welcoming Satan into your home. You may be saying, "I'm try-ing to do this family thing right, but it just isn't working." The problem may be that you're trying the wrong thing. The issue is not just that you're trying but *what* you are trying. Are you using your spiritual weapons to attack family strongholds, or are you using the world's methods and simply sprinkling a little Jesus on top?

It's like the couple who decided they needed to start doing things together, so they decided to go duck hunting. The couple inquired what they needed, and were told, "The main thing you need for duck hunting is a good dog." So they bought a hunting dog and headed out.

They hunted all day long but didn't bag one duck. Finally the husband looked at his wife and said, "Honey, we've got to be doing something wrong here. We haven't caught a duck yet."

His wife answered, "Well, I'm not sure, but maybe if we throw the dog up a little higher, he can catch one of 'em."

That's what a lot of Christian families are doing. They're trying, but they're using the wrong weapons. Check out Ephesians 6:10–17 and you'll read about the spiritual weapons God has given us. They are awesomely powerful and effective against Satan. Use them and take your family back!

THINK ABOUT IT

It takes spiritual firepower to defeat our spiritual foe. In Christ, we have all the fire-power we need!

ONE WHO UNDERSTANDS

All of us like sheep have gone astray, each of us has turned to his own way.
—ISAIAH 53:6

❧

ne of the hard realities of parenting is that our older children can make potentially life-changing choices that fly in the face of all we have worked so hard to teach them.

At times like this, it can be comforting to realize that even God, the perfect Parent, has to endure the choices of His children that violate His training. In other words, even perfect parenting does not prevent children from making wrong choices.

We are in good company when we experience pain over the bad choices our children may make. God understands our grief. The next time a child's decision or rebellion makes you feel that you've done it all wrong as a parent, remember that you can lead a child to wisdom but you can't make him think, as someone has so wisely said.

We're not suggesting that parents simply feel bad when children stray from the truth. There may be mistakes and failures on the parents' part that need to be dealt with honestly.

But when you have done the best job you know how to do, the best thing you can do is commit your children to the Lord.

God never loses track of where we are, and He is never late with His help. Lean on Him today, and hear His words of comfort.

PRAY ABOUT IT

Remember God's promise not to give you more than you can bear (see 1 Cor. 10:13). Thank Him today for His sufficient grace to handle any problem He permits to come your way.

WHAT MOTIVATES YOU?

Inasmuch then as I am an apostle of the Gentiles, I magnify my ministry.
—ROMANS 11:13

By the time Sunday morning is over at our church, I'm spent. After two sermons, I am physically and mentally wrung out. But no matter how tired I am, by the time I finish the second service and pronounce the benediction, if I feel like the message accomplished the goal the Holy Spirit had for it, I feel a sense of accomplishment.

The key to satisfying work is having the right job for the right reasons, which gives you the right reward. That's why you should always want to move toward what I call your motivated gifts or talent. Let me explain what I mean.

We have two kinds of abilities. The first is just raw ability to do a job, whether or not you're motivated to do it. You may hate doing it, but you can do it. The problem with unmotivated talent is that you only do it because you have to. There's no real feeling of accomplishment or satisfaction with it. At night you say, "I've got to get up and go do that again tomorrow."

In contrast, preaching is motivated talent for me. It's the idea "I get to do this again next week!" or "You mean people will actually fly me there to do this?" Nobody has to coax or beg me to preach; they have to beg me *not* to preach! That's what God wants to move you to. That's why you want to link up with Him.

Using your motivated talent in your work gives you confidence. David didn't know God wanted him to be king; he was just motivated to be God's top shepherd boy. So when the lion and the bear attacked his sheep, he killed them. When Goliath defied God, David was ready. He had already killed ferocious animals. This guy would be no problem.—TONY

THINK ABOUT IT

David's accomplishments as a shepherd gave him confidence to face deeper challenges. Can you look back and see how God has been preparing you for the challenges you face today?

THE POWER SOURCE

Apart from Me you can do nothing.

The night before He was crucified, Jesus shared some critical information with His disciples. He knew they would need supernatural help after His departure, so He spent a good bit of time teaching them about the Person and ministry of the Holy Spirit (see John 14–16). Four times, Jesus said a divine Helper would be sent after He left (see John 14:16, 26; 15:26; 16:7).

Then, right in the middle of these discussions, Jesus dropped on His men the statement recorded in John 15:15, telling them there was no way they could please the Lord or serve Him effectively by mere human effort.

Jesus' statement of helplessness apart from Him is for us too. If you have discovered your own spiritual insufficiency, you are a good candidate for the ministry of the Holy Spirit. If not, you are a good candidate for spiritual disaster.

In the original language of Scripture, the word Jesus used for the Holy Spirit, *Helper,* is a pregnant term. Some versions translate it *counselor* or *advocate,* because it literally means "one called alongside to help," that is, "to enable." Jesus knew His followers would need divine power to pull off what He wanted them to do. And He knew where they were going to get that power: from the enabling presence of the Spirit. This was very important, because whenever the disciples had needed help, Jesus had been there. When they were discouraged, Jesus had been there to encourage them. When they were defeated, Jesus had been there to pick them up. When they were afraid out on the sea, Jesus walked on the water and calmed their fears.

Whatever these men needed, Jesus had been there to provide. So when they heard that Jesus was leaving, their immediate question was, "Who is going to help us?" The answer is the same truth we cherish today: Jesus will continue ministering to and empowering His people through the Holy Spirit.

THINK ABOUT IT

The enabling power of the Holy Spirit works at home too. Apart from His ministry, we can't do marriage or family the way God intended.

BEING YOUR WIFE'S SANCTIFIER

We have been sanctified through the offering of the body of Jesus Christ.
—HEBREWS 10:10

***

*I*f a husband is going to live out God's kingdom agenda in his marriage, he must be his wife's sanctifier. This does not mean a husband can make his wife holy; only God can do that. I'm using the term *sanctifier* in a different sense. The word *sanctification* means to set apart for special use. That is, to place a person in a unique category, to take her from where she is to where she needs to go. The process of sanctification is what we call spiritual growth.

Paul said of Christ and the church, "That He might sanctify her, having cleansed her by the washing of water with the word, that He might present to Himself the church in all her glory, having no spot or wrinkle or any such thing; but that she should be holy and blameless" (Eph. 5:26–27).

Now, let me tell you what happens in a marriage. When a man marries a woman, he also marries her history and her family. He has to accept the good parts as well as the bad parts. The good parts he enjoys. The bad parts he may not discover until after the honeymoon.

It reminds me of the man who fell in love with a great opera singer after he heard her sing. They had a brief, whirlwind romance and were married. They went on their honeymoon, and the man was shocked when his new bride removed her wig, revealing a completely bald head. Then she removed her false teeth, top and bottom, took out her hearing aid and glass eye, and unstrapped a wooden leg. Her stunned husband looked at her and said, "Sing, woman, sing!"

A lot of men think that when they get married, the main job has been accomplished. But in truth, it's just beginning. A husband's job is to sanctify his marriage, to make it something special, something set apart. What Jesus is to the church, a husband is to be to his mate.—TONY

PRAY ABOUT IT

My brother, if being your wife's sanctifier sounds like a task that's too big for you, you've got the idea! Ask God for His strength to be His man today.

A GIFT TOO VALUABLE TO GIVE AWAY

Do not let immorality or any impurity or greed even be named among you, as is proper among saints.

—EPHESIANS 5:3

God puts a very high value on sexual purity. The Bible says it from beginning to end: Sex is His gift, to be reserved for and expressed within the covenant of marriage.

The reason people give sex away so easily is that they don't know how valuable sexual purity is in God's eyes. Stuff that you think is cheap you throw away. Stuff that is expensive, you hold on to.

When Lois and I first started dating, she told me, "Let's get the rules straight up front. I am giving myself to one man, and that is the man I marry. That's it. If you have any other ideas, you are not the man I want to marry."

I knew right then that Lois was the woman I wanted to marry, because she was telling me that she understood the value God placed on her, and on her purity too, and that commitment really attracted me to her.

This is the attitude of Scripture. In Bible times, it was a proud thing for a woman to be able to produce the evidence of her virginity and say to her parents and to all Israel, "I kept myself a virgin for my husband." Today, however, popular society makes a joke out of virginity. If you are a virgin, you are laughed at and scorned.

Not so in God's economy. In His view, a commitment to chastity before marriage is an act of consecration. Then the act of marriage is another form of consecration. Every time a husband and wife engage in sexual intercourse, they are saying afresh to each other, "All of me belongs to all of you." The sexual act within marriage is a continual recommitment to the covenant.—TONY

PRAY ABOUT IT

Even if your wedding night was many years ago, take time today to thank God for the special gift you gave to each other that night and from that point on.

THE SEASONS OF A WOMAN'S LIFE

Who knows whether you have . . . attained royalty for such a time as this?

—ESTHER 4:14

This verse from the life of Esther is the theme verse for my life, because Mordecai's statement to Esther reminds me that there are various seasons in a woman's life.

In order to relax and enjoy the season you are in right now, you have to believe that God's Word is true and that if you keep your part of the deal, He will definitely keep His part of the deal. Following the guidelines of Scripture is not always easy. During my season of staying home with my children, I had my share of struggles with persevering, as many young mothers do, especially since I wanted to use my gifts and abilities outside the home. But my staying home was a decision Tony and I made before the Lord, and I soon realized that I could use my gifts inside the home to manage rather than just maintain my household. Then, as the kids reached school age, I was able to use those skills outside the home part-time.

Paul spoke of the seasons in a woman's life when he instructed the older women to teach the younger women how to care for their families. This reminds us that there is constant need for reinforcement and encouragement. The Christian life was not meant to be lived alone.

Women especially need the encouragement and motivation of other women if they were not raised themselves according to biblical principles. All of this can be very foreign to them.

It is important for all of us to fellowship with other women who are in the same season we are in for support. This is where the body of Christ becomes so important. When a woman becomes isolated from other people, she is more vulnerable to the enemy's attacks. Your husband can be a great help here if he understands where you are in your life.—LOIS

TALK ABOUT IT

My sister, does your husband know the season you are in? Give him a window into your heart.

A DONE DEAL

[Cast] all your anxiety upon Him, because He cares for you.

—I PETER 5:7

Christians who make God's kingdom a priority reflect a heavenly rather than an earthly perspective. One place where a heavenly perspective comes into play is in the matter of worry. Peter invites us to "offload" all of our cares on God. And when we do that, we need to leave them there, not take them back. When we've done that, we don't have to worry whether God will handle the problem.

When our children express a concern to us and we say, "We'll take care of it," that means they don't have to think about it anymore. As far as they are concerned, it's a done deal. In fact, we often say to them, "Why are you worrying about that? Didn't I tell you I'd take care of it?"

In the same way, when God promises to carry your burdens, it's definitely a done deal! When you seek God's kingdom and His righteousness (see Matt. 6:33), He promises to add to you all the things you need—all the things that the non-believers are knocking themselves out trying to get. So you can be relaxed about your earthly needs, because God will supply your needs.

Let's face it. As Christians we worry by choice, not by necessity. Once you adopt a kingdom perspective, it changes everything.

Now, some believers love to worry, and they get mad at us if we say, "You don't have to worry. Everything is going to be all right."

They say, "Are you kidding? If you understood what I was going through, you'd be worried too."

Maybe, but we like what God says better: "Go get some sleep. You don't need to toss and turn in bed tonight. I'm staying up taking care of the problem, so you can rest."

THINK ABOUT IT

When was the last time you lost sleep through worry? Did worrying help or just wear you out? What are you going to do next time?

LOOKING IN THE RIGHT DIRECTION

*If then you have been raised up with Christ, keep seeking the things above, where
Christ is, at the right hand of God.*

—COLOSSIANS 3:1

Have you ever tried to drive with your eyes closed or while staring into your rearview mirror? Either situation can lead to a very nasty accident!

Obviously, you can't drive without looking ahead. It's OK to glance in the rearview mirror once in a while, but you have to get your focus right in order to drive. You have to be looking in the direction you need to go.

Many of us are getting lost and veering off the path in our spiritual lives because we are trying to move forward while looking in the wrong direction. We are looking at ourselves, at other people, at our circumstances, or even looking backward at the past.

But the only way we can move forward in our Christian lives is by fixing our focus firmly above, on the exalted Christ. He is to be the object of our focus.

Paul urged us to seek the things that are above because that's where Christ is and because we have been raised with Christ and seated with Him in "the heavenly places" (Eph. 2:6).

To put it another way, Paul was telling us to view earthly things through heavenly glasses. We need to use the lens of heaven to draw our conclusions about earth. We cannot afford to allow ourselves to make our daily decisions based solely on earthly thinking. Instead, we must function on earth based on the thinking of heaven. Paul makes that explicit in Colossians 3:2 when he says, "Set your mind on the things above, not on the things that are on earth."

Since we are seated with Christ in heaven, we can stand strong on earth because we are linked to the ruling authority of the universe. So we might say that how you stand is determined by where you sit!—LOIS

THINK ABOUT IT

Since Christ is exalted in heaven, we should exalt Him on earth by giving Him our total focus and obedience.

WORRY IS A CHOICE

In Thy book they were all written, the days that were ordained for me, when as yet there
was not one of them.

—PSALM 139:16

Worry isn't just a bad habit. It's a sin, because when you worry you are saying that while God may have the ability to keep you alive, He doesn't have the ability to clothe, feed, or shelter you.

Not only is worry sinful, it is also useless. There's one thing we need to know about our lives. Our days on earth have been appointed by God. That's not fatalism. That's biblical reality. God has allotted to all of us our life span, and when He's ready to take us home, no amount of jogging or oat bran or anything else will delay it one day. Those things will just help you look better on your way out. So if God has our days firmly in His hand, worrying about the next one won't do a thing for us.

You say, "But, Tony, I'm just a worrier. I can't help it." Yes, you can. Worry is a decision, a choice. You can decide not to worry. The Bible wouldn't command you not to worry if you weren't able to stop doing it.

The real issue isn't whether you worry. It's whether God is first. If He isn't, then you should be worried. Why? Because that means you are assuming the responsibility of providing for your own needs.

How do you know if God is first in your life and your marriage? One way is by how you handle your money. God says, "If you will honor Me first with your money and your time and your abilities, I will make what you have stretch further than you ever could."

As I have said before, God does not want our leftovers. Suppose God reversed things and gave us His leftovers. You wouldn't want leftover oxygen or water, would you? So let's give God our best, not what's left.—TONY

TALK ABOUT IT
You and your mate need to get together and decide what giving God your best means for you. Agree on the specifics of how you are going to honor Him.

RECAPTURING THE FEELING

Now abide faith, hope, love, these three; but the greatest of these is love.

—I CORINTHIANS 13:13

***

*B*rother, I suspect that when you were dating the woman who became your wife, you went all out to win her. You probably bombarded her with calls, notes, and gifts. You surprised her with stuff all the time. You were creative and spontaneous. You gave her every spare minute. But what happened once you were married? Often, a man stops honoring his wife after the wedding vows are exchanged. He stops making her feel special. She has to fend for herself emotionally. Her skills are taken for granted.

I often ask husbands, "When was your last date with your wife?" Now, by a date, I mean you come home and say, "Honey, I've got this evening all planned out. All you need to do is come along and enjoy yourself."

That kind of thing communicates honor and value to your wife. It tells her you've been thinking about her and that she's not just an afterthought to you.

Your wife is your equal in terms of her value as a human being and her spiritual value to God. She may be called to be submissive to your leadership, but she deserves honor as your fellow heir (see 1 Pet. 3:7). She may be not as physically strong as you are, but she is worthy of your honor. God's mandate must be reflected in the way you relate to your wife.

Now, don't misunderstand. Honoring your wife doesn't mean you two always see eye to eye. You may have to make a decision she doesn't agree with. But honoring her means you take her thoughts and feelings into account before you make that decision, because God may be showing her some things you need to hear.—TONY

TALK ABOUT IT

One way a husband honors his wife is by the value and attention he gives to her ideas and opinions. Wife, do you feel honored by your husband?

SEXUAL FASTING (DAY I)

Stop depriving one another, except by agreement for a time that you may devote your-selves to prayer, and come together again, lest Satan tempt you.

—I CORINTHIANS 7:5

The Bible says that, except for one specific situation, sexual intimacy is to be the norm within marriage. Just as single people aren't to act married, married people are not to act single.

Other than uncontrollable things like illness, the only situation in which intercourse is not to be a regular part of marriage is an agreed-upon period of time so the partners can give themselves to focused prayer. Let's talk about this special case.

First, consider the *agreement* part of this situation. This is not a unilateral decision; Paul says it must be by mutual agreement.

Second, the time is to be limited. After a husband and wife have devoted themselves to prayer, they are to resume normal sexual relations so that Satan doesn't tempt either partner because of a lack of self-control.

I call this commitment to temporary abstinence "sexual fasting." The Bible has something important to teach married couples here about a different kind of intimacy that can be as satisfying as sexual intimacy.

Fasting is giving up a craving of the body because of a greater need of the spirit. Most of us relate fasting only to food, a period during which we give up a meal, or perhaps a day's meals, and spend the time praying when we would normally be eating; we choose to do this because of a deep spiritual need in our lives.

If you have a need in your individual lives or in your marriage and you have never fasted over it, you have not fully addressed it yet. Fasting as a spiritual discipline is being rediscovered in the church today—and the Bible indicates it can extend to a married couple's sexual life.—TONY

PRAY ABOUT IT
Your decision regarding sexual fasting depends in part on the depth of your need. Pray about it together.

SEXUAL FASTING (DAY 2)

This kind does not go out except by prayer and fasting.

—MATTHEW 17:21

We are talking about a situation in which there is a deep spiritual need in your lives as a married couple, and in order to get that need met you give up a craving of the body.

In this case, the physical appetite you give up is not your hunger for food but your craving for sexual intimacy with each other. The two of you take the time that you would normally spend being *physically* intimate to be *spiritually* intimate with each other and with God.

We know from passages like Exodus 19:9–15 that when God was getting ready to meet with the children of Israel, one way He commanded them to prepare for this meeting was by abstaining from any sexual contact. There was to be total concentration, total focus on this spiritual invasion by God. So Paul was on solid biblical ground when he said a sexual fast is legitimate for a married couple.

One of the great things a husband and wife can do is to mutually agree to set aside sex so they can pray together rather than endure a sexual deprivation based on anger or wanting to punish the other person or anything like that.

Imagine the intimacy a couple will experience when they kneel together to plead with God to intervene in a difficult situation. Imagine a husband taking the spiritual lead to propose a sexual fast to his wife for the purpose of prayer together. That alone would revolutionize many Christian marriages!

If you need an intervention by God in your affairs as a couple or as a family, He calls on you to set aside time and sacrifice physical intimacy for spiritual intimacy with Him. In other words, cease your sexual activity for a while in order to fast and pray for the Lord's mercy and forgiveness. It works!

THINK ABOUT IT

Whatever need or burden you may be facing, it is appropriate for you to consider abstaining from sex by agreement for a time of prayer.

FEELING TRULY ALIVE!

For to me, to live is Christ, and to die is gain.

—PHILIPPIANS 1:21

❧

What is it that makes you come to life? On a practical, day-to-day basis, what gets you going and makes you feel truly alive? In other words, what is life to you?

Different things excite different people. If you were to tell a little girl, "We're going to the toy store," she would come alive. Say to your teenaged son, "It's time to go and get your driver's license," and chances are good that he will feel truly alive.

We all know that when we meet that special person we have been looking for all our lives, the mere mention of our beloved's name brings us to life. We become animated, maybe start acting a little silly, and perhaps even show pictures that no one really wants to see. Why? Because we have come alive.

With His disciples gathered around Him in the Upper Room, Jesus said, "I am the . . . life" (see John 14:6). Paul made the same statement when he said that Jesus Christ was his life. In other words, what got Paul going and made him feel truly alive was his relationship with his living Lord and Savior.

The same should be true for us as Christians. Is it? How do we know when our sense of "aliveness" in Jesus Christ is fading? One way is by a reduction in the amount of time we spend in His presence, feeding on His Word and communing with Him in prayer. When Christ becomes dim in our focus, life starts getting fuzzy, and we no longer feel alive. The cure for that sense of deadness is found in the Lord.

Do you feel really alive today? If not, maybe the problem is that Jesus is not the focus, the heartbeat, of your life.—LOIS

THINK ABOUT IT

One way to come alive spiritually is to make sure that Jesus Christ has first place in everything (see Col. 1:18). Is this the case with you today?

DON'T SETTLE FOR ONE LITTLE DRINK

He who believes in Me, as the Scripture said, "From his innermost being shall flow rivers of living water."

—JOHN 7:38

The story is told of a thirsty man who was staggering through the desert and came upon a little shack. Inside the shack, lo and behold, he saw a water pump! The happy man worked the pump vigorously, but no water came out. He slumped down by the pump, totally defeated.

Then his eye happened to spot a bottle propped in the corner. The bottle was full of water, and beside it was this note: "If you want water, you must pour the contents of this bottle into the pump to prime it. Then you will get all the water you need. Please refill the bottle before you leave."

The man was on the horns of a dilemma. Should he go ahead and drink the bottle of water, of should he risk pouring that precious, life-giving water into the pump?

This is the kind of choice we must make every day. In our marriages, each of us has the choice of satisfying our immediate needs—perhaps at the expense of our partner—or working toward long-term joy.

The thirsty man in that desert poured the water into the pump and started pumping. At first, nothing happened. But after a minute, water started gushing out. The man drank deeply, filled his canteen, and then refilled the bottle, writing at the bottom of the note, "Believe!"

THINK ABOUT IT

Are you settling for a drink of spiritual water now and then when God wants to give you a flowing river?

THE QUIETNESS OF GODLY SUBMISSION (DAY 1)

You wives, be submissive to your own husbands so that even if any of them are disobedi-
ent to the word, they may be won without a word by the behavior of their wives.

—I PETER 3:1

⸙

T he apostle Peter raised an issue faced by a lot of women who ask, "What am I supposed to do? My husband isn't even a believer!" Peter's advice actually takes a burden off the wife, because it says that God didn't call a wife to be her husband's pastor. She doesn't have to turn up the gospel radio station so her husband can hear the preaching and get convicted. She doesn't have to pin Bible verses to his pillow or slip Christian tapes into his car's tape player. Peter said the way a messed-up husband is won to the Lord is not by his wife's homiletics (preaching) but by her humility.

This takes a burden off the wife because, as most women can attest, the more a wife tries to change her husband by badgering or preaching at him, the worse he usually gets.

Do you know why? Because when a woman does that, she is messing with the one thing a man will not compromise on, which is his ego. A man will let his wife mess with a lot of stuff in his life, but not his ego.

Now, I'm not saying this is right. I'm just telling you that's the way it is. This is the way men are built. Many men want to make themselves look like more of a man than they really are. But if they were that much of a man, they wouldn't have to *talk* about themselves that much; their success would be obvious.

Men have egos, and those egos need to come under the Lordship of Christ. A wife's quiet submission helps clear the way for God to work.—TONY

THINK ABOUT IT
God can work on a man's ego better than his wife can. So what God calls the wife to do is get out of the way so He can get to her husband. Her quiet, godly behavior makes that possible.

THE QUIETNESS OF GODLY SUBMISSION (DAY 2)

If when you do what is right and suffer for it you patiently endure it, this finds favor with God.

—I PETER 2:20

G od can't get a husband's full attention when his wife is in the way. This does not mean that a Christian wife is to be speechless in her home. It does mean that she is to honor her husband's position even when she disagrees with him.

God says to the wife, "Be like Jesus in your home." The wife's example is the way Jesus bore up under His suffering. Peter wrote, "[He] committed no sin, nor was any deceit found in his mouth; and while being reviled, He did not revile in return; while suffering, He uttered no threats, but kept entrusting Himself to Him who judges righteously" (1 Pet. 3:22–23).

Jesus did not threaten people. He didn't manipulate them by using tears, a powerful weapon some women draw on to make their husbands bend to their will. When Jesus was mistreated, He committed Himself to God the Father. He took the suffering.

When you do it God's way, He makes it work. Christian wife, have you tried God's way to change your husband, or have you been fussing and nagging at him? If you've been fussing, you're telling God, "Don't bother trying to change my husband. I'll take care of it myself."

Instead of preaching, God wants "chaste and respectful behavior" (1 Pet. 3:2) from a wife. That word *behavior* means to stare at, to take a close look at. In other words, a Christian wife should make her husband stare at her in wonder by her loving, submissive attitude and reaction to him.

PRAY ABOUT IT

A wife can make her husband stare in wonder at her by the way she reverences and submits to him. But this doesn't come naturally. A wife needs to pray and trust God for this kind of grace.

THE QUIETNESS OF GODLY SUBMISSION (DAY 3)

Let not your adornment be merely external . . . but let it be the hidden person of the heart, with the imperishable quality of a gentle and quiet spirit.

—I PETER 3:3–4

❦

*J*nstead of giving her husband the leftovers of her energy, her emotions, and her attention after serving and looking good for the boss all day, a Christian wife who wants to lift her husband spiritually comes home from work wanting to know how she can serve her man. She looks for ways to help him.

The idea is to make him stare, to shock him with your support and submission, to make him say, "We're going to church next week" because he likes what he sees and wants to find out what's going on.

Now, I realize some women can say, "You don't know my husband. He will take advantage of me if I do that." God says, "Leave that to Me." That situation may not change for now. But the issue once again is, do you trust God, or do you follow what your mind and your emotions are telling you?

One thing women can do to please their husbands is to keep themselves as attractive as possible. When Peter wrote about "braiding the hair, and wearing gold jewelry, or putting on dresses" (v. 3), he was not telling women it's wrong to wear jewelry or nice clothes. He was urging them to keep these things in their proper perspective. Now, shopping is not my favorite activity. But Lois covers every rack in the store; when we go, we're out there all day. And some of those stores don't even have a chair so that husbands can sit down.

When it comes to fixing up the outer person, many women are meticulous. And that can be good. But the Bible says women are to give that same meticulous attention to their inner person as well. God says, "While you're at it, glamorize the inside too."

A gentle and quiet spirit isn't just attractive to your husband. It is "precious in the sight of God" (v. 4).—TONY

THINK ABOUT IT

The beauty a woman can buy comes and goes, but the beauty that's inside is imperishable. It is not going to fade.

THE QUIETNESS OF GODLY SUBMISSION (DAY 4)

In former times the holy women also, who hoped in God, used to adorn themselves, being submissive to their own husbands.

—I PETER 3:5

G od wants women to be consistent. If you're going to be an ugly person, don't camouflage it with beautiful makeup. But if you are going to take the time to look beautiful on the outside, make sure your inner spirit is looking beautiful too (see v. 4).

I know that many Christian women today often get bent out of shape whenever someone brings up the submission passage in 1 Peter 3:1–6. But I can't ignore it, because it is God's Word to me and my marriage, and also to you.

The most misunderstood verse in this section may be the last one: "Thus Sarah obeyed Abraham, calling him lord, and you have become her children if you do what is right without being frightened by any fear" (v. 6). This does not mean Sarah was Abraham's slave. It means she reverenced him. And by calling him "lord," a term of deep respect and honor, Sarah took her submission public.

Now, the context in which Sarah called Abraham "lord" is very interesting (Gen. 18:1–15). God came to Sarah and Abraham and told them they were going to have a baby the next year.

Sarah wondered about the promise, because pregnancy was an impossible situation for her. She was ninety years old, Abe was one hundred, and there was no hope in sight. But when God saw that Sarah reverenced Abraham, suddenly Abraham could do things no hundred-year-old man was supposed to do. As a result, Sarah got pregnant. When she called Abraham "lord," God gave her a miracle.

The lesson, my sister in Christ, is that when you reverence your husband, God can make him do things he couldn't do before. God can turn his attitude and his life around. If you do your part and get out of the way, God can reach your husband.—TONY

THINK ABOUT IT
One of the best things any wife can do for her husband is pray for him. When a godly woman goes to her knees, watch out!

LOOK FOR WORK, NOT EXCUSES

If anyone will not work, neither let him eat.

༄

P aul's directive to the Thessalonian church is some of the best advice ever given on the importance of work. In effect, Paul was saying if a man *can't* work, you help him. But if he *won't* work, you don't help him. When he gets hungry enough, he'll change his mind. That's why the church is not like the welfare system, which pays people not to work.

I'm an anti-welfare person. Welfare started out as a temporary, stopgap measure to help the farmers and then to help people through the Great Depression. That was good, but then welfare became a permanent institution that now rewards people for being irresponsible and lazy.

Throughout history, lazy people have made excuses for not working, and some of those excuses are pretty humorous. In Bible times, for example, a lazy man might have said, "There is a lion in the road! A lion is in the open square!" (Prov. 26:13). In other words, "Hey, I can't go to work; I might get eaten." Now let me lay a more modern excuse on you. In the nineties, a sluggard says, "There are no jobs out there." Why is that a sluggard's mentality? Because if you're a man, and especially if you know Christ, you were made to be a producer, not just a job finder.

There may not be any openings in your field, but a man who understands his responsibility before God does whatever it takes to provide for his family, even if it means flipping hamburgers for a time. Granted, it's not the best job. And it certainly isn't the best income. But it can be done with integrity—even with joy—to God's glory.

You are working for the Lord, not just for "the man." If the only time you work hard is when you know your boss is looking, you have an attitude problem. Work for the Lord's approval, and the other stuff will take care of itself.—TONY

TALK ABOUT IT
Want an interesting dinnertime conversation? Ask your kids if they like to eat, then read today's verse and discuss the importance of work.

WEEK FORTY-THREE—MONDAY

DON'T CALL HIM FATHER AND THEN WORRY

Do not be anxious for tomorrow, for tomorrow will care for itself. Each day has enough trouble of its own.

—MATTHEW 6:34

I don't know what's going to happen to my family and me tomorrow, but I know Someone who does. He knows all about tomorrow, and He tells me not to worry about what's ahead.

Jesus said if we will look after His concerns on earth—His kingdom and righteousness (see Matt. 6:33)—He will look after our concerns. That doesn't mean we can stay in bed tomorrow and forget about work. We still need to live responsibly, but Jesus' command not to worry about tomorrow means we can turn the worry over to the One who has already been to tomorrow and back.

Now, I'm not perfect at this; I worry sometimes, just like you do. But it's a sin for me to worry, because God says, "Stop worrying, Evans. It's a sin for you to call me Father and then act like I'm not going to take care of you."

Back in 1989, I had a lump that the doctor feared was cancer. The night before the surgery, as I lay on that hospital bed, was I worried about what I would wear the next day or what would be on the menu? Do you think I was worried about whether the roof would shelter me from the rain?

I assure you, I was not. In that hospital, the only thing that counted was God and my relationship to Him. Praise God, the lump was not cancerous, and I left the hospital. God was saying to me, "Evans, I gave you your life back. So don't insult Me by worrying about whether I'm going to feed you tomorrow. I'll feed you until I'm ready to take you home."

Put God first, and you can stop worrying.—TONY

THINK ABOUT IT

Since about 90 percent of tomorrow's worries never materialize, why waste today worrying about them?

LETTING THE WORD BE AT HOME

Let the word of Christ richly dwell within you.

—COLOSSIANS 3:16

❧❧❧

*I*s God's Word at home in your heart? The word *dwell* in today's verse means to make oneself at home. Paul doesn't just want us to hear the Word but to give it access to every part of ourselves.

We are really telling a lie when we say to our guests, "Come on in and make yourselves at home." We don't mean that literally. They aren't free to go into our bedroom and look in our closets or open our desk and examine our personal papers. What we usually mean when we say, "Make yourself at home" is, "Come into this specific room and stay right here."

But if Christ is going to be the Lord of our lives, we can't place restrictions on Him. We have to say, "Lord, check the closets, go into the attic, look inside the desk, and show me what I need to throw away or rearrange. Make Yourself completely at home."

Now, when the Lord God starts making Himself at home in our hearts, some painful "redecorating" decisions will have to be made. God's Word will show you some things that need to be thrown out. It will set your house in order, even though the process may hurt. But God hurts us only to heal us.

Letting the Word be at home in you means coming before God with honesty and openness, ready to act on whatever He reveals to you. Colossians 3:16 goes on to say that we must also come to God in an attitude of teachability and worship, with a heart that is full of "psalms and hymns and spiritual songs, singing with thankfulness in your hearts to God."

This "attitude of gratitude" is critical. When you invite God to make Himself at home, begin by thanking Him for what He has already done.—LOIS

PRAY ABOUT IT
Invite God to make Himself completely at home in your heart today. Don't seal off any room or nook He may want to explore.

HELPING YOUR HUSBAND AS A PARENT

She rises also while it is still night, and gives food to her household, and portions to her maidens. . . . She is not afraid of the snow . . . , for all her household are clothed with scarlet.

—PROVERBS 31:15, 21

godly wife can help her husband both *parentally* and *personally.* Why does God ask a woman to make her home a priority? Because the job of the home is to raise the next generation of godly seed, and Proverbs 31 says the "excellent wife" cares for her children. If a woman is away from home so much that she cannot assist her husband in parenting their children, she's not fulfilling what God has called her to do.

She has to take care that the pull of the outside world doesn't keep her from being an effective wife and mother.

In other words, don't let your job interfere with your duties at home. If somebody has to work overtime, let it be the husband.

A Christian wife helps her husband, not only by helping him parent their children, but also by taking care of herself, her person (see Prov. 31:17, 22). She takes pains to look good, both for herself and for him. Her man is excited to go home. This is what happens when the wife's priorities follow the guidelines of Proverbs 31.

Instead, here's what often happens: The woman gets up every day and gets dressed up because she wants to look good on the job. She knows the boss doesn't want haggard-looking people walking around the office. And when this woman gets to the office, she takes care of the boss, because he has her money in his pocket. Meanwhile, her husband comes home and has to fend for himself.

It's OK for the office to get in on what a woman does to enhance herself for her husband, but that's secondary. A wife who wants to help her husband strives to make him look good by taking care of herself.

TALK ABOUT IT
We have too many women working overtime outside the home and working "undertime" in the home. A Christian wife helps her husband by being the manager of the home.

THE PLUMBER

She is your companion and your wife by covenant.

—MALACHI 2:14

A marriage can get clogged up with junk, just like a kitchen sink. A lot of stuff can go undetected for a while, but eventually the problem begins to build, and before you know it, the sink—or the marriage—is completely clogged.

At this point, the husband needs to do what a plumber does; he unclogs the backup so that things flow properly again.

Husband, when your marriage gets backed up, when the pressure begins to build on your wife, you're to come in with the power of love and minister to her until the backup is gone and everything is flowing freely again. A husband is his wife's sanctifier, the way Christ is the church's sanctifier (see Eph. 5:26–27). The husband's love is to be a sanctifying agent to help cleanse and heal the troublesome things she may bring into the marriage.

Maybe she was abused by her father. Or maybe she was raised by a domineering mother. That stuff won't disappear just because a woman gets married. Our wives need our sanctifying love.

The result of a husband's sanctifying work is a wife who has "no spot or wrinkle" (v. 27). These are very picturesque terms. *Spot* means defilement from outside. *Wrinkle* has to do with internal aging.

The church has spots, external stains from the world, and wrinkles, the external signs of internal aging and decay. Jesus said His job is to wash off the spots and remove the aging. That is the husband's job in his marriage.

This means that when your wife needs strength, you are her strength. When she needs encouragement, you are her encouragement. When she needs joy, you are her joy. When she needs peace, you are her peace.

THINK ABOUT IT
Husband, when you love your wife like this, she will be eternally young because she's got a sanctifier in the house!

WAITING FOR THE REAL THING

How beautiful is your love, my sister, my bride! How much better is
your love than wine.

—SONG OF SOLOMON 4:10

***

God created Adam and Eve as opposite yet complementary, sexual beings with a natural attraction for each other. When Adam first saw her, he understood right away that they were created for each other. And when God joined that first pair in marriage, there was no hesitation or shame in their union. Theirs was the first and only perfect marriage, because sin had not yet polluted everything.

Anything God creates is intended to produce ecstasy and not guilt. When Adam and Eve came together sexually they had no remorseful memories that made them think, *I should not have been there. I should not have thought that. I should have not done that.* Obviously, they were virgins before their marriage, so they had no reason to feel shame.

The entrance of sin into the world did not change God's sexual standards. Men and women are still expected to be virgins before marriage.

But today men, in particular, make excuses for their sin by saying, "Well, I'm a man, and you know how men are." No, you don't set the standard; God does. I'm really concerned about this, because America is producing a generation of young men and even boys who are like my dog. When my dog wants to satisfy his sexual desires, he goes looking for a female dog. His standards aren't very high. All he is concerned about is that his partner is a female.

You may be saying, "Tony, we're concerned too, but what can we do about it?" We can begin, of course, in our own homes with our kids, teaching them God's standards for love and sex. If you don't have a son, there are probably boys you can reach in your extended family, in the neighborhood, and at church. If you have a daughter, you can teach her high standards too.

Use every ounce of influence God gives you!—TONY

PRAY ABOUT IT

Pray that Satan's counterfeit for God's gift of sex will be exposed for what it is and that young people will wait for the real thing.

DON'T REVERSE THE PROMISE

Seek first His kingdom and His righteousness; and all these things shall be added unto you.

—MATTHEW 6:33

Here's a New Testament principle that ought to brighten your day: Christians who prioritize God's kingdom each day will have their needs met. That's what Jesus said.

How can anyone improve on a promise like that? It's impossible. So let us ask you a question. Why do we reverse the process so often? So many times we say by our actions if not by our words, "Lord, I'm going after all the things I need and want in life, and whatever is left over of my time, talent, and treasure, I will use to seek Your kingdom and Your righteousness."

At other times, we say, "Lord, I'm going to worry about all these things because frankly, I'm not sure I can trust You to provide for me and my family."

But according to Jesus, that orientation to life is characteristic of people who don't know Him (see Matt. 6:32). Jesus asks you to put Him first in each decision and commitment of your marriage, your family life, and your life in the church and the community.

That's what makes you a kingdom Christian. A kingdom-focused person asks of every situation, "What would please God in this situation?" (see 1 Cor. 3:23, 10:31).

Do you want a way of life that will bring you rest of body and peace of heart? Nothing will help you relax more than knowing that you have a heavenly Father who says, "If you will put Me first, You can leave your daily needs in My hands."

How can we learn to seek God's kingdom today and not worry about tomorrow? The secret is to live life one day at a time. God only gives you the help you need for today. So you don't worry about how you are going to make it tomorrow, because when you get there, God's grace and provision will be there to meet you.

PRAY ABOUT IT

What are your worried about that might come up tomorrow? Get a headstart by praying about it today.

OVERCOMING SPIRITUAL ANEMIA

Those who wait for the LORD will gain new strength.

—ISAIAH 40:31

⟢━━━━⟣

*A*nemia is a physical condition in which there is a reduction in the number of red blood cells, the amount of hemoglobin, in the bloodstream. The symptoms of anemia are weakness, headaches, fatigue, and irritability. The anemic person is usually unable to pursue a normal level of physical activity.

There is such a thing as spiritual anemia too, and it is not limited to the so-called layperson. It also afflicts people who are involved in active ministry of all sorts: pastors, pastors' wives, missionaries, etc.

The cure for spiritual anemia is the same for the pastor as it is for the person in the pew. "Those who wait for the LORD" are the ones who experience renewed strength. Waiting for the Lord means spending time in His presence, in prayer and in reading and studying His Word. Many people want to see the Lord's power in their lives, but they aren't willing to follow His "prescription" for overcoming spiritual anemia: waiting in His presence.

Sometimes we try our own cure. We figure that if we go to more church services, we'll start feeling fine. Going to church is great, but Sunday and Wednesday won't help you much if you are never on your knees or never open your Bible the rest of the week.

Here is another similarity between physical and spiritual anemia: The anemia sufferer probably won't see miraculous results after just one dose of medicine. The patient needs to obey the doctor and follow the prescribed treatment, and after a while he or she will start feeling better.

The same is true with devotions. If you are having trouble being regular in daily devotions, keep at it, because you know that's what God wants. When you are obedient, the power will come.

THINK ABOUT IT
Spending time with the Lord is the surest way to recharge your spiritual batteries and plug into the source of power every day.

GOING FOR THE CROWN OF GLORY

When the Chief Shepherd appears, you will receive the unfading crown of glory.

—I PETER 5:4

❧

*T*he Bible says that Jesus Christ has a very special reward waiting for those who make Him look good by their lives. The apostle Peter wrote to the church at large to exhort the leaders in Christ's body to carry out their ministry as shepherds under the leadership of Jesus Christ, the "Chief Shepherd." Those who shepherded God's flock in the right spirit and for the right reasons could expect to be rewarded by Christ for their faithful service.

What is the attitude and motive Christ wants from His servants? We're to "shepherd the flock of God among you, exercising oversight not under compulsion, but voluntarily, according to the will of God; and not for sordid gain, but with eagerness; nor yet as lording it over those allotted to your charge, but proving to be examples to the flock" (1 Pet. 5:2–3).

Although this instruction was written primarily to pastors and other shepherds who lead God's flock, any Christian can win this crown by helping new believers grow up in Jesus Christ. The church should not only be a place where new believers grow up, it should be a maternity ward where new Christians are born, a nursery where those babies begin growing.

Those who help other believers grow up spiritually will be rewarded by Christ for their work with the "crown of glory." *Glory* means to show off or put on display. God is going to show off those believers who invested their lives in the lives of others. These faithful ones will be put in God's Hall of Fame, so to speak, honored with a specific blessing for those who make discipleship the heartbeat of their Christian lives.

We like that word *unfading* because a person's glory or honor can fade really quickly down here. You may find yourself being cheered one minute and booed the next. But when Christ rewards us with this crown, we won't have to worry about the applause fading away, because it will be the applause of God.

TALK ABOUT IT

Have you ever thought that you are to be a discipler of your mate? You should be setting an example for each other and urging each other on to maturity in Christ.

DON'T BOTHER GOD

The one who does not love his brother whom he has seen, cannot love God whom he has not seen.

—1 JOHN 4:20

⬧

The title and verse of today's devotional may seem kind of hard-hitting, but there's a reason. In a familiar verse we have talked about several times this year, Peter told husbands that if they were not living with their wives in the way God expected, their prayers wouldn't get any higher than the ceiling (see 1 Pet. 3:7).

In other words, my brother, if there is no dynamic spiritual relationship between you and your wife, your relationship with God will lose much of its dynamic too. When you become a husband, you no longer have a singular relationship with God. He doesn't see two people anymore. He sees one person, one flesh. And because this is so, husbands need to pray *with* their wives, so that both can enjoy the spiritual riches of God's kingdom plan and His kingdom inheritance together.

So the question is not, will your marriage have a spiritual component? The question is, what will be the *quality* of your spiritual relationship as husband and wife?

If your marriage needs to be turned around spiritually, I want to challenge the husband: Let the turnaround begin with you. Wife, if your husband is trying to pray with you, don't turn him down. Help him and encourage him, because God is not going to help him apart from you.

My brother, if you turn the right way, your wife will follow your lead. And when God sees you turn, He will turn a fresh ear to your prayers. This is the mind-set of a man who wants to relate to his wife according to a kingdom agenda.—TONY

THINK ABOUT IT

Generally, you can tell a lot about a man by looking in the face of his wife. She is his mirror.

HOW TO MAKE YOUR HUSBAND SECURE

She does [her husband] good and not evil all the days of her life.
—PROVERBS 31:12

*O*ne of the marks of a godly woman's home is that her husband can feel secure because he has confidence that she will do what is right for him and for her family.

A lot of women read Proverbs 31 and wonder how all of these virtues could ever be true of them. One thing is certain: A solid, growing, and spiritually mature marriage takes time. But you have vowed, "Till death do us part." So relax and enjoy your mate, because if it is the Lord's will, you have a lifetime to lovingly work on the various adjustments and challenges that marriage and family bring.

Things might be tight in your marriage financially, emotionally, or in other ways right now, but a wife can still do her husband good by keeping the commitment she made on her wedding day. As Corrie ten Boom once said, "There is no pit so deep that He is not deeper still." This is a great lesson for a married couple to learn. There is no trial so deep that a husband and wife cannot meet it together in the strength God provides.

My sister in Christ, the best way I know to make today's verse a reality in your home is to remember that you are your husband's helpmate. You are his completer, not his competitor. A wife is functionally subordinate to her husband. She has a head who covers her (see 1 Cor. 11:3), although she is equal with her mate in essence and spiritual value.

A woman who honors her marriage commitment and knows how to accept God-given authority in her life will do her husband and her family good.—LOIS

PRAY ABOUT IT
Pray together today that God will help both of you make your marriage a good reflection of Him.

A DECLARATION OF WAR

Our struggle is . . . against the rulers, against the powers, against the world forces of this darkness, against the spiritual forces of wickedness in the heavenly places.

—EPHESIANS 6:12

❧

You are at war! In fact, no war in history can compare with the battle that you, your mate, and your family are fighting. And this war can be either the cause of your greatest joy as a Christian or the source of your deepest pain. The war we are talking about is the spiritual warfare that you became a part of on the day you trusted Jesus Christ as your Savior. This war affects your relationship with your spouse, and there is no way you can avoid the conflict. There is no bunker or foxhole you can crawl into that will shield you from the effects of this cosmic battle between the forces of God and the forces of Satan.

Because this warfare is first and foremost spiritual and not physical, the degree to which we will be successful is the degree to which we are prepared to understand and fight this battle on a spiritual level. Perhaps a definition will help. Spiritual warfare is that conflict being waged in the invisible, spiritual realm that is being made manifest in the visible, physical realm.

In other words, spiritual warfare is a battle between invisible, angelic forces—a battle that impacts you and me. So the cause of the war is something we can't see. But the effects are very visible in the kinds of problems we face every day.

It's hard enough to fight an enemy we can see. It's much harder to fight what we can't see—but this is exactly the kind of enemy our marriages face. A spiritual battle requires spiritual armor. That's why Paul followed his classic statement on the nature of spiritual warfare with a description of the Christian's armor (see Eph. 6:13–17).

PRAY ABOUT IT

Paul follows his discussion of the armor by exhorting us to "pray at all times" (v. 18). Why don't you and your spouse arm yourselves with prayer right now?

HOW MUCH DO YOU DESIRE GOD?

His delight is in the law of the LORD, and in His law he meditates day and night.

—PSALM 1:2

⬥

*B*eing consistent in spending personal time with God is the ultimate test of your desire to know God. Regular time alone with God draws us closer to Him.

One benefit of regular devotions is that through the study of God's Word, we learn of the many spiritual blessings He has given us (see Eph. 1:3) and what must be done to attain them. Personal devotions are to the soul what regular meals are to the body: sustenance and nourishment. If we don't eat daily, we become physically weak and even sick. The same will happen to us spiritually if we fail to nourish our souls in God's Word and in prayer.

Spending regular time with the Lord also helps give us the assurance, comfort, guidance, and strength we need each day.

What are some reasons for failing to have regular devotions? One reason is lack of time. But if Jesus could find the time to pray despite the incredible demands on Him (see Mark 1:35), we have no excuse. Finding time for devotions is a matter of priority, not simply a matter of time.

Some people say the Bible is too difficult to understand. Many study helps are available, but it's amazing how much more understandable the Bible becomes when you simply start reading and studying it regularly.

Another hindrance to regular, meaningful devotions can be unconfessed sin in your life. If that's the case, ask God to forgive and cleanse you (see 1 John 1:9) and then move on.

If lack of desire is a problem, ask God to give you a hunger for His Word. But while you are asking, *do* something. Start spending time in the Word in obedience to God, and the desire will come. Make time with God a priority, and He will meet with you!

PRAY ABOUT IT

Devotions are a deliberate decision of your will, just like your salvation was. You made a decision to follow Christ; now make a decision to know Him intimately!

WHAT'S THE BIG SECRET?

If we have food and covering, with these we shall be content.

—1 TIMOTHY 6:8

❦

One of the great rewards for faithful stewardship—giving to God the best of our time, talents, and treasure—is contentment. Yet contentment is so elusive that the world has been chasing it for centuries and still hasn't found it.

The apostle Paul called it a "secret" in Philippians 4:12 but not because God is hiding it from us. Contentment is a secret because it can only be found when we do things God's way. In fact, in the very next verse of Philippians, Paul reveals the secret to contentment: "I can do all things through Him who strengthens me" (v. 13). The secret to being a contented steward is to have such a dynamic relationship with Jesus Christ that it doesn't matter what your circumstances are.

The reason this is a secret even to a lot of Christians is that we haven't slowed down long enough to learn it. God can't teach us this lesson when we're knocking ourselves out to get ahead and don't have time to listen.

You may be saying, "But Tony, it's a dog-eat-dog world out there, and I'm one of the dogs. It's tough making a living. I've got to scratch and scrape just to keep up sometimes, let alone get ahead. I really don't have time to sit around trying to be super-spiritual about this thing."

I hear you. But remember the principle Jesus enunciated in Luke 12:15: "Beware, and be on your guard against every form of greed; for not even when one has an abundance does his life consist of his possessions."

Learning to live contentedly with what God provides frees us to pursue His kingdom agenda. And that's when life really begins to get exciting.—TONY

PRAY ABOUT IT
Do you and your family have food and clothing for today? Praise God for it! Are you feeling envious of others? Better pray for contentment.

AN UNBEATABLE TEAM FOR GOD

She extends her hand to the poor; and she stretches out her hands to the needy. . . .
She opens her mouth in wisdom, and the teaching of kindness is on her tongue.

—PROVERBS 31:20, 26

---

*E*arlier we discussed how a Christian wife helps her husband parentally and personally. She also helps her husband ministerially. We're not talking solely about pastors' wives here. The picture here is of a wife who serves alongside her husband in their ministry for the Lord. She's busy helping her husband help others.

One result of this wife's helping hand is that her husband acquires a solid reputation. The husband of the Proverbs 31 woman was one of the elders at the city gates (see Prov. 31:23), where the elders conducted business and governed the land. In other words, the guys at the office should know that a Christian man is where he is and is able to do what he does because he has a wife who helps him get it all together. Just before I go to the office or to the church to preach, Lois checks me over and makes a few adjustments. If I'm looking good when I arrive, it's because she helped me look good.

Now, I know what some women are thinking at this point. "But what about me? I don't always want to be in the background." The woman in our text wasn't an invisible person. Verse 28 says her children and her husband blessed her and praised her.

Husband, teach your children to praise their mother; teach them to say, "Thank you, Mom, that I'm warm on cold days. Thank you for the food you prepare. Thank you for everything you do." How do children learn that? By hearing Dad praise his wife.

My brother, if you have a wife like this, you should "talk her up" all day long: "Thank you. Can't live without you. Need you. Enjoy you. Don't want to go to sleep without looking at you one more time. You're the first person I want to see in the morning." Go public with this woman!—TONY

PRAY ABOUT IT

Nothing will draw a couple closer together any better or faster than serving the Lord together.

BEING YOUR WIFE'S SATISFIER

He has brought me to his banquet hall, and his banner over me is love.

—SONG OF SOLOMON 2:4

A husband who wants to love his wife according to God's kingdom agenda must be his wife's satisfier. When Solomon and his Shulammite bride celebrated the joy of each other's love, his bride's speeches show that she felt satisfied and protected—and she was talking about more than just their sexual relationship. The apostle Paul gave us the New Testament version of this idea when he said that husbands need "to love their own wives as their own bodies" (Eph. 5:28).

What we need today is a group of Christian men who know how to satisfy their wives. Now, when most men hear the word *satisfy,* they think *sex*. And some men will brag about how many women they can satisfy. But any man who talks that way doesn't know what he's talking about. A real man is one who can commit himself to his wife and love her with a steady commitment so that after fifteen, twenty, thirty, or fifty years, his wife can still say, "I'm satisfied."

Paul explained the way to do this is to love your wife the way you love your own body. So just as a man works out to make his body look good and does things to satisfy his needs, he is to help his wife look good externally and feel fulfilled and satisfied.

There are too many dissatisfied wives out there today because there are too many unsatisfying husbands. Changing this situation starts with you, my fellow husband. It has nothing to do with what your wife does in return. We're talking about biblical love here, which loves—period.

A man who is determined to satisfy his wife won't stop even if his efforts are not met with equal love. The first thing on a husband's kingdom agenda is to love his wife by being her savior, sanctifier, and satisfier.—TONY

TALK ABOUT IT

Ask your wife how you're doing as a satisfier. Encourage her to be specific in pinpointing areas where you're doing well as well as areas where you can improve.

HONORING YOUR HUSBAND

Sarah obeyed Abraham, calling him lord, and you have become her children if you do what is right without being frightened by any fear.

—I PETER 3:6

Today's verse often upsets women because they feel it puts them in a demeaning position. But when you read the verse in its context, it becomes obvious that God's Word is not assigning godly women a demeaning role at all.

If you know Sarah's story in the book of Genesis, you realize that she was not a passive, "wallflower" saint. She was a woman of strength and dignity. Yet Sarah understood that God had assigned Abraham the role of leadership in their family, and she honored Abraham for that.

Sarah honored him even though he had weaknesses. In fact, Abraham was far from perfect. He had made a number of mistakes. He had been a wimp when he needed to be strong before King Abimelech.

Despite Abraham's shortcomings, the Bible says Sarah honored his headship in the family. The term *lord* was a word of respect for the husband, not a term of humiliation for the wife.

And here is the best part. When Sarah obeyed God by honoring Abraham, she received a miracle. God gave her the desires of her heart (see Ps. 37:4), and when she was ninety years old and childless, she had a baby.

What miracle are you asking God for in your marriage or family? Perhaps God wants you to begin honoring your husband's position before He will give you that miracle.

Some wives may say, "But if I honor my husband in this way, he will take advantage of me." Go back to the last part of the verse above. If you do what is right, you need not be frightened by any fear.—LOIS

THINK ABOUT IT
When you honor your husband, that frees God up to work with him.

THE REAL ENEMY

The great dragon was thrown down, the serpent of old who is called the devil and Satan . . . and his angels were thrown down with him.

—REVELATION 12:9

❧

*I*f you have any doubt about who our spiritual enemy is, this verse identifies him and his demons quite clearly. Satan is the real foe, so we make a grand mistake if we think other people are our enemies.

People can be bad, no doubt. But they are merely conduits for this greater battle. Satan has been very successful in getting us to fight people rather than the source that is causing them to be the way they are.

Everything we see in the visible, physical realm is either caused, influenced, or provoked by something in the invisible, spiritual realm. Your five senses are not the limit of reality. This means that if you are going to wage successful spiritual battle, you need a "sixth sense"—a keen awareness of the spiritual realm. This awareness begins with your world-view.

Your world-view is simply the lens through which you perceive reality. It has to do with the presuppositions that determine what you believe and the way you look at life.

There are really only two world-views. One is called the natural, materialistic, or scientific world-view. It says that mankind, by his own reasoning, can figure out how the world works. This view leads quite naturally to agnosticism and atheism because it believes you don't need God as long as you have test tubes, microscopes, and telescopes.

The second world-view is the spiritual world-view, which says there is a realm outside of the physical. This view is very popular today, but unfortunately it is often not a biblically based, theistic view that believes in the one true God. Instead, too often it involves horoscopes, palm readers, and all sorts of New Age teaching. This is not the world-view of the Bible.

We need to keep our heads and our hearts in the Word, asking the Holy Spirit to reveal the truth to us. Then we'll be ready for spiritual battle.

THINK ABOUT IT
Are you and your mate using the Word to evaluate the world-views that confront you?

EVERY PART OF US BELONGS TO CHRIST

Now you are Christ's body, and individually members of it.
—I CORINTHIANS 12:27

◆━━◆

Our bodies and our spirits are closely linked, and both belong to the Lord. Paul wrote in 1 Corinthians 6:15, "Do you not know that your bodies are members of Christ?" In verse 14, Paul had just referred to God's resurrection power, which someday will "raise us up" from the dead. He wasn't talking about our spirits, which never die, but our bodies. So Paul was saying that since our bodies have significance beyond the grave, what we do with our bodies now also has significance beyond the grave.

If we really believe that God's power is so great that He will transform our dead bodies someday, then we must also believe that His power is great enough to help us control our bodies today. Anyone who does not believe that does not understand the resurrection power of Jesus Christ.

What this means is that we do not have to be owned by our passions. And it means that, for the Christian, sex is a spiritual issue.

Maybe you think this discussion doesn't apply to you since you are already married and have a legitimate outlet for the expression of your sexual desires. But it doesn't mean that you are beyond the problem of sexual temptation or the sin of fantasies and all the other stuff. And Paul's message tells you God can help you deal with those problems.

You have probably deduced by now that when it comes to Christian marriage, the passion of our hearts is that you will protect and defend and thoroughly enjoy your marriage. But we also want you to understand that the secret to a fulfilling marriage goes far beyond just the quality of a couple's sexual performance.

We husbands and wives must understand that our bodies belong not only to each other (1 Cor. 7:4) but to the Lord. Our spirits are His too. We are whole beings, which means we can't separate our behavior into neat categories.

PRAY ABOUT IT
Ask God to help you treat your sexual relationship as a holy thing, which it is!

AN UNBEATABLE FORMULA FOR PEACE

Let the peace of Christ rule in your hearts.

—COLOSSIANS 3:15

---

hat has to happen in your life for the peace of Christ to rule in your heart? The answer is very simple: The peace of Christ will rule in your heart only when you are in God's will.

How do you know when you have found the will of God? Many aspects of His will are clearly revealed in His Word. For example, "This is the will of God, your sanctification; that is, that you abstain from sexual immorality" (1 Thess. 4:3). There is no confusion about God's will in this area!

There are many verses in the Bible that spell out God's will. But in the areas where His will is not specifically stated, there are steps we can take to find His will and experience His peace. The first step is found in Colossians 3:16: "Let the word of Christ richly dwell within you." God's Word is the greatest source for discovering His will and finding the peace He promised.

A second step is to make sure that you are acting in the name of Jesus, for His glory and honor (see Col. 3:17). When Jesus is the motivation for what you do, you won't get too far off the path.

A third means of finding God's peace is prayer. The Bible tells us not to worry about anything but to pray about everything. Then it promises, "The peace of God, which surpasses all comprehension, shall guard your hearts and your minds in Christ Jesus" (Phil. 4–7).

Here's a fourth step to finding God's will and His peace: "Humble yourselves, therefore, under the mighty hand of God, that He may exalt you at the proper time" (1 Pet. 5:6).

It's an unbeatable formula. When you are exalting Christ, praying about all things, and letting the Word and the name of Christ be your guide, His peace will be yours.

PRAY ABOUT IT
Why not commit your greatest need to the Lord in prayer today? It could be your first step toward finding God's peace.

SATISFYING MARITAL INTIMACY (DAY 1)

As a loving hind and a graceful doe, let her breasts satisfy you at all times; be exhila-rated always with her love.

—PROVERBS 5:190

❦

Some people think the apostle Paul was a self-righteous single person who looked down on those who could not control their passions. Not so. It's possible that Paul was married at one time, because he had been a member of the Sanhedrin, the Jewish ruling council, whose members were required to be married. Whether Paul was an exception to the rule or a widower, we don't know. We do know that he spoke very forthrightly about the subject of marital intimacy.

In 1 Corinthians 7:3, a passage we have encountered before in these devotional studies, Paul wrote, "Let the husband fulfill his duty to his wife, and likewise also the wife to her husband." This word *duty* can cause great consternation. What did Paul mean? Is marital intimacy supposed to be a *job?*

We believe Paul was talking about the distinction between sexual intimacy between Christian couples and sexual intimacy between non-Christian couples. Although we can't make a hard-and-fast rule in every case, I think that, in general, intimacy between non-Christians is primarily self-generated, by individuals think-ing, "This is what I want." But intimacy between two Christians is designed to be *other*-generated by individuals believing, "This is what my mate needs." It doesn't happen this way in every case, of course, but it's the ideal. By the way, the order of Paul's wording is very important. It's the husband's responsibility to take the lead, and his wife's calling to respond.

Many men have said to me, "I would love to fulfill my duty to my wife, but she won't let me." That could be because you are offering to fulfill a need she does not have. One challenge in building true physical intimacy is understanding what the other person needs. What a woman needs starts in the morning, not at night. It starts in the kitchen and not in the bedroom. It begins with her emotions and not with her body. We husbands need to relearn that constantly.—TONY

PRAY ABOUT IT
When some husbands say they want to meet their wives' needs, they are talking about something far different than what their wives understand by that phrase. Is that true in your marriage?

SATISFYING MARITAL INTIMACY (DAY 2)

Husbands, love your wives, just as Christ also loved the church and gave Himself up for her.

—EPHESIANS 5:25

T he husband who is serious about meeting his wife's needs will imitate the self-sacrificing love of Christ. In fact, we husbands are commanded to do so. Now, most of us husbands will not be called on to give our lives for our wives. But you would think some husbands were being crucified by the way they react when told they need to be more sensitive to their wives—to talk with them more, compliment them more, date them regularly, and show them care and affection.

Listen, my fellow husband. If the only time your wife has your undivided attention is at 10:00 P.M. when you want to be intimate, you are not fulfilling your duty to your mate. If the only time you are going to compliment, recognize, and value her is at 10:00 P.M., when you have not met her emotional needs that began at 10:00 A.M., you are not fulfilling your duty to your mate.

Most of our wives were attracted to us, at least in part, because of what we did during the dating period, when one thing we were able to do was to "rap," showering them with compliments and being smooth with our words. (I must admit that I was among the best at this!) Another thing a lot of dating men are good at is making women feel special, planning little surprises, showing courtesies such as opening the car door and softly closing it behind her. Now, some wives are lucky to get in before hubby drives off.

Brother, the attraction that made your wife want to marry you was not your physical attributes. It was the fact that you met a need in her. Are you still meeting the needs she feels?—TONY

THINK ABOUT IT

When a wife's needs are being met in a marriage, physical intimacy is usually not a problem.

SATISFYING MARITAL INTIMACY (DAY 3)

No one ever hated his own flesh, but nourishes and cherishes it.

—EPHESIANS 5:29

❧

Wives tell us they need affection and a sense of security, communication and a sense of being cared for and esteemed. When these needs are not met, it's no mystery that a wife's passion for sex dies.

Not so with men. Men don't have to have all of that relationship stuff. You can make a man mad at 10:00 P.M., and at 10:05 he's fine. You make a woman mad at 10:00 A.M., and if that mess is not fixed, she may not be fine at 10:00 P.M. a month from now!

We men have a long way to go in learning the art of intimacy with our wives. We need to learn that for a woman, intimacy involves the whole person and the whole house. It involves the compliment you make about the meal, how you come in the door from work, and how you treat her when she comes home from work, if that's the case.

Many couples who tell me they have a physical problem really have an intimacy problem, a relational blockage. Because of this, they cannot get the physical part of their marriage on track. In fact, I would say that married couples who have a good relationship connection but know little about sexual intimacy can have better intimacy than a couple who knows all about the technical aspects of sex but has a poor relationship.

Husband, to nourish and cherish your wife means your duty is to her, not to yourself. When some men say, "I want to meet her needs," what they really mean is, "I want her to meet my needs." The issue for a husband is his wife's needs. Until he is willing to take the time and make the investment to understand his wife and her needs, he will never be able to meet them.—TONY

THINK ABOUT IT

A husband who says he can't figure out what his wife wants can start by thinking about the ways he takes care of his own flesh. His wife would enjoy that same care.

SATISFYING MARITAL INTIMACY (DAY 4)

Eat, friends; drink and imbibe deeply, O lovers.

—SONG OF SOLOMON 5:1

I've had a lot to say to husbands over the past three days, but now let's turn things around and say that meeting needs and nourishing intimacy in marriage is a two-way street.

If a husband is meeting his wife's needs, her duty is to reciprocate, to respond. She does this by coming under her husband's authority, or control. This is what the word *authority* means in 1 Corinthians 7:3–4, where Paul describes the duties of wives and husbands in their physical relationship.

The wife relinquishes control of her body to the touch, the care, the caress, and the love of her husband. Then as the husband responds to his wife's response, he also relinquishes control of his body. When these two people are intimate, there is a giving of themselves, a vulnerability, a yielding of control. Sex should be the ultimate act of selfless giving rather than a selfish act done to fulfill one's own needs.

The Song of Solomon contains the Bible's most unblushing description of sexual intimacy in marriage. Chapter 4 describes the buildup to intimacy in great detail, and the beauty of it is that you see the self-giving between Solomon and his wife, the mutual yielding of their bodies.

Read that chapter together and notice that the intimacy begins with Solomon's compliments, words of admiration, and appreciation for his bride, not with the physical act of sex. But when the moment of intimacy occurs, God Himself issues the invitation of today's verse, an invitation to the lovers to enjoy one another.

Satisfying marital intimacy is a matter of meeting each other's needs and of yielding control of your body to your mate. Rather than stifling freedom and spontaneity, such a commitment allows for the full expression of each one's person.—TONY

TALK ABOUT IT

Can each of you honestly say to the other, "I relinquish control over my body because you are fulfilling your duty to meet my needs"? I hope so!

RETURNING TO YOUR FIRST LOVE (DAY 1)

I remember concerning you the devotion of your youth.

—JEREMIAH 2:2

〜⋘⋙〜

*J*udging by the music our secular culture keeps churning out, you would have to conclude that we are in a love crisis—and have been for quite some time. This worldly crisis is twofold: First, no one seems to know how to keep love alive, how to keep the flame lit. Second, everyone seems to be stepping out on his or her true love.

Well, the church has a love crisis too. We have a hard time keeping our first love for Jesus Christ in its rightful place. Unfortunately, this is not a new problem. The risen Jesus Himself described it to a group of first-century Christians in the church at Ephesus (see Rev. 2:4).

Because we are imperfect people in an imperfect world, it's easy for us to get our priorities messed up. And the place where we often mess up is in getting our eyes and hearts off of Christ, our first love, and on to something else.

This week, we are going to talk about what it means to leave our first love and how we can recapture it. Along the way, we'll discover that many of the principles for recapturing our first love for Christ will also help in rekindling the flame in our marriages.

As soon as you realize you've made a wrong turn and headed off in the wrong direction, you want to return to the right road. But before you can get back to where you're supposed to be, you have to see where you are, figure out how you messed up to get where you are, and retrace your steps. Tomorrow we'll discuss how to identify and deal with the attitudes and actions that can get us off the track.

PRAY ABOUT IT

All of us need our love rekindled from time to time. If your heart feels cold, ask God to ignite it this week!

RETURNING TO YOUR FIRST LOVE (DAY 2)

I, brethren, could not speak to you as to spiritual men, but as to men of flesh, as to babes in Christ.

—I CORINTHIANS 3:1

We are talking this week about the biblical mandate Jesus Christ has given us to keep our love for Him in first place—and to return it there, if necessary. This means that anything that comes between us and our love for the Savior is a "love stealer."

One of the greatest love stealers is what the New Testament calls *carnality.* Simply stated, carnality is that spiritual state where a born-again Christian knowingly and persistently lives to please and serve himself or herself rather than Christ (1 Cor. 3:1–4).

Whether it's in our individual lives, our family life, our church life, or our life in society, a lot of what is wrong with us is attributable to our own carnality. The problem is that too many of God's children are trying to step out with Christ and with the world at the same time. The result is a situation that leads to unanswered prayer, emotional and physical weakness, loss of peace, loss of joy, lack of stability, and all manner of other ills.

The solution for this problem—the way to return completely to our first love—is spelled out in Revelation 2:5, "*Remember* therefore from where you have fallen, and *repent* and *do* [repeat] the deeds you did at first" (italics added).

We'll explore these three steps in detail as the week goes on. They create a powerful formula, not only for personal spiritual renewal, but for revival in your marriage and your family and in the church at large. As a pastor I'm convinced that if enough of us as individual believers would take Jesus' exhortation seriously, we'd have revival!—TONY

THINK ABOUT IT
Our mates would not—and should not—tolerate our divided loyalty in marriage. How much more does Jesus deserve our undivided love and commitment?

RETURNING TO YOUR FIRST LOVE (DAY 3)

I love Thee, O LORD, my strength.

—PSALM 18:1

When Jesus told the church at Ephesus to "remember therefore from where you have fallen" (see Rev. 2:5), it's clear that He wanted those early Christians to remember the days when their love for Him had been in first place, where it was supposed to be.

Since there is no question that Jesus Himself is to be the object of our first love, we need to remind ourselves today who Jesus really is. Jesus Christ stands unique among all men in all ages. He claims unique authority over the lives of all those who call themselves children of God. Jesus Christ alone is Lord, above and beyond any other authority or name that can be named.

So when Jesus Christ demands our first love, our undivided loyalty, and our total commitment, He is demanding nothing more than what is His right and prerogative. So the first step in restoring the primacy of our love for Him is to *remember* what that first love was like.

Marriage offers a good analogy of this. When two people get married, at first they are starry-eyed, beside themselves with joy and enthusiasm for their mate. The whole world looks wonderful to them, and they expect their lives together to be nothing but bliss.

At some point, however, they wake up to the rather disturbing reality that being married is not necessarily all they had thought it would be. They discover there's a little bit more to it than they had anticipated. They're still committed, but now the thrill is gone.

Many of us have found this to be true in our Christian lives. We got saved and thought it all was going to be bliss, just victory after victory and showers of blessings. But when the hard times came, our love began to cool.

If that's your condition today, don't let your love stay cold.

PRAY ABOUT IT
Pray that God will light a new flame of love in your heart . . . beginning today.

RETURNING TO YOUR FIRST LOVE (DAY 4)

Those whom I love, I reprove and discipline; be zealous therefore, and repent.

—REVELATION 3:19

*T*here's a great deal of joy in being a Christian; even better, there's eternal bliss awaiting us in heaven. But the Christian life here on earth is not a tiptoe through the tulips. Salvation fixed a lot of our problems, but it also raised a whole new set of issues and left some of the old ones around for us to deal with too.

Just as two people in a marriage can have their fellowship interrupted, their intimacy negated, and their closeness canceled because of problems, so we as Christians can have our fellowship, our intimacy, our closeness with God interrupted by sin. That interruption doesn't cancel the relationship. But sin has come between God and us, and the intimacy is lost. The only cure is repentance.

God calls on people who are in relationship with Him to change their minds about sin. That's the basic meaning of the word *repent*. It means changing your way of thinking from the previous way to the proper way. Repentance is crucial if we are going to restore harmony where there is chaos, if we are going to return to our first love for Christ.

It's possible to be saved but not be in fellowship with the Savior. Repentance is the second step we must take to restore our fellowship with Christ and put a new bloom on our love for Him.—TONY

PRAY ABOUT IT

When sin comes between you and Jesus Christ so that your intimacy with Him is lost, the only cure is repentance. Talk to Him about it today.

RETURNING TO YOUR FIRST LOVE (DAY 5)

Set your mind on the things above, not on the things that are on earth.

—COLOSSIANS 3:2

Third part of Jesus' command in Revelation 2:4–5, which tells us to return to our first love for Him, is what I have termed *repeat*. After *remembering* and *repenting*, we need to repeat again "the deeds [we] did at first."

Today I want to focus on what I think is the starting point for this repeating: your mind.

There is nothing more important to us than our minds, because as Christians we are supposed to think with the mind of Christ—that is, with brand-new, spiritually informed minds. A Christian mind is so ordered by the Word and will of God that the dictates of heaven completely penetrate it, and the mind instructs the feet. The result is a walk on earth that reflects the new mind received from heaven.

You may have heard the adage that someone is "so heavenly minded he's no earthly good." That person has missed the point, because the purpose of our being heavenly minded is so that we can be of *plenty* earthly good! We are to think with a divinely directed mind so that the world can see the kingdom agenda lived out by God's people.

When you make the things of Christ your focus, they become the stimuli through which the Holy Spirit informs you of God's will.

If we are going to think with Christ-centered minds, that condition must become a way of life for us every day. We cannot be sacred on Sunday and secular on Monday. We are to be sacred all day every day, because we are all ministers under God.—TONY

TALK ABOUT IT

Read the definition of a Christian mind again and talk together about how well your thinking reflects the mind of Christ in your marriage and family.

RETURNING TO YOUR FIRST LOVE (DAY 6)

You were formerly darkness, but now you are light in the Lord; walk as children of light.

—EPHESIANS 5:8

❧

*Y*esterday we talked about thinking with Christ-centered minds in response to the third part of Jesus' command that we regain our first love for Him. This third part of the command tells us to *repeat,* to do again, the works we did for Christ when our love for Him was red hot. Today we continue our focus on how we can repeat our "first love" fervency.

The New Testament calls our daily Christian life our "walk." To return to our first love for Christ, we must make sure that what is in our new minds gets transferred to our earthly feet. Ephesians 4:17–31 is a very insightful passage describing what it means to translate the thinking of our new minds into our everyday "walk." We encourage you to read these great verses sometime this weekend.

Paul began this passage by writing, "This I say therefore, and affirm together with the Lord, that you walk no longer just as the Gentiles also walk, in the futility of their mind." Notice how Paul links the mind with a person's walk—in other words, his course of living, his lifestyle, his orientation.

When you walk, you put one foot in front of the other in order to make progress toward a particular destination or goal. It's a process. You don't get where you're going in one giant step, but you walk step by step toward your goal. Paul used the idea of walking to explain the step-by-step process of moving from where we are to where we ought to be going. The Christian life is not an airplane ride; it's a walk. We don't "jet" to spiritual maturity.

When a baby gets his mind and his feet functioning together, he starts walking. That's the same challenge we face as believers in returning to our first love for Jesus Christ. We need to get our minds and our spiritual feet working together!

PRAY ABOUT IT
The Christian life is not a free ride; it's a costly but very rewarding walk.

AVOIDING THE EXTREMES

If Thy presence does not go with us, do not lead us up from here.

—EXODUS 33:15

❧❧❧❧❧

*A*s Christians trying to get the right mix in our efforts to strengthen our marriages, families, and communities, we must walk a fine line between two extremes. One extreme is the belief that God is sovereign and does whatever He pleases, so why should we try to do anything? When He wants to move in marriages, families, and communities, it will just happen. The other extreme says that God has left some things up to His people, so if we don't do something we can't expect Him to act by Himself.

This is the old argument about divine sovereignty and human responsibility. Where does one end and the other begin?

The situation in Exodus 33 helps us understand. Verse 15 is part of Moses' prayer concerning Israel's entrance into Canaan. He didn't want the nation to move until he had the assurance that God would move with them. God gave Moses that promise (see v. 14), but the people still had to get up and go.

When it comes to working for change in any area of life, Nehemiah is a great model. His story shows that God definitely arranged things so Nehemiah would have some real "clout" when he went back to rebuild Jerusalem (see Neh. 1–2).

Nehemiah needed timber for his rebuilding plans, but he couldn't have gotten access to the king's forest by his own scheming alone. Instead, God decided Nehemiah needed some of *His* royal timber, so He simply moved Artaxerxes to draw up the necessary papers. That wood belonged to God, not to the king of Persia. But Nehemiah still had to ask.

Nehemiah had a plan, but it depended on God's sovereign power. Nehemiah's responsibility was to be ready when God, in His sovereignty, said it was time to move.

THINK ABOUT IT

A good formula for balancing our responsibility with God's sovereignty is the old adage that says, "Work as if everything depended on you, and pray as if everything depended on God."

LOOKING THROUGH GOD-COLORED GLASSES

If God so arrays the grass of the field, which is alive today and tomorrow is thrown into the furnace, will He not much more do so for you, O men of little faith?

—MATTHEW 6:30

*J*esus says if we don't trust God for our daily needs we possess "little faith." So how do you know if you have little faith? One way you can know is by the questions you are asking. In verse 31, Jesus says that "little faith" people wring their hands in worry and ask, "What shall we eat?" "What shall we drink?" "With what shall we clothe ourselves?"

Today the questions may take another form: "How am I going to make the house payment next month?" "How in the world are we going to make it if I get laid off?" "Where is the money for these hospital bills going to come from?"

The questions may be different, but the effect on our lives is the same. Spending all of our time fretting about our needs takes us out of the realm of faith. We're not recommending a "Pollyanna" approach in which you simply view life through rose-colored glasses. But it *is* possible for you and your mate to live in peace today even if things are rough right now.

How? By replacing our rose-colored glasses with *God*-colored glasses. Does this mean we just sit back, fold our hands, and let God do everything? Hardly! In Matthew 6:33 Jesus tells us to actively seek the kingdom of God and His righteousness. That word *seek* means we're to strain, to exert real effort.

We have work to do, all right! But instead of straining to fulfill our own needs and desires like the unbelievers do (see v. 32), we are to work hard for God.

TALK ABOUT IT
Recall a time when God met your needs in a special way. Relive the moment together, thank God for it again, and tell the kids the story.

A UNIQUE PERSON

The fellowship of the Holy Spirit, be with you all.

—2 CORINTHIANS 13:14

～～～～～

There is a lot wrapped up in the name *Holy Spirit*. The Spirit is *holy* because He is God, totally separate from everything that is unlike God. This title also focuses attention on His primary work in the life of believers: to progressively conform us to the image of Christ, the process we call sanctification (1 Pet. 3:13–16).

The Holy Spirit is *spirit* because He is non-material. Both the Hebrew and Greek words for *spirit* mean "wind, breath." The Holy Spirit is the very breath, or wind, of God. And like the wind, He wields great power, even though He is invisible. So you can't relate to Him simply by trying to use your five senses.

It is difficult trying to explain an invisible reality because it's like trying to explain electricity. You know electricity is there. You know it is powerful. But trying to explain it can be tough. So it is with the Holy Spirit. But Jesus made it clear that the Holy Spirit is knowable. We who know Christ can know the Holy Spirit.

Why doesn't the world know the Holy Spirit (John 14:17)? For the same reason you cannot pick up radio stations if you don't have a radio. Radio waves are going through the air all the time, but you need a receiver to pick up the signal.

The world does not have a spiritual receiver. But if you know Jesus Christ, He has implanted within you a receiver to pick up heaven's signals so you can tune in to the very voice of God. So in the midst of discouragement, fear, loneliness, insecurity, or even sin, we can tune in to the Holy Spirit.

The Holy Spirit is part of our lives because He is a Person who lives within us.

THINK ABOUT IT

If the Holy Spirit lives within each partner in your marriage and within each member of your family, His love and power and holiness ought to be evident in your home life.

PUT YOUR MASK ON FIRST

Like newborn babes, long for the pure milk of the word, that by it you may grow in respect to salvation.

—I PETER 2:2

When you are in an airplane preparing for takeoff, the flight attendant instructs you on how to use the plane's oxygen system in case of emergency. You're told to put on your own mask first before you try to help a small child or anyone else needing assistance. The reason is obvious. You won't be much good to your child when you're gasping for air yourself.

The same principle is true in our spiritual lives. We cannot minister to others when our own souls are gasping for air because we have neglected our personal time in the Word and in prayer. The great nineteenth-century Christian statesman George Muller once said concerning his personal devotions:

> The first thing to be concerned about was not how much I might serve the Lord, or how I might glorify the Lord, but how I might get my soul into a happy state, and how my inner man might be nourished. The first thing I did after having asked in a few words the Lord's blessing upon his precious Word was to begin to meditate upon the Word of God, searching into every verse to get blessing out of it: not for the sake of the public ministry of the Word, not for the sake of preaching on what I had meditated upon, but for the sake of obtaining food for my own soul.

Again and again, God clearly teaches the necessity for personal, consistent exposure to the Scriptures. Our verse for today exhorts us to hunger for the Scriptures the way a baby craves milk in order to grow.

Someone has said that you cannot give out what you have not first taken in. Take time to nourish your own soul in God's precious Word, and you'll have something to give to others.

PRAY ABOUT IT

Trying to make it without time in God's Word is like trying to exercise while holding your breath!

THE IMPORTANCE OF THE HEAVENLY PLACES

There was war in heaven, Michael and his angels waging war with the dragon.

—REVELATION 12:7

*I*n order to understand the concept of spiritual warfare, we have to address it through the lens of the spirit with the help of the Holy Spirit. The apostle Paul tells us this great, cosmic battle between the forces of God and the forces of the devil is being fought "in the heavenly places" (Eph. 6:12). And we learn from today's verse that this battle erupted in heaven as the angel formerly known as Lucifer tried to unseat God from His throne.

In the Bible, the word *heaven* describes three levels of existence. The first heaven is the atmosphere that surrounds the earth, the environment in which we live. The second heaven is what we commonly refer to as outer space, the stellar heavens where the stars and planets exist. This is also a realm in which angels operate, because in the Bible angels are called stars. The third heaven is the throne room of God, the place we normally think of when we hear the word *heaven*. This is the heaven Paul was referring to in 2 Corinthians 12:2.

The third heaven, or "the heavenly places," is the heaven most frequently mentioned in the Bible. It is the primary location of spiritual warfare—the control center of the universe.

Understanding how to tap into the heavenly places is crucial to waging victorious spiritual warfare. If you are engaged in a spiritual battle and need help to win, the help you need is with God the Father, who is in the heavenly places (see Eph. 1:20). But if you don't know how to get to heavenly places, you won't know how to get to the heavenly help you need to win the battle in earthly places.

Once you understand that our warfare is in the heavenly sphere, you can begin changing what happens on earth.

PRAY ABOUT IT

If it has been awhile since you checked the condition of your spiritual armor (see Eph. 6:13–17), do an inspection today.

TRANSFORMING THE CULTURE

You are the light of the world. A city set on a hill cannot be hidden.

—MATTHEW 5:14

* * *

Most Christians agree that our culture is going in the wrong direction, but we disagree over what to do about it. There's a great model for community transformation in the Book of Nehemiah. The story describes a community gone bad, a community plagued by devastation, injustice, family disintegration, and everything from robbery to bad interest rates to employment problems, as well as severe problems in marital and other relationships.

Sounds a lot like America today, doesn't it? Our communities need to be rebuilt—but they need rebuilding from the inside out. That means just electing the right people or passing the right laws won't do the job. The church must lead the way in transforming culture.

The Book of Nehemiah tells us about a remarkable man who knew God and knew what his community needed, and was able to bring them together. Very few people are nation builders; even fewer are nation *re*builders. But Nehemiah was just that. He was an Israelite living as part of an exile community many years after Israel was carried off to captivity in Babylon. He was a trusted adviser to Artaxerxes, the king of Persia (see Neh. 1:11).

One day some relatives came to Nehemiah to tell him about the shameful condition of Jerusalem. When Nehemiah learned about the degradation of his homeland, the first thing he did was pray. The prayer recorded in Nehemiah 1 shows that Nehemiah definitely knew how to pray. He prayed on behalf of himself and his nation, asking God to forgive their sins and to give him an opportunity to turn things around. Nehemiah also knew that God could work through the Persian government, because he asked God to give him favor before King Artaxerxes in his plan to rebuild Jerusalem.

You may not be in a strategic position in the world's eyes, but if you know God, you can play a significant role in transforming your world.

PRAY ABOUT IT

The prayer of Nehemiah 1:4–11 is a great model for us to pray on behalf of ourselves, our spouses, our families, and our nation.

WHAT'S YOUR PASSION?

Those who want to get rich fall into temptation and a snare and many foolish and harmful desires which plunge men into ruin and destruction.

—I TIMOTHY 6:9

*D*o you have a passion to get rich? Be careful, because that desire has a snare in it. You know how a snare works. The hunter covers it with brush and uses bait to lure the animal. Just when the animal thinks he has a meal, the trap has him.

That's how money works. You think you have it, but in reality it has you. How do you know if money has you? Ask yourself what is number one in your life, God or gold?

The problem is that the love of money doesn't make you more Christlike. Instead, "the love of money is a root of all sorts of evil" (1 Tim. 6:10). Don't misread that. Money itself is neutral. The problem is in the heart, not in the paper.

You know you love money if your passion for it outweighs your passion for God. You know you love money when you have to choose between money and God, and money wins. You know you love money when your career keeps you off your knees, out of the Word, and out of fellowship with the saints.

This is why God required His people to give Him a tenth of their income as a minimum and why He required it to come out first. He wants to help us learn not to love money but to love Him. Stewardship is His way of making us think of Him first.

Go to God and say, "You're going to be number one with me. I'm going to be Your steward and give You my best. And I'm going to trust You to fulfill Your Word and take responsibility for my needs."

THINK ABOUT IT

Once you understand that you can't shortchange God and come out OK, and once you see that you can't outgive God when you put all you have in His hands . . . then putting Him first will be no problem for you.

KEEP THE FIRE IN THE FIREPLACE

If therefore the Son shall make you free, you shall be free indeed.

—JOHN 8:36

❧

*Y*ou have probably heard preachers say that true freedom is never doing what you want to do but what you ought to do. That's especially true when it comes to sex. I hope the two of you have discovered the wonderful freedom you have to express yourselves within the healthy, God-given boundaries of your marriage.

Let me illustrate this principle with one of my favorite analogies about freedom: In the game of football, the sidelines are designed to contain the game and make it interesting, not ruin it. Suppose the halfback grabs the football and decides, "I don't feel like being tackled today. I am not into sidelines. I think I'll run up into the stands, out into the concession area, into the parking lot, come around to the other side, run back through the concession area, down the bleachers, back onto the field, and across the other team's goal line."

That's not freedom. And it's certainly not a football game.

The football analogy breaks down a little bit when we apply it to sex, because it *is* possible to have sex outside the boundary God has set. But it is *not* possible outside of His rules to enjoy sex the way God designed it to be enjoyed. I say this to help you appreciate the wonderful, *freeing* boundary God has set for the expression of our sexuality. It's called marriage.

Sex is like a fire. Contained in the fireplace, a fire keeps everybody warm. Set the fire free, though, and the whole house burns down. Like a beautiful fire contained within a fireplace, the gift of sex contained within a marriage generates warmth and pleasure, not destruction.—TONY

THINK ABOUT IT

Only God could have designed a boundary that is more freeing and more enjoyable than having no boundaries at all!

WHAT DO THESE STONES MEAN?

These stones shall become a memorial to the sons of Israel forever.

—JOSHUA 4:7

I hope your home is filled with stacks of what I call "Joshua stones." You may recall the story of Israel's memorial stones described in Joshua 4. After the nation had miraculously crossed the Jordan River at Gilgal to enter the Promised Land, God commanded Joshua to send twelve men—one from each tribe—back into the river to gather one stone apiece.

Joshua did as he was commanded, and then he used the twelve stones to build a memorial to God's care and protection. The idea was that as future generations of children saw the stones and asked their parents, "What do these stones mean to you?" (Josh. 4:6), the parents could retell the story of God's faithfulness. Thus a godly heritage would be passed down from generation to generation.

We need "Joshua stones" in our lives too. When Tony and I established our own home, we had many occasions to see God answer prayer and provide for our needs. As the years passed, we learned to trust totally in God the same way we had seen our own parents trust Him. Tony and I have often recounted to our children the ways God has met our needs and answered our prayers when we were facing impossible situations. These times have helped build "stones of remembrance" in our children's hearts that give them something to hold on to when they face their own hard places.

Your children need to hear stories of God's deliverance and provision in your lives individually and as husband and wife. Did He make a way where there was no way? Tell your kids about it, and tell them more than once.

Our children are now old enough to see God's hand at work in their own lives, and they are telling Tony and me the stories of their own "Joshua stones."—LOIS

PRAY ABOUT IT

Relive one of your favorite "Joshua stones" remembrances with your family then thank God afresh for His deliverance.

ENJOY LIFE WITH YOUR WIFE

Enjoy life with the woman whom you love all the days of your fleeting life which He has given to you.

—ECCLESIASTES 9:9

I'm as guilty as anyone when it comes to being absorbed with my job. I know what it is to spend so much time at the church that I find Lois discouraged when I come home. She's disappointed because while I have ministered well at church I am too tired to minister well at home.

Lois didn't marry my ministry. There was no church, national ministry, radio broadcast, or conferences when we got married. It was just Lois and me. For a husband, making a priority commitment to his wife may mean making some hard decisions. But imagine what it would mean to a wife for her husband to tell her, "I'm committed to you. If I have to give up some things or back off at work, I'll do it."

Obeying God's Word in this area means that when a husband goes home from work, he goes home to his second job. Many men expect that when a wife comes home from work, she's coming home to her second job. She's supposed to get something on the table and clean and make sure everyone, including hubby, is taken care of. Then she's supposed to have enough energy to meet her husband's physical needs at night.

A wife and mother can't just come home and turn on the TV or pick up the newspaper and expect someone else to carry the load. She needs a husband whose attitude is, "We're in this together, so when I come home, I come home to work too." What kind of work? Whatever kind of help the wife needs at the time.

Sometimes a husband's "job" is as simple as calling his wife in the middle of the day to say, "I can't get you off my mind today." Husband, making your wife feel special and cared for will pay better benefits than any job!—TONY

THINK ABOUT IT

Your wife was given to you to be your partner, not your slave. God wants you to live in the intimacy of that partnership. When you've got that right, there is nothing on earth more satisfying.

HEAVENLY WARFARE, HEAVENLY RESOURCES

[God] raised us up with [Christ], and seated us with Him in the heavenly places, in Christ Jesus.

—EPHESIANS 2:6

⚜

*T*he Book of Ephesians is loaded with important principles for fighting the daily spiritual battle you and I face with our adversary the devil (see 1 Pet. 5:8). Paul told the Ephesians—and us—that our battle is against wicked spiritual forces "in the heavenly places" (Eph. 6:12), so we had better know what heavenly resources are available to us there.

Our greatest resource is Jesus Christ Himself, who is seated "at [God]'s right hand in the heavenly places" (Eph. 1:20). When you accepted Christ, you were transported to that same sphere. Even though your body is limited to earth, your spirit, which should be controlling your body, is operating in a wholly different realm—the heavenly places.

Our real existence is what happens in our spiritual lives, not what happens in our bodies. In our spirits we are already residents of heaven; someday we'll be residents of heaven in our bodies too.

Spiritual rulers and authorities also exist in the heavenly places, according to Ephesians 3:10; these are angels. Satan has a whole host of evil angels called demons he can use for spiritual attacks. So anything that hell can bring against you and your marriage is the result of satanic activity in the same realm in which God operates.

You and I are no match for the power and deceptiveness of Satan and his army. We need the power of God to neutralize Satan's attacks against us. We can be thankful that God has established His throne in heavenly places, because there's a war going on out there, pitting His kingdom against the kingdom of darkness. And there is no question that the kingdom of God and His King, Jesus Christ, are firmly in charge.—TONY

THINK ABOUT IT

Jesus' eternal victory is already assured. Our challenge is to tap into His victory rather than trying to battle Satan on our own.

FIRST THINGS FIRST

I and my father's house have sinned. We have acted very corruptly against Thee and have not kept [Thy] commandments.

—NEHEMIAH 1:6–7

❧

T he debate among believers about the best way to reclaim America and transform our culture is likely to heat up even more as we approach the twenty-first century. But before we start applying various fixes to the problems around us, we need to spend some time with Nehemiah. He was an Israelite living in an alien culture, serving a pagan king, and mourning the destruction and degradation back home in Jerusalem.

Nehemiah 1 teaches us an important principle about transforming culture. He understood that the deterioration of culture is first and foremost a spiritual issue that involves the family ("my father's house"). He knew that until the spiritual dynamics have been addressed in the home, the social, economic, or political realms in the wider culture cannot be properly addressed.

What this means is that we must start changing the things that need to be changed in *our* house as we wait for God to start changing things in the White House. True cultural transformation will begin when our homes are transformed to model the spiritual solutions our culture needs to see.

This transformation may be slow in coming, but it will happen if we are in God's will. According to Nehemiah 2:1, it took four months for Nehemiah to begin to see an answer to his prayer about the desperate condition of Jerusalem.

Waiting on God to move is a whole lot different than waiting on someone downtown to push papers or someone in Washington to cut red tape. But the transformation of society is primarily a spiritual issue that is rooted in the family, so until God shows up and transforms our marriages and our homes, our culture will not really change.

PRAY ABOUT IT

Seeing America transformed may seem like the impossible dream. But God issues this challenge: "[If] My people who are called by My name humble themselves and pray, . . . then I will . . . heal their land" (2 Chron. 7:14).

WHAT WILL THEY REMEMBER MOST?

Encourage one another day after day, as long as it is still called "Today."

—HEBREWS 3:13

❧❧❧

*O*ne of the most important things your children should know about you is that you are always ready to encourage them. This does not mean you have to ignore their sin or disobedience. The inevitable times of disobedience require discipline, and we need not be slow in applying the "rod" when it is called for (see Prov. 13:24).

But too much criticism, even when delivered in the right spirit, is still too much. We all know that the Scripture commands children to be obedient to their parents, "for this is well-pleasing to the Lord" (Col. 3:20). But with the very next stroke of his pen, the apostle Paul warned fathers not to exasperate their children, lest they "lose heart" (v. 21).

I think Paul specifically mentioned fathers here for two reasons. First, even though mothers are very much a part of a child's upbringing, in the Bible it is the father who is responsible to oversee the home. Second, as Tony often points out, in many homes it is the father who tends to be more critical and demanding of the children.

Of course, children need correction. But part of the skill of parenting is balancing criticism and correction with genuine encouragement and praise. My hope is that when our children put our criticism and encouragement side by side, they will see that what dominated our conversation was encouragement.

Instead of exasperating or embittering our children, let's equip them with encouragement every chance we get!—LOIS

PRAY ABOUT IT

Since it is still called "Today," try not to let this day end without your kids hearing an encouraging word.

GOING FOR THE CROWN OF JOY

Who is our hope or joy or crown of exultation? Is it not even you, in the presence of our Lord Jesus at His coming?

—I THESSALONIANS 2:19

The crown of joy is the reward to be given for faithful evangelism. Jesus Christ is going to give a higher level of joy to those people who spent their time and energy winning others to Him.

When was the last time you won somebody to Christ—or even tried? If evangelism has not been a part of your Christian walk, you can change that right away—and your own life will never be the same. For one thing, you'll experience a joy you didn't think was possible. If you are not regularly sharing your faith, you are not a joyous Christian, because God's greatest joy comes when people are won to Christ. Jesus said a party breaks out in heaven every time a sinner comes to Him.

For most of us, effective evangelism doesn't just happen. It has to be a planned part of our lives. A man we know told us he joined the local Rotary Club a few years ago for the express purpose of being around lost people so he could witness to them. This friend planned at least one witnessing occasion every week, so that at the end of a year he had witnessed to at least fifty-two people.

What decision have you made to place yourself next to non-Christians so you can win them to Christ? Don't just invite your friends to church so the pastor can evangelize them. Win them to Christ yourself, add them to your crown of rejoicing, and then bring them to church to be trained and discipled in the faith.

Someone may say, "I don't have the gift of evangelism." Too bad! We all have the spiritual responsibility to share our faith with lost people. And that gives us the incomparable privilege of seeing a lost person pass from death unto life.

THINK ABOUT IT

When you arrive in heaven, will there be anyone at the gates to welcome you because you were responsible for their being there?

A BATTLE FOR GLORY

Whether, then, you eat or drink or whatever you do, do all to the glory of God.

—I CORINTHIANS 10:31

❧

Revelation 12:7–12 describes an invisible warfare that is being waged in heaven between the forces of God and the forces of Satan. Someday that war will break out on earth as never before. Notice that although this conflict is angelic—the archangel Michael and the holy angels are fighting Satan and the angels who rebelled with him (see Rev. 12:7)—they are fighting over the earth. So the war in heaven directly affects what is happening here.

We are in the midst of an angelic conflict, a satanic rebellion, in which Satan is seeking to bring this whole world under his domain. That means when you were born again and became a member of the kingdom of God, you were born into a war.

We are surrounded by our spiritual enemy, but the battle is not for land or anything physical. This cosmic battle is for *glory.* The issue is, who is going to get the glory in this universe? Who is going to be worshiped? As Lucifer, Satan was the highest-ranking and most beautiful angel God ever created (see Ezek. 28:12–17). But Lucifer let his exalted status and his beauty go to his head, and he got tired of being number two in the universe. So he challenged God for the glory in creation.

God's response was, "My glory I will not give to another" (Isa. 48:11).

With that, the conflict called spiritual warfare was begun.

Praise God the outcome has never been in doubt, but the battle goes on every day in our personal, family, church, and community lives. That's why it is so crucial that as believers, we do *everything* for the glory of God (see also Col. 3:23).

PRAY ABOUT IT

If there is something you are doing for your own glory or simply because you think God expects it of you, you need to get that fixed!

THE KING AND THE KING OF KINGS

The king's heart is like channels of water in the hand of the LORD; He turns it wherever He wishes.

—PROVERBS 21:1

Nehemiah may not have had the Book of Proverbs to read like we do, but he knew the truth of today's verse. An Israelite exile serving Persian King Artaxerxes, Nehemiah was confronted with a situation we also face today: the deterioration of his community and the families that were a part of it.

Nehemiah was a man of God, so he took the problem to God first. God gave Nehemiah an opportunity to present his plea for Jerusalem to the king (see Neh. 2:1–5), and when he approached the king, Nehemiah did something very interesting. He did not mention Jerusalem by name. He talked about the home of his ancestors, but he said nothing about Jerusalem.

Artaxerxes had previously ordered a halt to the rebuilding of Jerusalem because he got word that if Jerusalem were rebuilt the people would stop paying taxes. Nehemiah knew this history, and he understood the politics involved. So he just talked about the plight of his people.

Now, the king was no dummy. He knew what city his cupbearer was talking about. What Artaxerxes didn't know was that his heart was in the Lord's hands. God knew exactly the right time for Nehemiah to bring up the subject to the king! He arranged things so perfectly that when Nehemiah let the king know what was on his heart, the king was open to the suggestion—despite his political problem with Jerusalem.

Notice also Nehemiah's prayer (v. 4). Nehemiah was *talking* to the king of Persia while he was *praying* to "the God of heaven." Nehemiah was dealing with two kings. One king was in control of the Persian Empire. But the other King was and still is controlling heaven and earth. Nehemiah was about to make a request that the earthly king do something about Jerusalem. But first he asked the King of kings to do something about the earthly king.

THINK ABOUT IT

Since God controls the affairs of a country, let's go right to the top with the problems in our homes!

298

A HAND IN YOUR FACE

Your adversary, the devil, prowls about like a roaring lion, seeking someone to devour.

—I PETER 5:8

C an you imagine basketball star Michael Jordan coming back to the bench and saying, "I could score a whole lot easier if I didn't have that other guy out there putting his hand up in my face all the time"?

Michael's coach could tell him, "Michael, if there were no opponent, it would be easy to score. We're paying you millions to score with that guy's hand in your face."

As Christians, we have an opponent in our face too. Whenever you decide to do something significant for God, Satan will show up, usually in the person of people like Sanballat and Tobiah (see Neh. 2:10ff).

Everything wasn't rosy for Nehemiah and his rebuilding project in Jerusalem. Two opponents, Sanballat and Tobiah, surfaced early in the project and planned to thwart, physically and spiritually, Nehemiah's every move to rebuild Jerusalem. Not everyone wants their culture transformed by the influence of godly people!

It upset Sanballat and Tobiah greatly to learn that Nehemiah had come to seek the welfare of Israel. They took it upon themselves to stop him. In the same way, Satan's job is to keep God's people from carrying out God's will.

By the way, this isn't just true for the big projects like rebuilding a community. Satan's job is to destroy you and your family because he knows that families populated by committed Christians are the foundation to transforming society.

Nehemiah wasn't afraid of his adversaries, but neither did he take them lightly. For the rest of his rebuilding project and well beyond it, he kept a close eye on those characters.

Following Nehemiah's example, we need not fear Satan and his demons. Instead we need to resist and overcome them in the power of Christ.

PRAY ABOUT IT

Once you understand what Satan is up to, you will make this declaration against your enemy: "Not today. Not me, not my marriage, not my family, not my community, because we are submitting ourselves to God."

THE MOTHER WHO SAVED A NATION

The woman conceived and bore a son; and when she saw that he was beautiful, she hid him for three months.

—EXODUS 2:2

❦

oday we're going to talk about a heroic woman who saved a nation. The nation was Israel, the baby was Moses, and the mother was Jochebed— although her name is not even mentioned in the Exodus 2 story of her son's birth and preservation. In fact, Jochebed's name doesn't appear until Exodus 6:20, when God is speaking to Moses from the burning bush on Mount Horeb and Moses' lineage is outlined.

You probably know the background of this story. Israel was in slavery in Egypt, and the people were multiplying. So Pharaoh gave orders to kill all the male Hebrew babies as soon as they were born. But the Hebrew midwives refused to do so, and they became heroines of faith themselves.

It was into this kind of oppressive and dangerous culture that Jochebed gave birth to Moses. Imagine the courage it took for a woman like Jochebed to hide her baby and evade this ungodly attempt to annihilate God's people. Jochebed exhibited the kind of faith that has always characterized godly mothers.

When the Bible says that Jochebed hid Moses when she saw that he was beautiful, it doesn't mean she just thought her baby was extra pretty. The word and the text indicate that when Jochebed looked at Moses, she saw a baby who had the hand of God on his life. God gave her insight that this little boy was very special.

If you are familiar with the noise a baby can make, you know how hard it must have been for Jochebed to keep Moses hidden for three months. But God helped Jochebed, and her faith was rewarded. And Moses grew up to become Israel's deliverer. Thus the fate of a nation can be traced back to a mother's lap.

PRAY ABOUT IT

Mother and Father, pray for your children every day. Stand by their beds at night and pray for them. Kneel down with them and lift them by name to God. They'll never forget it.

LIVING WITHOUT MASKS

Blessed are the pure in heart, for they shall see God.

—MATTHEW 5:8

In His Sermon on the Mount, Jesus Christ commended people who are without *hypocrisy*, people who don't wear a mask or play a role that hides their real personality or intentions.

God wants us to be real, to be men and women whose lives are transparent. These people don't have hidden agendas. What you see is what you get. What they say is what they mean. They are like Nathanael, the disciple of Jesus "in whom is no guile" (John 1:47).

None of us is pure in heart by nature. Spiritual purity is only possible when we put our faith in Christ. So we are not just talking about *nice* people here. The pure in heart are *transformed* people.

Being pure in heart doesn't make a person perfect, of course. But even when people like this make mistakes, they don't try to hide. They say, "I was wrong. It was my fault. I'm sorry."

Wouldn't it be great to be married to someone whose heart was pure—a person you could trust, someone whose heart was an open book before you? We hope you are married to a person like that. Better yet, we hope *you* are becoming a marriage partner like that! The pure in heart will not only see God themselves, but they will help other people see God because they're not blocking the view by their hypocrisy.

It's easy to look good at church, where everybody is dressed really nice and acting really nice. But the masks come off at home. That's one reason getting married and having children is so stressful for some people. It forces them to drop the pretense and come clean.

THINK ABOUT IT

If you want to see God at work in your life, allow Him to purify your heart from sin and pretense.

STAY CLOSE AND GET FED

Draw near to God and He will draw near to you.

—JAMES 4:8

❧

Some friends of ours like to feed the birds when they go to the beach. On one occasion, they tell us, a large flock of birds gathered to receive the food the couple had brought; the birds ate and then left. Our friends went back to their beach chairs to relax then later got up to feed the birds again. And again, the birds returned for food, ate what they wanted, and left.

But in between the feedings, our friends noticed that one little bird remained behind when the others left. They gave this little one more food. And the more food they gave him, the closer he stayed to them. This went on all day. Every time they turned around, they saw this little bird waiting patiently for more food. And they did not disappoint him.

What a wonderful picture of the hunger we should have for God! The psalmist used the imagery of a timid, thirsty animal to depict the intensity of desire we should have for God: "As the deer pants for the water brooks, so my soul pants for Thee, O God" (Ps. 42:1). James said if we will draw near to God, He will draw near to us.

When we draw near to God He satisfies our thirst with the water of life and feeds us with the living bread. When that begins to happen in our lives, people will begin to wonder how we can have so much peace, joy, and contentment in our hearts.

The answer will be that we have learned to stay close to God.—LOIS

TALK ABOUT IT
Those same friends challenged us to spend twenty minutes a day with the Lord for twenty-one days to build up a habit of meeting with Him. Why not take this challenge as a couple over the next three weeks?

CHOKING ON THE DETAILS

Do not be anxious for your life, as to what you shall eat, or what you shall drink; nor for your body, as to what you shall put on.

—MATTHEW 6:25

*J*esus told us not to let the details of life get us all knotted up. Did you know that the word *worry* is from a word that means "to strangle"? Worry chokes us. It cuts off our emotional and spiritual air supply.

But worry is also like fog. It's a lot of smoke and almost no substance. Jesus told us not to worry about the things of little substance—what we are going to eat or drink or wear. Then He closed His admonition with this question: "Is not life more than food, and the body than clothing?" He was saying if we want to worry, we should worry about whether we are going to wake up tomorrow.

Jesus' point was that if God gives us life, He's going to sustain that life. If we wake up tomorrow, that means God has obligated Himself to take care of us for at least one more day. Jesus was helping us get things in the right perspective. When we go to bed at night we've already got the next day planned. Most of us don't worry about whether we are going to wake up tomorrow. We worry about how we are going to pay the bills tomorrow, how we are going to straighten out this or that problem tomorrow, how we are going to get our work done tomorrow, where the money is going to come from for the kids' braces tomorrow.

But these are just details. Jesus wants us to focus on loving and serving Him first. When we do that, He'll worry about what is second, third, and fourth.

PRAY ABOUT IT

Check over your worry list (don't say you don't have one!). Is anything there too big for God? Then quit worrying!

EYEBALL-TO-EYEBALL ATTENTION

He who finds a wife finds a good thing, and obtains favor from the LORD.
—PROVERBS 18:22

A husband needs to study two things: the Bible and his wife. Both are difficult to interpret. Any man will testify that it takes work to understand a woman. That's why we have to study our wives; and you can't study something without giving time to it.

Remember, God built a complex circuitry into women. That circuitry includes hormones that are on the move. So each month, you need to be aware of what is happening to your wife. The week before her menstrual cycle, she may be a little bit more sensitive, perhaps a little more irritable and more easily frustrated, depending on her temperament. But in a few days she'll probably bounce back with renewed energy.

A husband who really wants to know his wife will be a little more understanding, a little more tender, a little more conversational during this time. It's not always easy to be an understanding husband. But it's worth the effort, because in the process of knowing your wife, the two of you will grow closer together.

Knowing your wife means you have to make some adjustments. For example, you may have to give up some television programs or get your news some other time besides the evening newscast because that time of the evening is when you say, "Honey, I'm ready to listen. Tell me anything you want me to know, because when I learn it, I'm going to use it to love you better. You've got my undivided attention."

That's a big change from reading the newspaper or watching TV while you "listen" to your wife. But if you want to know what makes her tick, you need to give her eyeball-to-eyeball attention.

THINK ABOUT IT
There are "some things hard to understand" (2 Pet. 3:16) in both your Bible and your wife—but both will richly repay your careful study.

YOU DON'T HAVE TO GIVE IN

How then could I do this great evil, and sin against God?

—GENESIS 39:9

⁓⊰⊱⁓

One of the most successful people in history at overcoming sexual temptation was a handsome young man, probably in his midthirties, still a virgin and committed to God. His name was Joseph, and his story is found in Genesis 37–50.

Consider Joe's background. He was from a dysfunctional family. His brothers were murderers, adulterers, and connivers who sold Joseph into slavery. His father, Jacob, was a polygamist. Yes, Joseph was from a troubled family, but he turned out fine.

Does this mean you can come from a messed-up family and still turn out fine? Yes, it does. Does this mean you can recover from abuse and give yourself fully to your mate? Yes, it does. Does this mean you don't have to give in to sexual temptation in any form? It certainly does, because the God who helped Joseph do these things is your God too.

If you're thinking Joseph had to be a nerd to be this clean sexually at his age, you're wrong. Genesis 39:6 tells us, "Joseph was handsome in form and appearance." The brother was cool! Besides this, Joseph had some money in his pocket because he had a good job, the top position in the house of Potiphar, an important Egyptian official. But Joseph was God's man, and as a result, he was able to remain strong when Mrs. Potiphar threw herself at him.

Now, this was one needy woman. She told Joe, "I'm being neglected, and I need a man; I need you."

But Joseph did not let somebody else's passions control his decisions. His answer to Mrs. Potiphar, quoted in the verse above, shows that he understood that sexual sin, like all sin, is ultimately sin against God.

Once you get that perspective on sin and temptation, it will help keep you on target.

TALK ABOUT IT

Are you helping each other avoid sexual temptation? Check out the things you read and watch and the places you go to make sure you aren't putting temptation in each other's path.

IT'S SHOW TIME

[God] delivered us from the domain of darkness, and transferred us to the kingdom of His beloved Son.

—COLOSSIANS 1:13

───※───

oday's verse is one of the great statements about our spiritual freedom in Jesus Christ. But you may be wondering, "If God has set me free, why am I still in bondage to the devil in my daily life? If I'm on the winning side, why am I losing so often?"

Many believers suffer defeat in spiritual warfare because they are trying to fight Satan in their own strength. But Satan isn't afraid of you at all! He's not afraid of me either. However, he cannot stand up against God for even a second. This is why Paul wrote, "Be strong in the Lord, and in the strength of His might. Put on the full armor of God, that you may be able to stand firm against the schemes of the devil" (Eph. 6:10–11).

No matter where you are in your Christian walk right now, it is not too late to put on the armor of God, pick up your God-given weapons, and join the battle. In fact, as a child of God you are already a member of His army!

But one of our problems today is that we have too many Christian civilians and not enough Christian soldiers. Some of us simply want to jump into a soldier's uniform when we run into a problem, rather than understanding we *are* already soldiers who are supposed to be in uniform at all times because we are in a war.

We are at war, but it's not like other wars. Christ has already won this conflict! All we have to do is enlist, put on our fatigues and our boots, and pick up our weapons, because it's show time!

As a married couple, don't forget to help each other get armed for battle.

PRAY ABOUT IT

We need to pray from a position of victory, not just for victory. Thank God today that you are free in Christ and that in Him you have spiritual victory.

THE ESSENCE OF CHRISTMAS

She will bear a Son; and you shall call His name Jesus, for it is He who will save His people from their sins.

—MATTHEW 1:21

Surely any couple can appreciate what Joseph and Mary were up against as her pregnancy became known (see Matt. 1:18–19). If you two have been married for any length of time, you are probably old enough to remember an America in which pregnancy outside of marriage was still cause for shame and even ostracism from polite society. Joseph was experiencing these kinds of feelings in a much stronger way because of the strict Jewish culture he lived in. Mary was a candidate for embarrassment, too, even though she certainly knew where the baby had come from.

Joseph did not want to disgrace Mary publicly, so he was arranging to divorce her "secretly" when the angel appeared to him and laid out God's wonderful plan. The angel's words, quoted in today's verse, captured the essence of Christmas. This is what the joy of the season is all about.

Notice Joseph's response to the angel's message (v. 24); it was a response of faith. Joseph believed God so completely and unreservedly that he totally reversed his plans. Instead of divorcing Mary, he married her and became her partner in carrying out the will of God.

God could do this miracle through Joseph and Mary because they were righteous people. The Holy Spirit was free to do His thing because they were a godly couple. Neither Joseph nor Mary was perfect. But the driving passion of their lives was honoring God in their attitudes and actions.

Those who have a heart for holiness are good candidates for God's miracles. Imagine what God could do if He could find a righteous couple like Joseph and Mary today!

THINK ABOUT IT

Joseph's high standard of morality would not allow him to compromise. Mary was a woman of godly character. And they were both obedient. Is there a Joseph and Mary in your house?

SO BE IT, LORD

He will reign over the house of Jacob forever; and His kingdom will have no end.

—LUKE 1:33

❦

The story of the angel's visit to the Virgin Mary in Luke 1:26–38 has to be one of the most beautiful and powerful texts in all of Scripture. Mary needed a Savior just like we do today (see v. 47). As we said yesterday, Mary was righteous, not sinless.

The angel Gabriel came to Mary in the sixth month of her relative Elizabeth's pregnancy with John the Baptist. Both births would be miraculous, with one huge difference. John was conceived through the normal means of human conception, although it was miraculous that a couple as old as Zacharias and Elizabeth would have a baby.

But Mary, of course, was a virgin. Jesus' birth was a miracle of God from beginning to end. This helps to explain why Gabriel did not rebuke Mary for asking a question (v. 34) the way he rebuked Zacharias (see Luke 1:18). Mary asked a very innocent question. After all, she knew she was a virgin. Besides, her response in verse 38 shows that she was not expressing doubt or unbelief.

Jesus could not have a human father because He had to be a perfect Man to die for the sins of imperfect people. He had to have a Father who was perfect, and God alone meets that criterion. So in Jesus we have the perfect God-Man, full humanity and full deity in the same Person.

Mary believed God over against her physical circumstances. She did not know how, but she did know *Who*. We need to note that. Too many of us are trying to figure God out. But He's under no obligation to explain every detail to us. All we need to know is that He is accomplishing His program through His people.

Mary's question was, "How is this possible?" When God answered her, all she needed to say was, "So be it, Lord."

PRAY ABOUT IT
When you know God, you don't necessarily have to know how He's going to accomplish His plan in your life. You just have to know that He is going to do it. Tell Him today you're willing to do anything He wants you to do.

WHEN GOD IS READY TO MOVE

She gave birth to her first-born son; and she wrapped Him in cloths, and laid him in a manger.

—LUKE 2:7

❧

If you're familiar with the cultural and religious context of the times in which Jesus was born, you know that He was born into a chaotic world. First-century Palestine was an occupied land under Roman domination. The political and governmental environment was one of endless intrigues and plots and revolutions.

The mighty Roman Empire was the bully of the world into which Jesus was born. Rome crushed nation after nation to expand its rule and then taxed its subjects until they were bled dry. The Roman authority in Judea was a crazy and very powerful man named Herod the Great, whose cruelty was already legendary. He even had members of his own family killed when he suspected they might be plotting against him. This evil ruler held Judea in his iron grip, and as an occupied people, the Jews had little choice but to submit. Obviously, tensions were always high.

The religious scene wasn't much more encouraging. Prior to the announcement of Jesus' birth, no one in Israel had heard from God for nearly four hundred years. There were no prophets and no miracles at that time, and there was little true worship of and reverence for God. It seemed that nobody was really looking for the Messiah to come. Things were a mess.

Then God said it was time for His Son to come, and the political and cultural mess no longer mattered. God moved men and nations to accomplish His plan. Mary and Joseph offer us one example of this truth. They had to get to Bethlehem so Jesus would be born there and fulfill Scripture. No problem. God just said, "Tax time," and the job was done.

When God gets ready to move, don't worry about the mess around you. Just make sure you're ready.

PRAY ABOUT IT

If God hasn't answered your prayer yet, don't stop praying. When He gets ready to act, obstacles are irrelevant.

SOMETHING TO GET EXCITED ABOUT

Today in the city of David there has been born for you a Savior, who is Christ the Lord.

—LUKE 2:11

⁘

*T*here's a painting by the great artist Rembrandt that says it all for me at Christmas. The scene is the manger of Bethlehem. The painting focuses my attention exclusively on the Baby, because Rembrandt painted a shaft of light that falls on the baby Jesus and illuminates Him alone. Other figures appear in the scene, but Rembrandt wrapped them in the shadows so that all the attention goes to Jesus. Focusing all of our attention and adoration on Jesus is exactly what God the Father has in mind for us, especially at Christmas.

We know from the famous story in Luke 2:8–20 that the shepherds had the right idea. A great choir of angels filled the sky while the little band of ragged shepherds looked up in terrified wonder. But the shepherds caught on right away and quickly got into the spirit of this Christmas thing. They wanted to worship this new King, so they went running off to Bethlehem with real joy and anticipation in their hearts. We need to go running to Bethlehem with them!

What I especially like about these guys is that ordinarily they had little to get excited about. Shepherds in that day were on the bottom rung of the career and social ladder of the day. When they got excited that first Christmas it wasn't because they thought they were going to get some presents. They didn't get pumped to go see baby Jesus because they heard the manger was all lit up with pretty lights. And they weren't looking for an overweight man in a red suit. They focused totally on the Messiah; all they wanted was to worship Him.

If all you and your family had this Christmas was Jesus, would it be enough to send you jumping for joy? I pray it would!—TONY

THINK ABOUT IT

If your family can't get excited about Jesus this Christmas, better check out how you're celebrating the holidays. Some adjustments may be in order. Maybe your Christmas celebration needs a fresh focus on Jesus.

BORN JUST DOWN THE ROAD

Where is He who has been born King of the Jews? For we saw His star in the east, and have come to worship Him.

—MATTHEW 2:2

*T*he Magi were professional astronomers. But they were more than just stargazers, because when the magnificent star appeared they knew the true God was up to something. So they began a trip that took them well over a year and maybe as long as two years. No price was too high, no inconvenience was too great, to keep them from finding this King of the Jews and worshiping Him.

What a stir these intriguing men must have caused when they finally arrived in Jerusalem! They were from the East, which meant they were Gentiles, yet they were seeking a King who would rule over the Jews. King Herod himself got shook up when these guys pulled into town, perhaps because there may have been far more than just three of them and certainly because of their inquiries about a newborn king. If you are king and some folks show up to worship another king born in your own neighborhood and you don't even know who he is, you are going to be a little upset!

So Herod called in the local preachers, the "chief priests and scribes of the people" (Matt. 2:4). He must have been stunned to learn that they already knew about the new King's birth. They said, "Oh yeah, He was born just down the road a few miles in Bethlehem. Says so right here in Micah 5:2."

These preachers knew the Bible, but they weren't even looking for the Messiah. Jesus had been born down the street, but they hadn't even bothered to check it out. They didn't want to be inconvenienced.

Do you take time to worship Jesus, even when it's inconvenient?

THINK ABOUT IT
You will know you are getting serious about worship when neither the inconvenience nor the price of worship can stop you from worshiping God.

THE PERFECT POSITION FOR US

They came into the house and saw the Child with Mary His mother; and they fell down and worshiped Him.

—MATTHEW 2:11

Ｔt's interesting to me that Herod called the Magi to a secret meeting and then sent them to Bethlehem to check out this new King. Why didn't Herod send his own men to investigate? Why did he ask these "tourists" from a foreign country to go instead?

Perhaps the king figured that if his own court preachers had kept this thing quiet this long, he wasn't going to let them mess up now. Besides, Herod knew that as Jews, these religious leaders would not like what he had in mind for the new King once he located Him. So Herod sent the Magi to Bethlehem.

These men were driven by a passion to worship the true God. As a result, they also enjoyed His guidance. God led them to Jerusalem by means of His star, the brightness of God's glory. Then, when the Magi were in Jerusalem, God used an ungodly king and ungodly preachers to lead the wise men to the next step.

There's a great principle here. God's guidance is such that if you follow what you do know, He will show you what you don't know until you get where you are supposed to go.

The Magi started out knowing only that God was telling them, "Just go west, boys." The specifics came later, at just the time they were needed.

And notice when the Magi got to where they were going, they fell on their knees in worship of God's new King. Being on our knees before God is the perfect position for us to be in as we seek His will.

PRAY ABOUT IT
God will never show you the specifics of His will if He can't trust you to obey Him in His general will. Pray that God will give both of you a heart of obedience whether you are facing a new year—or just a new week.